Profitable Conveyancing

Other titles by Law Society Publishing:

Excellent Client Service
Heather Stewart
1 85328 777 6

Lexcel Practice Excellence Kit (3rd edn)
The Law Society and Michael Moore
1 85328 911 6

New Partner's Guide to Management
Simon Young
1 85328 776 8

Practice Management Handbook
Edited by Peter Scott
1 85328 915 9

Profitability and Law Firm Management (2nd edn)
Andrew Otterburn
1 85328 820 9

Profitable Conveyancing

A Practical Guide for Residential Conveyancers

Stephanie Dale

The Law Society

For Bob and Cynthia

ISBN 1 85328 862 4

Published in 2005 by the Law Society
113 Chancery Lane, London WC2A 1PL

Typeset by J&L Composition, Filey, North Yorks
Printed by TJ International Ltd, Padstow, Cornwall

Contents

About the author and contributors

Stephanie F. Dale

After gaining an MBA and Diploma in Marketing, Stephanie established Customised Marketing in 1987, primarily providing marketing consultancy advice to national property developers to gain planning permissions for major commercial and residential developments. In the early to mid-1990s, in addition to being a senior marketing lecturer she also lectured in law, and further developed the marketing consultancy to work almost exclusively with law firms. After training delegates from many FTSE 100 companies in London, she established Customised Professional Development in 1997 to provide CPD training for solicitors in addition to consultancy. She is a Law Society authorised trainer on management, marketing and client care topics for national, London-based and high street firms. She regularly writes articles for the legal press.

Contributors

Michael Debens qualified as a solicitor in 1982, becoming a partner in Atkins Walter and Locke of Dorking, Surrey in 1986. He joined Downs in 1991 when the two Dorking firms merged. He has 20 years' experience in commercial and property law, including large scale projects both in the UK and overseas. Michael is both Head of Property and Head of Administration for the firm.

Rupert Kendrick is a former partner of a medium-sized law firm. He is the author of *Managing Cyber-Risks* (Law Society Publishing, 2002) which examines strategies for law firms wishing to manage Internet risk. He is a director of risk management consultancy Web4Law, and editor of the quarterly publication, *Managing Risk*. He writes widely on IT and Internet issues for law firms.

Malcolm Price was admitted as a solicitor at 21 and spent the next 14 years primarily in residential conveyancing. In the 1980s he moved into retail development, helping one of Europe's largest retail investors buy or develop regional shopping centres on mainland Europe. In 1996 he became Managing Partner of BPE, which quadrupled in size within eight years, during which he oversaw the creation of a legal IT software company. He is now Chief Excutive of volume conveyancer BPE Homemove LLP.

Foreword

Michael Garson

If fools went not to market, bad wares would not be sold.

The author has set herself an unenviable task as she offers a set of tools sharpened for the new and changed marketplace across the varied and uneven patchwork that is the property market – an environment which is barely recognisable from that just ten years ago.

Since 1997 there has been an active programme of government-led reform initiatives. Radical reforms prescribed by the Land Registration Act 2002 are 'work in progress' and yet to be fully developed. E-conveyancing is gradually shaping the new environment in which practitioners will operate in the future, while current Land Registry and Stamp Duty Land Tax procedures impose on the current generation of practitioners a transitional regime fraught with frustrations and false trails.

Over the same period markets have developed in response to growing consumer spending power. Since the recession of the early 1990s specialisations have taken root in the property markets as elsewhere in the economy, with the rejuvenation of inner city living in loft and dockland areas. Affordable and shared equity housing for key workers is being developed in response to political initiatives and lifetime mortgages and home reversion plans are the response to changing needs of the ageing population.

Within the liberal professions structural changes are the response to pressure for greater competition and accountability to the public through Parliament and its regulating agencies. Changes to the framework for regulation of legal services at a high level are likely to be recommended by Sir David Clementi in early 2005 and be followed by a decision in the next Parliament later that year. Over time there will be inevitable changes to supervision with a new rewrite of professional practice rules to frame the way in which services may in future be delivered. In the meantime providers of professional services must now respond to Money Laundering Regulations, and revised Solicitors' Practice Rules for conflict of interest and referral payments. The open market insurance regime has since 2000 brought a new emphasis on risk management which bears heavily on the structure of organisations in an era of rising consumer complaints which bring into question the model of service that conveyancers offer to their public.

The changes so far have taken place in largely benign economic conditions as the private housing market has for many seen a doubling of price and the new rules and procedure have yet to be tested in volatile or negative market conditions. A sudden change to the balance of supply and demand, be it geographic brought about by employment changes or sectoral caused by demographic shift, remains to be seen. As I write the challenge looms ever closer of the introduction of Home Information Packs, which along with other changes demands that solicitors undertake the reskilling which is a prerequisite of using modern IT.

The author brings to this array of moving targets a number of solutions for practising conveyancers and also of help to a wider audience of professionals involved in the property market as the techniques are relevant to a full spectrum of ages, background and experience. Stephanie has set out to capture in this handy reference book the basic ingredients necessary to construct a thoroughly modern model for delivering professional services. She has achieved that goal in a way that enables readers to pursue their own route to success while competing effectively with others who share the same ethical values and professionalism.

The author brings to bear that degree of detachment which is so necessary and valuable for practitioners locked into their local markets and working within prescribed organisational structures. Views and preferences are expressed which will serve to challenge the preconceptions of those with established practices and raise confidence in those who are about to embark.

Much time is presently given across the country to considering how best to market for business using old or new media. Some firms still hold back, questioning whether the response can be cost-effective for them. Whichever side of the fence the reader stands it is undeniable that we are all affected by clients being sufficiently motivated to return to an existing adviser, to experiment with a new one, or neither. What gives rise to perceived marketing success differs in almost every instance. Despite this, great importance attaches to a better understanding of the factors that affect those client decisions. For that reason alone Stephanie's skills and her sharing the experience of the marketing industry will be of interest and value to all readers.

'Helping clients' has been the traditional service model for solicitors; but where in the past clients may have been captive they have now to be wooed. Informed clients will no doubt be better clients. To adopt the political imperative of the moment, like it or not, we in the conveyancing market will need to acknowledge that 'we are all sales people of our wares and things look a lot different from the other side of the counter.'

Problems such as referrals payments and government intervention are intractable, and over the span of a generation changes yet to come will further 'move the goalposts' or even 'remove' the pitch. In the shorter term, Stephanie Dale has laid out a rich selection of the efficacious strategies that are needed for practitioners to thrive in this transitional period and dissected them to be easily absorbed by the busiest of conveyancing practitioners.

September 2004

Acknowledgements

My first acknowledgement and thanks go to Ben Mullane, commissioning editor at the Law Society, for persuading me to write this book, and for his ideas, patience and sense of humour.

I would like to thank the contributors to the book, Mike Debens, Malcolm Price, Rupert Kendrick, and also Mark Slade for his helpful input. Their additional advice and insights have been invaluable.

Thanks also go to Michael Garson for writing the foreword and for enjoyable, lively discussions.

Special thanks go to all the firms who have allowed me to use them in examples, in particular BPE solicitors in Cheltenham, Fidler & Pepper in Nottinghamshire, Heseltine Bray and Welsh in Barnsley, Withy King in Bath, Conveyancing UK in Sutton Coldfield, Gard and Co. in Plymouth, Goldsmith Williams in Liverpool, the Centre for Interfirm Comparison and Bath Design Centre.

Sincere thanks for their time, advice and patience when editing chapters and making interesting suggestions go to Mike Debens of Downs Solicitors, who has provided a generous fount of knowledge, also Lesley Alberici of Conveyancing UK, Jane Tyler, Debbie Thorp, Win Coulthard, Fiona Starkey of the Bath Design Centre and copy editor Hilary Scannell.

Numerous additional people have provided advice, recommendations and pointed me in the right direction.

Grateful thanks go to my unique family for their support and astonishment. For her presence, I thank Bridie, and for his constancy, I thank Roger.

Final thanks go to Captain John K. Coulthard Royal Navy for his encouragement and love and without whom little worthwhile is achieved.

Stephanie Faith Dale
2005

Introduction

This book analyses the two components of profitablity, costs and income generation, within a residential conveyancing context. The challenges facing the conveyancing market provide opportunities to exploit and threats that firms will want to take steps to minimise. Standing still is not a long-term option in business.

Who is this book written for?

Profitable Conveyancing is written for solicitors, and licensed conveyancers in small and medium-size firms who are responsible for residential conveyancing work. It will particularly interest heads of residential conveyancing departments, practice managers, managing and senior partners responsible for the future direction of the firm, for costs and for new business development. Solicitors aiming to become partners will gain an insight into the business management aspects of maintaining and increasing fee income in a residential conveyancing department.

How to use this book

Chapters have been written to enable readers to dip into individual ones for reference purposes. Each stands alone. Where relevant, references direct the reader to other chapters.

A brief description of the chapters

The first three chapters focus on planning for the future, managing costs and using IT to improve profitability. The first, 'Planning for success', shows firms how to undertake a strategic planning review in order to decide the future direction of their practice and of the residential conveyancing department. The chapter provides a significant part of a strategic review by investigating the external challenges facing firms and offers a list of strategic options available to conveyancers.

The second chapter, 'Costs, pricing and product', analyses the decisions to be made on when to spend and when to refrain, depending on the selected structure of the department and target client type. A table showing profitability and costs for a conveyancing department for firms with six or fewer partners in the Midlands provides a benchmark for similar firms.

'Using IT to improve profitability', Chapter 3, gives an overview of available technology and the benefits of various software systems. It provides a guide to writing an IT or an information communication technology plan and includes a case study of the chapter author's personal experience of developing a case management system.

Ten of the remaining twelve chapters offer ideas, inspiration and guidelines on generating fee income from existing and new clients. Chapter 4, 'Direct marketing to gain and retain clients', looks at how direct marketing is used and where new potential clients can be sourced. Chapter 5, 'How to save money on advertising', describes the different types of advertising and suggests how to write a good advertisement.

Chapter 6, 'Relationship management and building brands', recommends how to manage existing clients to generate fee income. It suggests ideas to encourage staff to cross-refer clients to give a better service and how to develop strong brands to reassure clients and increase profitability. Chapter 7 on 'Brochures, flyers and newsletters' offers practical guidelines for producing publicity literature, including how to save costs in design, printing and distribution and how to write a newsletter that will attract attention and fulfil its purpose.

Chapter 8, 'Networking', focuses on the growing importance of the topic and how to do it effectively and enjoyably. Chapter 9, 'Profile-raising activities', continues with the theme of raising one's profile with practical ideas on how to get better known through using public relations techniques.

Chapter 10, 'Evaluating marketing activities', provides essential ways to assess what works and what does not to assist in directing marketing budgets to activities that produce desired results. 'Converting telephone callers into clients', Chapter 11, helps a firm train its staff to encourage callers to use the firm and so be more cost effective.

Chapter 12, 'Managing clients' expectations', describes what behaviour clients like and dislike about the actions of solicitors. It recommends low cost ways to manage clients' expectations to avoid problems that may give rise to complaints. The following chapter, 'The client's perspective', expands on the concept of managing clients' expectations by seeing the firm as clients may see it. It discusses the differences between buying products and buying services from a law firm.

Chapter 14, 'Complaints avoidance', considers the causes of complaints and how to avoid them. The final chapter, 'Internet and e-conveyancing', reviews the framework for e-conveyancing and looks at future developments.

Recommended further reading and suggested websites are provided as sources of additional information.

1

Planning for success

KEY POINTS

This chapter will

- explain the process of strategic planning
- describe how to do a strategic review
- recommend the content of business plans
- provide an overview of external challenges facing conveyancing departments
- show how to assess internal strengths and weaknesses of your firm
- offer a list of strategic options
- suggest how to set objectives
- remind firms to keep Practice Rule 15 and terms of business information up to date

For many firms, there is mounting pressure on margins, increasing competition fighting for their client base and decreasing client loyalty. The need to have a strategic review and a clearly defined business plan is critical in such an environment.

What is a business plan?

A business plan sets out what the firm will do to achieve a goal within a specific time frame. It records the results of the strategic planning review that analyses the current state of the organisation and the business environment within which it is operating. It states the objectives of the business and provides a strategic plan to achieve these objectives in the first year and a less detailed one for the following three to five years.

The business plan provides a benchmark against which the firm can assess its progress.

A recent survey found that only 13 per cent of law firm partners strongly agreed with the statement 'Our firm has a well-developed business strategy based on a clear understanding of the firm's strengths, competitors' weaknesses and clients' future business advisory needs' (report from Wheeler Associates and McCallum Layton, 'One for all, and all for one?' 2004).

A business plan covers the following strategic planning stages:

1. Where are you now? This includes the external pressures and influences on the firm and allows for the internal strengths and weaknesses of the practice.
2. Where do you want to be in the next three to five years (including position in a market, financial position, organisational structure, etc.)?
3. What steps will you take to get there and why? This should include a consideration of the alternatives.
4. How will you ensure you achieve your objectives? This should include evaluating actual results against planned ones at agreed points and the corrective steps to be taken.

Writing a business plan

A business plan may be written to persuade a lender or investor (where allowed) to provide funds or to provide an operational guideline for the firm as a whole. It may be compiled to ensure that all departments work towards achieving the corporate goals or to gain approval for a major activity.

Before writing a business plan you should consider for whom you are writing and what they will want to get out of it. A single business plan will not be suitable for all audiences. It may need a different focus or a change in the level of detail included according to who will read it. These differences may be more pronounced depending on whether the business plan is intended for an external audience or an internal one.

One of the key benefits of undertaking a strategic planning review and writing a business plan is the actual process of doing it.

It provides the opportunity for partners to stand back and look at their business afresh. It helps them to reassess what they want from the firm and consider what they want it to be known for in the future. It motivates them to generate ideas and to question current activities. It provides a process for agreeing the future direction and the objectives of their firm.

The process of writing the business plan can raise staff motivation. Where staff are encouraged to become involved and there are open channels of communication, it helps them to understand where the firm is going and why. It can increase their commitment to achieving the resulting objectives.

Here is a summary of business planning stages:

1. Determine why you are writing the plan.
2. Decide for whom the plan will be written.
3. Define the business the firm is in.
4. Describe the external business environment in which the firm operates now and the changes likely to affect the firm and its clients over the next three to five years. Identify and assess opportunities and threats.
5. Assess the internal strengths and weaknesses of the firm compared to its competitors from the perspective of clients and referrers.
6. Summarise key points from (4) and (5) in a SWOT analysis (strengths, weaknesses, opportunities, threats).
7. Formulate the partners' goals for the firm and for individual departments.
8. Develop a strategy to achieve the goals for individual departments (include the impact on finance, marketing, human resources (HR) and IT.
9. Assess the strategy against (6) above and make any amendments necessary. Write operating plans.
10. Determine costs, revenues and cash flow in detail for year one and prepare an overview for the following three years.
11. Gain agreement for the plans.
12. Use the plans as a blueprint, while continually assessing the market in which the firm operates for changes that might affect the firm and its clients. Act on variations from planned results.

Preliminary issues to answer before you begin

Presentation

A business plan needs to be concise and easy to follow. Summaries can give directions of where to find more detail in the appendix. An example of a typical layout for a business plan is given in Appendix A.

Implementation problems

It is worth at this point considering the reasons why plans may fail to be implemented in organisations, so that these can be taken into account during the planning process.

The reasons for failure include weak support from the senior and managing partners or the task being delegated to a planner or person with insufficient authority. Lack of support among staff that may be due to lack of involvement, poor understanding and communication can also result in failure to implement plans. In addition, confusion over the expressions and terms used or poor specification with too much or too little detail causes problems. Other reasons for failure include insufficient time being given for implementation or a loss of interest when short-term gains are not quickly apparent. If the business plan is seen as a once-a-year ritual less attention may be paid to its implementation.

When is the strategic review going to be done?

A complete strategic review should be done approximately every three years with an update every year. This enables the firm to stand back periodically and assess the implications of medium- to longer-term changes. It allows the firm to take potential changes into account in its business planning with the aim of avoiding issues taking the firm by surprise in a potentially damaging way.

The outline plan produced will cover years two to five, with more detail in the earlier years than the later ones.

A one-year plan will consist of the budget, marketing, IT, personnel and training plans.

Who is going to lead it?

The planning review has to be led by a senior person to ensure that the right message is given to everyone that this is an important and serious undertaking. Ideally the managing or senior partner will lead it.

Who will be involved?

A good cross-section of people will be required. It can help to have a small team consisting of the managing or senior partner, heads of departments and managers of non-legal departments such as finance and marketing. If the lead partner is aged 50 plus, another partner in their late 20s or early 30s should be involved. Also be aware that the experience of some partners may be restricted to working for their own firm for many years and they may find it difficult to be objective or consider new directions. Try to ensure that the people selected represent different parts of the firm. Keep the committee small in order to achieve more.

It can help to use external consultants to undertake part of the process, for example to analyse staff questionnaires, as people are often more forthcoming if they know their views are being given to an independent person. Furthermore, internal staff may not have the experience to carry out an analysis of potential clients' future needs. An additional area where an external consultant can be used is facilitating partner 'away days'. Consultants can often raise issues that partners feel uncomfortable about, and question aspects that need bringing out into the open, because they are not involved with the politics or group dynamics. They can give an independent perspective.

How is the strategic review to be carried out?

Consider organising an 'away day' to examine the external influences on the firm and have a brainstorming session, employing the services of an independent consultant. Send a confidential questionnaire to all staff. The aim is to discover how they think the firm is operating; what problems there are; what could be done better and how it could be done better; what the firm is good at doing; how they think the firm is viewed from the outside and ideas they have for its future development.

The purpose of this is to get everyone involved at an early stage. The information gleaned can be quite revealing. The results can be used to assess the strengths and weaknesses of different departments.

The other information required may be gathered from a combination of the following methods:

- an analysis of client satisfaction questionnaires;
- an audit of everyone's skills
- appraisal reports;
- interviews with heads of departments and a cross-section of staff;
- analysis of financial data;
- approaching professional contacts for their frank opinions of the firm compared to other firms.

How will it be communicated?

Make an announcement to everyone in the firm explaining what is being done and the reasons for it. Tell everyone the benefits to be gained, what will happen and who is on the committee. Explain what is expected of them and when, and emphasise how important each person's input is to make a success of it.

Hold a staff meeting when the strategic plan is ready to be presented. Parts of it may be confidential but the more that can be shared, the more staff will see how their earlier involvement has helped to develop it. It will increase their understanding of their role in the achievement of it.

How long will it take?

The timescale to undertake a strategic review is often underestimated. Typically, it may take up to six months to do thoroughly, sometimes longer. The implementation of the entire plan rarely takes less than three years.

The gathering of information for the business plan will assist firms in gaining accreditation for Investors in People. See Box 1.2 on p. 19 and **www.iipuk.co.uk** for further information.

What business are you in?

Theodore Levitt argued that declining industries became that way because they focused too much on the product and not enough on the market within which they operated. As a result, organisations were taken by surprise by environmental change, found it difficult to respond and often either lost market share or went into liquidation.

> The failure is at the top. The executives responsible for it, in the last analysis, are those who deal with broad aims and policies . . .
>
> The railroads did not stop growing because the need for passenger and freight transportation declined. That grew. The railroads are in trouble today not because the need was filled by others (cars, trucks, aeroplanes, even telephones), but because it was not filled by the railroads themselves. They let others take customers away from them because they assumed themselves to be in the railroad business rather than the transportation business. The reason they defined their industry wrong was because they were railroad orientated instead of transportation-orientated; they were produce-orientated instead of customer-orientated.
>
> 'Marketing myopia', *Harvard Business Review*, 38 (July/August 1960) 24–47

Being 'customer orientated' means monitoring the changes in the wider environment in which your firm operates, understanding the effect of these changes on the needs of your clients and potential clients, and keeping an open mind about the business you are in to serve these needs. It may mean looking beyond providing legal services.

BOX 1.1 What business are conveyancers in – or could be in?

The home moving business?

If this is the case, then other aspects of moving home come within the potential scope of practice.

The personal solutions business?

If it is the 'solving people's problems' sector, then other problems could fall within the firm's sights, such as transfers of equity, tenancy agreements, declaration of trusts, filling in tax returns, investment and pensions advice, where the firm is able and permitted.

The personal services business?

If the business is to help people's lives be better (part of which is moving home), other ways of helping people could be included in the business, such as arranging home cleaning, ironing, maintenance of home and vehicles, decorating, separation and divorce, wills, business start ups and business consultancy advice, careers advice and life coaching.

External issues: where are we now?

The analysis of the wider environment requires three factors. The first is the skills of those involved to be able to stand back, analyse the environment and to make realistic forecasts. The second relates to the culture of the practice and the willingness of partners to give sufficient importance to the process of reviewing the internal and external environment. The third is the motivation to respond actively to the findings of the review. Many a review has been done and then ignored or not given sufficient emphasis, to the detriment of the firm.

The first part of strategic planning is to answer the question 'where are we now?'.

Make an assessment of the external influences affecting different departments including the conveyancing department. These influences can be divided into the macro-environmental factors that affect all businesses and the micro-environmental factors that affect your particular practice and the departments within the practice. It is necessary to assess

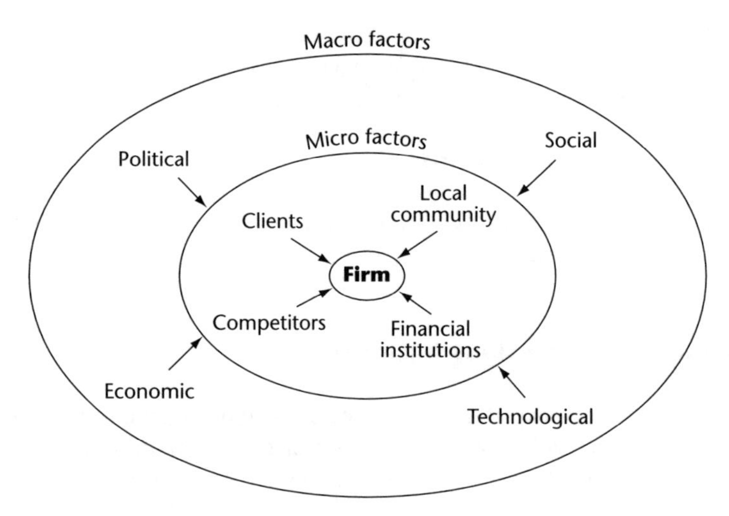

Figure 1.1 Environmental influences

factors affecting all departments, as cross-referral of clients from other departments may produce a significant turnover for the firm's conveyancing department.

Macro-environmental factors

Consider the issues and potential issues likely to affect all firms over the next three to five years. Pay particular attention to long-term trends rather than snapshot figures. Review the implications of the issues raised under the following general headings (PEST):

- Political;
- Economic;
- Social;
- Technological.

Political influences

Political influences include government policy, laws, regulations and directives. Examples affecting conveyancers may include the following:

- introduction of the Home Information Pack, giving estate agents considerably more influence over clients selling property to direct them to use specific solicitors or licensed conveyancers on their panels;
- the Law Society allowing (at the time of writing) the payment of referral fees leading to estate agents and other introducers of business

wanting fees to be paid. Some practitioners fear that this will decrease profit margins and others believe that placing referral agreements on a firmer footing may help to establish a more consistent level of workflow for a fee;

- an e-conveyancing drive to make home moving a faster process, leading to the necessity to invest in suitable computer hardware and software and have the skills in place to take e-conveyancing in the firm's stride when it fully happens;
- implementation of legislation, including the Land Registration Act, the Stamp Duty Land Tax, and the Commonhold and Leasehold Reform Act. These require training time for staff and more time spent on each conveyancing matter, increasing the costs of doing the work;
- the impact of the Clementi review regarding the regulation of the legal services sector could have a significant impact on the industry and firms within it;
- the potential introduction of so-called 'Tesco law' enabling employed solicitors to provide legal services for the general public. This may lead to the introduction of supermarkets and large businesses into the conveyancing industry, resulting in increased competition and tighter margins;
- money laundering requirements placing greater responsibility and therefore costs on solicitors.

CASE STUDY **Legal help and triple Clubcard points at Tesco**

The 'Tesco law' took a step closer to reality this week after the supermarket giant launched an on-line legal store offering shoppers the chance to buy self-help legal solutions alongside their groceries.

Tesco has linked up with legal DIY publisher Lawpack to provide a range of DIY kits and forms covering 17 legal topics, such as accident claims, property and employment law, 'at great value prices'. There is a 30-day money-back guarantee.

Triple Tesco Clubcard points are available on some of the products, while there are special offers on the likes of the 'DIY Separation & Divorce Kit', currently £7.49.

Tesco.com chief executive Laura Wade-Grey said: 'Tesco wants to demystify the law by offering shoppers simple and easy to understand legal products.' However, Tesco would not be drawn on its longer-term plans for legal services if the market is liberalised as a result of the Clementi review.

[2004] *Gazette*, 24 June

Economic influences

Economic influences include interest rates, the state of the economy, employment rates and the levels of salary needed to attract good staff. Those factors affecting conveyancers potentially include:

- rising interest rates to stem house price inflation;
- the Home Information Packs, expected to cost several hundreds of pounds, which may discourage some home owners from selling;
- the wage demands of staff leading to lower margins;
- the consolidation of practices as firms merge to take advantage of economies of scale (potentially lower costs and higher margins);
- demand for housing outstripping supply, pushing up prices and forcing out first time buyers. This is linked to panic buying or selling if the market changes;
- buy-to-let purchases for investment and pension purposes;
- high level of remortgages and parents remortgaging to help children with deposits to get on the housing ladder;
- a growth in equity release schemes.

Social influences

Social influences will include:

- the difficulty of finding and attracting good quality staff;
- more people attending university and expecting to walk into a high paid job leading to less willingness for university-educated people to start at the bottom and work their way up. This may lead to difficulty in attracting the right kind of staff for particular posts;
- single-person households and single-parent households increasing in number, leading to continuing demand for more housing;
- an increasing number of people opting to live together rather than marry. As more cohabitees break up than married couples, this may lead to more demand for conveyancing services;
- knowledgeable and demanding clients, leading to the need to provide information more often, but possibly with less personal contact.

Technological influences

Technological influences potentially affecting conveyancers include:

- the development of e-conveyancing promises faster transactions and possibly reduced costs, particularly in terms of volume of paper used and higher margins. The development of the National Land Information Service (NLIS) considerably speeds up property searches, shortening the time between offer acceptance and exchange of

contracts. Property searches are submitted and results are provided electronically;
- competitors offering potential clients the ability to request conveyancing quotes online and the use of case-tracking facilities on the Internet to attract them;
- the ability to provide conveyancing services to distant clients;
- estate agents and building society referrers of transactional and bulk remortgages increasingly insisting on compatibility of software to enable them to interrogate mutual client files to assess progress made;
- the growth of panel managers driving the need to have compatible software;
- with the ownership of land now based on computer records at the Land Registry, there is no longer a need to store deeds, leading to reduced storage costs. It also opens up the possibility of virtual offices, home working and flexible working through the use of technology. In the future, this may lead to the reduction in costs of providing office premises for staff leading to higher margins.

Micro-environmental factors

Micro-environmental factors that specifically affect your firm include:

- clients and potential clients;
- the local community;
- financial institutions;
- competitors.

Clients and potential clients

Data on existing clients will be available internally. Useful information includes a profile of the client types who generate turnover in your firm.

EXAMPLE **Profiling existing clients**

- 68 per cent of turnover is from couples buying a home who are middle to senior management with children leaving home;
- 18 per cent of turnover is from couples buying their second home in their mid to late 30s;
- 14 per cent of turnover is from a mixture of first-time buyers who tend to be the children of long-established clients, older people downsizing and singles buying their first homes;
- of all clients, 66 per cent are existing clients or resulted from recommendations. This figure is down from 74 per cent two years ago.

It will also be useful to identify trends in turnover from particular geographical areas; from particular referrers; according to the purchase price of properties; and from client types or segments.

It is useful to work out whether the firm's market share in the locality is increasing, static or decreasing over time. Details of the number of properties sold by type over the previous quarter are available from the Land Registry (**www.landreg.gov.uk**). From the firm's own data of the number of properties it has conveyed in the previous quarter, it is possible to work out its market share.

For potential clients, local population trends are required rather than snapshot figures – 2001 census data are available for geographical areas. As time progresses, this information becomes increasingly out of date.

Economic development units at local, county or unitary authorities are sometimes able to provide population projections and breakdowns. Caution should always be used when dealing with statistics as they may be out of date, or based on only a small or biased sample. Information which will be of use includes:

- socio-economic breakdown (occupations/business sectors and salaries);
- geo-demographics (area age/gender breakdown);
- migration into or out of the area for work and living purposes;
- employment rate;
- skills and level of education;
- social structure.

This information needs to relate to the typical clients the conveyancing department currently attracts or plans to attract.

EXAMPLE **Client analysis**

A developer completes a new housing estate in the town where your practice is located. The new development has attracted predominantly young families.

Your clients are mainly people buying their third or fourth home, in middle to senior management occupations, with children leaving home. It is therefore unlikely that you will benefit from potential clients on the new housing estate.

If your firm wants to attract these younger people, it will need to change its marketing tactics and possibly its image.

The local community

Issues to take into account and their implications include housing prices and trends, which will have an impact on fees quoted. The economic outlook for businesses in the area and a breakdown of business types and sizes is another issue to be aware of. It will give an indication of the number, type and likely income levels of employed people in the region who will potentially require conveyancing services.

The type of proposed residential development in the area will dictate the age and incomes of the people likely to move into planned new homes and therefore the levels of potential fee income.

The attitude to businesses generally by the local authority needs to be considered. For example, does it encourage or discourage the development and expansion of businesses and employment? Some regions may benefit from government grants to encourage development. This may lead to longer-term growth in the area leading to potentially increasing fee income.

Where an enterprise area is due for development this can have a bearing on the local property sales and the rental market. Some buyers, particularly investors, tend to favour properties in disadvantaged areas to save paying stamp duty. This can provide an opportunity.

Financial support

There is little point in having strategic plans to expand or change the direction of the practice if the partners have little access to funds to financially support those plans.

Partners need to consider whether retained profits, provision of additional capital from private sources or access to loans and overdraft facilities will be sufficient to enable the plans to become reality.

Competitor analysis

The impact of competition ought to be assessed regularly and taken into account when planning for your firm's future. The more knowledge a firm has about its competitors, the better placed it will be to take advantage of an opportunity or to counter any threats.

A competitor may be vulnerable if it has any the following characteristics:

- a lack of cash and/or poor access to extra funding;
- higher operating costs than its competitors;
- operating in a sector with poor growth;
- over-reliance on one segment of the market or on one or a small number of clients;
- staffing problems (e.g. poor retention, low morale, inability to attract quality applicants);
- predictable;

- taking their eyes off the ball;
- complacency.

From a list by J.H. Davidson (1987) *Offensive Marketing,* Penguin

Consider not only competitors, but also whether your own firm or any of its departments has a combination of any of the above characteristics.

Assess competitors' strengths or weaknesses in the marketplace compared to your own. Which are hungry to develop their conveyancing fee income and which client types are they targeting? Consider the implications for your own firm. These will depend in part on whether you focus on local clients or aim for national ones, possibly through an effective website which appears high up on search engines and provides competitive fees.

Internal issues: where are we now?

Figure 1.2 illustrates the issues to consider when examining where your firm is now as part of the strategic planning review process reported in the business plan.

The factors within the firm that are likely to influence its ability to meet the challenge of the external pressures are identified in the diagram. Each needs to be assessed to determine whether they are a strength or a weakness. A single area can potentially be the weakest link which causes the under-performance of the firm.

Figure 1.2 Internal issues to assess

Skills – the reputation of the firm

Consider how the firm is perceived by its clients. Do they think it has specific areas of specialisation? How do these compare with the actual areas of specialist knowledge and the areas of weakness or less experience? Assess whether the partners and staff have the necessary skills and experience to provide for the future needs of clients and the firm.

How will you assess these? By:

- staff appraisals and interests;
- analysis of staff questionnaires (these may be confidential and anonymous);
- analysis of responses given by clients to a research questionnaire;
- asking the senior partner to call key clients and ask for their frank opinion;
- surveying the firm's professional contacts to assess their views of the firm compared to other firms;
- asking support staff if clients have made any comments on the firm's performance to them;
- analysing complaints made by clients;
- evaluating the results and cost-effectiveness of the firm's marketing activities.

Staff numbers and adaptability

A firm's greatest asset is its people. Potentially, they are also its greatest liability. The selection, training and retention of the right staff provide the core strength of a practice. Staff need to be flexible and willing to react positively to changes affecting the firm.

Is the training in the firm directed at identified existing and future needs? Is there a willingness to constantly learn or are there pockets of resistance? Are the ratios of support staff to fee earners appropriate for the type and level of service given to target clients?

BOX 1.2 Investors in People

A number of firms have gained the Investors in People award to help make the most of their greatest asset. Investors in People (IIP) is an award given to firms that invest in their people in order to achieve their business goals. Over 34,000 organisations in the UK have gained the award by attaining the key principles of the IIP standard.

The benefits of IIP, according to the IIP organisation, are that it helps to improve earnings, productivity and profitability and it helps employees to be customer focused. It increases motivation through greater involvement and aids the reduction of costs and wastage. It gives firms a competitive advantage through improved performance.

Go to **www.iipuk.co.uk** for further information.

Office procedures

Office procedures need to be assessed to see if they are delivering what is required.

Consider how effective the systems are. Do they provide timely, easy to understand and actionable information? Do they do what they are supposed to do? Rather than looking at snapshot figures, analyse trends. For example, how efficient is the credit control system across the entire firm – measured by the average number of days it took to get paid compared to last year and trends in the value of work in progress?

Office procedures include the use of case management, practice management and document management software. How much of the software is utilised in terms of (a) identifying the people using it effectively and (b) the range of functions not used of which the software is capable?

BOX 1.3 Best practice standards

Lexcel

Lexcel is the Law Society's practice management quality mark. It is specifically written for solicitors and aims to improve the standard of management in practices. It is a risk management and business improvement tool.

Lexcel was revised and updated in 2003 to incorporate additional risk management procedures. The changes in the Practice Management Standards (PMS) relate to client care, risk management and complaints handling. The modules of the new standard include structures and policies; strategy, the provision of services and marketing; financial management; facilities and information technology; people management; supervision and operational risk management; client care; and file and case management.

Go to **www.lawsociety.org.uk** for further information.

ISO 9000 Family, 9001:2000

ISO 9000 is a group of internationally accepted quality management standards laid down by the International Organisation for Standardisation. It is based on business processes where the emphasis is on improvement and meeting the needs of clients.

The ISO 9000 model has eight quality management principles:

1. customer focus;
2. leadership;
3. involvement of people;
4. process approach;
5. systems approach;
6. continual improvement;
7. factual approach taken to decision making;
8. mutually beneficial supplier relationships.

Go to **www.dti.gov.uk/bestpractice** for more information on how the ISO standards can help improve your firm.

Structure and hierarchy

Typical structures are flat or hierarchical. The structure and hierarchy divides tasks and provides the coordination between them. Does the chosen structure do this effectively? Is the structure and hierarchy appropriate to the ways of working in the conveyancing department and for teams? It may be that different teams need different structures. The remortgage team may, for example, work better in a relatively flat structure with a team leader and fee earners/paralegals.

Leadership style

The style may range between the extremes of autocratic to abdication. Which style is used and to what effect?

Identify particular managers who are better or worse at managing. Assess their methods of communicating and openness and the reactions of their staff to them. Ask staff what they think the managers could do differently to help them achieve more and be more productive.

Culture and desire to plan for the future and act on those plans

Culture is described as 'That's the way we do things around here'. Is the culture helpful or hindering in terms of getting tasks done and do people feel part of the firm's 'family'? Assess staff turnover figures, absenteeism levels, the atmosphere of cooperation or the underlying current of conflict. Ask people who have recently joined the firm or the department to describe the culture. Once people have been in a culture for some time it is harder for them to stand back and identify it.

History of strategy pursued and results it generated

Look at what happened in the past when a strategic planning review was undertaken and changes made. What were people's reactions to it and were any problems encountered when subsequently implementing plans? What lessons can be learned to help avoid similar hindrances in the future?

Location of office

Is the location of the office(s) beneficial to attracting and retaining clients? Question whether it would be better to have the back room function carried out in lower cost office premises on a business park with a smaller office in a town or city centre for visibility.

Layout and adaptability of the office

The layout of the office in many firms is determined by the building's constraints. A 'rabbit warren' of rooms may not be ideal, but tends to be a fixed feature in older properties.

When considering the firm's plans for the next three to five years, this is the time to stand back and consider how appropriate is the layout. How flexible is it to adjust to the needs of the future?

Would it be better to have open plan offices? They help team working and make it easier to cross-refer clients internally between departments. The disadvantages are the noise and potentially increased interruptions.

Internal interruptions can be avoided by having a system whereby a card is placed on the person's desk. A red card means 'do not interrupt me unless it is very important'. A yellow card means, 'I am busy, but can be interrupted if necessary'. A green card means 'I am available/desperate to speak to anyone!' Where space allows, a quiet room can be used for concentrated thinking time where silence is maintained for that purpose. Separate interview rooms are reserved for client meetings.

Key values and aspirations

These are the fundamental values around which the firm is built. Why do people work for the firm? What do partners, staff, clients and professional contacts say are the core values and aspirations of the firm? Are they the same? Are they the ones you want the firm to have in the future and be known by?

Financial

In considering the firm's finances you may need to:

- assess trends in profitability by service type/department, branch and client group;
- consider the internal funding capability and access to external funds that may be needed to achieve the new strategy;
- identify how costs can be cut. Have an open mind before evaluating the effect of decisions;
- assess the fee earner to support staff ratios and the turnover to staff cost ratios for each legal service area; consider tasks that could be done by lower cost support staff; train support staff to undertake more repetitive and routine tasks with supervision; analyse how a department allocates tasks and critically assess whether the most cost-effective and knowledgeable people are doing the task;
- question everything you do and how it is done; think the unthinkable;
- assess partner and staff performances. Salaries account for the major part of a firm's overheads. Assume no position is guaranteed. 'A partner is for life' is no longer definite. Some may possibly be losing motivation, others may be bored with doing the same thing year after year. Are there any not willing to change with the times and who may think they can get away with letting the technological or culture changes needed pass them by? Partners or staff may be becoming out of touch or complacent;
- assess whether you need more partners to raise fees and so create either more salaried or equity partners, or whether you need to lose some because of overcapacity;
- analyse the buildings costs and consider the extended use of technology to let people work from home; investigate digital dictation and better use of existing case management software to allow home-working; consider the benefits of flexible working to retain staff and reduce staff hiring and associated training costs;
- critically assess the hardware and software packages you currently have in terms of whether they could do more functions, which with a little training, would help you save time and make a better use of the investment.

Productivity

To work out the firm's productivity you need to:

- assess the profitability of fee earners against other fee earners adjusted to allow for the types of file the person has, where possible; evaluate the income produced by individual and team members compared to the costs of servicing the income: turnover to staffing costs gearing (this also relates to investment (or costs of) in-staff training and in resources to aid productivity);

- assess people's time management and consider sending fee earners on a time management course and support staff on personal effectiveness seminars to increase the productivity of teams.

In addition to costs, productivity relies on having the right people, with the right qualifications and skills for the future and with the right attitude.

In the Royal Navy, people appointed to roles are considered in terms of whether they are SQEP – suitably qualified and experienced personnel. A person may be two of the three, but still not be SQEP. Consider your own personnel in the conveyancing department. How many of them are SQEP? How many will you need to be SQEP to face the challenges of the future? What will you need to do to get sufficient SQEP people?

Pricing

The flexibility of how legal services are priced will depend on the types of services offered, clients' willingness to pay or shop around, their loyalty to the firm, the level of expenses plus profit margin required and the strength of the competition. See Chapter 2 on costs, pricing and product.

SWOT analysis

The SWOT is the firm's key internal strengths and weaknesses compared to its competitors, which relate to the external opportunities and threats presented.

This is a summary of the 'Where are we now?' analysis of the firm. It aims to pinpoint only the key issues which are pertinent to the firm in deciding its future direction. It will enable the partners to see more clearly ahead to agree the medium- to longer-term objectives for the practice.

The aim is to build on strengths to take advantage of the opportunities and to counter threats and minimise weaknesses.

EXAMPLE **Residential conveyancing department SWOT**

Strengths/weaknesses

The conveyancing department is staffed by highly skilled, client-friendly people. Compared to near competitors, the ratio of one solicitor to four part-qualified fee earners puts the firm in a strong position to maximise profits and contain costs. The extensive use of case management software by all team members enables the department to increase the case load per fee earner without increasing costs. Should the case load require additional staff, existing support staff under training could step in to become fee earners under the close supervision of the partner in charge.

To reduce costs in order to fund potential referral fees, the firm will need to increase the ratio of one solicitor to five part-qualified staff.

While the conveyancing department works efficiently, it is weak in terms of its professional contacts in the area. This is due to the departure of the previous partner who had the contacts and the new partner being new to the area (although the senior partner is well known and has built long-term relationships with local estate agencies, IFAs, bank personnel and surveyors).

Opportunities/threats

It is projected that the introduction of Home Information Packs will give estate agents considerably more influence over clients to direct them to particular solicitor firms. National and regional chains of estate agents will increasingly have panels of firms they will want their clients to use. Unless a firm is on these panels, it may suffer considerable loss to its conveyancing fee income over the next three years. Alternatively, if the firm is on panels, it could experience a substantial increase in the number of cases it receives – at a price.

The introduction of referral fees will most probably drive down margins as referrers demand payment. Where bulk work can be agreed with a referrer for a fee, this will smooth out peaks and troughs and should increase overall productivity.

Limiting factors

Limiting factors facing firms when deciding their future objectives need to be listed to ensure that plans take them into account.

Limiting factors facing residential conveyancing departments could include:

- access to qualified and experienced staff in a tight recruitment market;
- the capital cost of buying case management software suitable for part-qualified and unqualified staff to use that limits risk management issues;
- office space shortage for expansion in the current building; and
- access to funding for the costs of moving premises.

These are likely to lead to the need for additional funding.

Assumptions

When writing a business plan, assumptions have to be made regarding the trading period covered. These need to be highlighted. If the reality turns out to be different from the assumptions made, alterations can be made to the business plan.

Assumptions for the residential conveyancing market may include:

- a slow increase in interest rates gradually tempering house price rises;
- an increase in unemployment, particularly in manufacturing areas, leading to reduced demand for housing, resulting in stagnation of property prices and lower volumes of conveyancing clients;
- the leap in personal debt, leading to increased levels of bankruptcies and increased repossessions. This in turn will lead to more properties on the market, leading to further price reductions;
- further investment in property as an alternative to pension investment in equities as the stock market continues to underperform, leading to more 'buy-to-let' purchases;
- alternatively, 'buy-to-let' landlords off-loading their properties when it appears property prices have peaked creating a significant increase in supply causing prices to slip and fewer people wanting to move;
- rises in remortgages as 'rate-tarting' becomes more widely acceptable and expected;
- remortgages increasing as parents take equity from their homes to help offspring to get on to the property ladder;
- remortgages increasing as people consolidate debt;
- increased bureaucracy requiring more time to be spent on each file as evidenced by the Inland Revenue Stamp Duty forms. This will result in lower profitability or higher costs passed on to clients which may lead to lower volumes of work;
- further new non-legal entrants, such as major supermarkets and organisations with substantial numbers of clients (energy firms, banks, insurance companies, etc.) aiming to slice up the conveyancing market affecting margins and volumes.

Goals

Once the strengths and weaknesses have been assessed against the opportunities and threats, the next decision is to decide where you want the firm to be or how you see the firm in the strategic planning period, say three to five years.

Two types of objective need to be decided. The first are the client/service type objectives which relate to what you want the firm to be known for in relation to its competitors and in terms of its reputation. The second are the 'corporate objectives' which generally relate to financial return.

The first step is to consider partners' personal goals or their requirements from the firm.

Partners' goals

Before discussing the strategic objectives for particular departments, it is important for partners to have a frank and open discussion to reveal what they personally want and need from the firm. It is useful to have this discussion during a partners' away day.

BOX 1.4 Partners' goals

Income needs are likely to be different depending on the age and commitments of the partners. Some may have substantial mortgages and school fees to pay or expensive hobbies they pursue which require significant incomes.

The pension provision partners have made is likely to influence when a partner wants to retire. This needs to be broached.

Both the above factors may influence a partner's attitudes towards investment in the practice. Partners coming up to retirement will be less willing to agree to substantial investment in capital projects when they are unlikely to see the return on them.

A younger partner looking towards decades of employment may prefer the investment now to put the practice in a strong position for the future.

The amount of capital partners have to invest and the amount of internal reserves are key to funding arrangements and costing potential investments.

Plans to reduce working hours, work part-time or to leave the practice in the next three to five years also need to be discussed.

Partners' objectives for the firm and their individual working lives are likely to vary and it cannot be assumed that everyone will have the same objectives.

Future reputation

From discussing partners' goals, the discussion should lead on to deciding an overall view of the firm – how do you want it to be seen, what do you want it to be known for in the next three to five years? What do you want its reputation to be for? It may be quite different from what it is known for now.

The SWOT summary will guide the partners in looking at the firm as a whole and deciding its medium- to longer-term goals. It may indicate, for example, that if the trend for legal aid payments/publicly funded work continues, the firm cannot make a profit out of it in A, B and C departments. If the firm is currently known in the area as being an excellent legal aid criminal litigation firm, it may have to decide to change direction and to build up its marine, commercial and conveyancing reputation in order to stay viable.

It helps if partners write down how they would like to see the firm in the next three to five years.

EXAMPLE **Aspirations of a conveyancing practice**

Partners' objectives

- to be a key supplier of remortgaging services to a major building society;
- to provide a specialist personal service to clients with properties valued over £750,000;
- to become a national firm by ultimately opening branches in Newcastle, London and Bristol specialising in bulk conveyancing transactions.

Corporate objectives

These are likely to relate to financial issues such as:

- to have gross fees of £250,000 per equity partner;
- to have a net profit of 25 per cent excluding partners' notional salaries;
- to have ratios of support staff to fee earners/partners of less than one to one;
- to have ratios of support staff to legally qualified conveyancers of seven to one;
- to have fee earner to equity partner ratios of eight to one.

Objectives hierarchy

Once the firm's objectives are agreed, the department's objectives directly contribute to the overall objectives. The team's objectives contribute to those of the department and in turn the individual's objectives contribute to the team's goals. All goals should be clearly stated and understood by those responsible for achieving them.

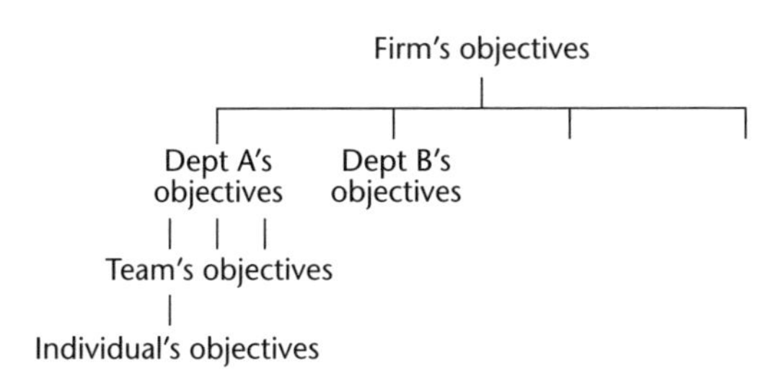

Figure 1.3 Firm's objectives

Strategic options

For the purpose of the internal plan, treat each department as a separate business unit.

A number of strategic options are available to achieve corporate objectives. Marketing objectives feed in to the corporate objectives. They relate to the range of services and the client type selected to generate turnover. The marketing objectives in Figure 1.4 show four strategic options, known as the Ansoff matrix. Additional strategic options are listed below.

	Existing clients	New clients
Existing services	Market penetration	Market development
New services	New services development	Diversification

Figure 1.4 Ansoff Matrix showing marketing objectives

Market penetration

Market penetration involves selling more of the existing services to existing clients. For example, this can involve a focus on increasing the volume of cross-referring clients across departments or doing more proactive marketing to existing clients.

The internal referral rate of clients to colleagues in other departments can improve if the practice is more client focused. Consider changing the internal structure of the firm away from being department led to being client led. Change the orientation to the needs of clients rather than the needs of the administrative structure of the firm. Think of whole-life client needs in a proactive way, rather than just responding to clients' immediate demands.

Market development

Develop the market by selling existing services to new clients. For example, expand the remortgage side by linking up with a regional building society. Focus on a new geographical area or new client type, such as first time buyers, people who buy listed properties, people in their 30s with growing families or people with properties valued at over £500,000.

New services development

An example of selling new services to existing clients is to investigate setting up an estate agency to counter the threat of estate agents using in-house conveyancers. Alternatively, the firm could set up alliances with the providers needed to complete a Home Information Pack or provide inheritance tax advice to people over 50.

Diversification

It is important to take an entrepreneurial approach to doing business. If you run a successful law firm, you are running a successful business. Your management skills can be applied to running different kinds of businesses. The risk of starting a new business will be lower if it is closely related to your current business.

Consider vertical integration of services offered – provide for the other needs of your clients at the time, just before or just after using your service.

EXAMPLE **Providing home moving solutions**

Rather than just providing conveyancing legal services, provide solutions to the problems and stresses faced by busy people moving home.

Target client type

- people aged 30–45 living in ?? postcode areas;
- those with total household income of £40,000 plus;
- professionals or management career people with little spare time.

Clients' needs identified

Clients may need:

- a new home locator;
- a home seller;
- a mortgage/finance source;
- legal services;
- a home makeover to sell their property;
- new home alterations/building/planning consents, decorations and soft furnishings, new furniture/kitchens/bathrooms/bedrooms, electrical and plumbing services;
- new schools researched;
- home help;
- to inform friends and contacts of the new address;
- a party planner for the house warming party;
- to research new areas for sports and activity clubs, transportation routes, doctors, dentists, local shopping and home delivery;
- to research religious centres.

Volume conveyancing

If you opt to increase volume, the attraction will be many clients and hopefully lower operating costs. Provision of volume conveyancing is achieved by standardising procedures and employing part-qualified or unqualified paralegals to undertake most of the work under the supervision of a solicitor or other legally qualified person. A case management system will be required to drive files through. See Box 2.1 on pp. 44–5 on the Direct Conveyancing Association.

High value, service orientation for a smaller number of clients

With a high value, service orientation objective the work is likely to be provided by qualified staff throughout, with clients having direct access to their solicitor. The provision of a close personal service will be the cornerstone to achieving the objective.

Increase cost-effectiveness

Increased turnover and maintaining or reducing the costs of servicing work will increase cost-effectiveness. This could involve the greater use of supervised lower-cost unqualified staff, or newly or part-qualified staff, for routine parts of transactions. The ratios of support staff and paralegals to solicitors or partners could increase. Aggressive marketing campaigns to gain more conveyancing fee income serviced by the existing staff is another approach that could be taken to achieve the objective.

Exit the market

Some legal services currently provided are unlikely to be profitable over three to five years. What are the profitability, potential volume and value of clients and costs trends? Address the issues of whether time and financial effort would be better spent on developing more profitable business and exiting from some areas.

To do this consider the 'loss leader' effect and how deleting one service may seriously affect the profitability of another. For example, deciding not to work for less profitable first time buyers may lead to reducing the number of clients who return to the firm in the future after using it for their first home purchase.

Specialise by client type

One tactic is to specialise by selecting target client types and to differentiate the firm from their perspective. Focus on a type of client such as veterinary surgeons, dentists, hairdressers, garage owners, etc. Alternatively, separate clients into groups of people with similar needs. Think how you can differentiate the firm in that specific group's eyes.

You could also create a new brand within the firm to differentiate the practice from others in clients' minds, such as Midlands Retail Solicitors or Lawyers for Accountants, part of ABC Solicitors. Offer a range of services specifically for the target clients which include conveyancing.

Specialise by property type

Another potential objective involves focusing on types of properties such as converted, listed or leasehold properties. Establish a brand that gives the firm a competitive advantage in the eyes of clients and referrers as being a specialist in that area.

For example, develop a brand specifically for clients wanting rural or listed properties. Consider the services those clients are likely to need and create a brand through the name, e.g. Rural Properties Solicitors, part of XYZ Solicitors or Listed Buildings Lawyers, part of ABC Solicitors. Use the brand name on brochures, advertising, in articles published in newspapers and county magazines, on letterheads and signage. The aim is to differentiate the firm from other firms in the clients' eyes by providing a specialist service to selected target clients.

SMART objectives

Objectives ideally need to be written using the SMART acronym, which stands for:

- Specific – the objective is clearly stated. It does not have the word 'and' in the sentence. If it does, it should be broken down into two separate objectives.
- Measurable – the objective has figures or measurable qualitative criteria within it. If the objective is measurable, it takes away the potential for subjectivity in determining whether it has been achieved.
- Achievable – the objective is challenging, but within reach with effort and determination.
- Relevant – to the firm, the department and the individuals charged with achieving the objective.
- Timescale – the objective should have an exact date in it.

EXAMPLE

SMART objectives focusing on particular types of clients or properties

- to increase fee income from transactional conveyancing clients with properties valued at over £350,000 by 17 per cent by 30 June 200X;
- to reduce leasehold conveyancing files to 23 per cent of the total, down from 36 per cent at present by 31 December 200X;
- to exit from the market for clients buying properties under £100,000 by 30 September 200X;
- to increase fee income by 19 per cent from clients referred from other departments by 28 February 200X;
- to gain X number of new clients from mortgage brokers who are not currently referring work to the firm by 5 April 200X.

Evaluation of objectives

A prioritised list of objectives and their implications for the firm can now be assessed. The list is then narrowed down and operational plans with the tactics to achieve the objectives are determined. These are then costed and the strategic options and tactics are either reviewed or the operational plans are put in place.

Operational plans

Operational plans state how the objectives will be achieved and at what cost (see Table 1.1).

EXAMPLE **Residential conveyancing**

You are the partner in charge of residential conveyancing. You are concerned that with the introduction of the Home Information Pack, estate agents will have an even greater influence over clients, directing them to panels of solicitors. The introduction of permission to pay referral fees is also likely to cut margins significantly.

Strategic options

- market development: expand the remortgage side by linking up with a regional building society;
- new service development: investigate setting up an estate agency to counter the threat of estate agents using in-house conveyancers.

In addition, to minimise the threat of having to pay referral fees, reduce costs on each file. Investigate the introduction of a hosted (web-based application software provider) 'ready to go' case management system whereby lower cost supervised paralegals can be used to drive files through the system. This will reduce risk and substantially cut costs. You aim to have one solicitor or legal executive to eight support staff. Your current ratio is one to two.

Tips for operational planning

Operational plans state how the strategic options will be achieved and at what cost.

Table 1.1 Operational plans chart

The following table is a simplified example of operational plans for IT, human resources and training, marketing and finance in respect of the above, for the first few months.

	IT case management	HR and training	Marketing	Finance
January	See three case management providers that use a web-hosted system.	Assess potential staffing needs and skills if case management is implemented.	Identify and target key personnel in leading local building societies and those with HQs in the area. Meet to discuss business development. Research to assess viability of setting up an estate agency. Investigate franchise options. Competitor analysis survey.	Cost IT providers, how and when to make payments and investment tax relief available. Cost out marketing, training and recruitment. Cost out setting up an estate agency. Work out break-even level, investment, working capital requirements, sales forecasts and cash flows. Organise additional funding, if required.
February	Research what other conveyancers' views are of the preferred case management system.		Aggressive marketing campaign to attract and retain clients to/for conveyancing planned for spring. Assess estate agency premises if needed. Develop relationship with building society staff.	Reach a decision on setting up an estate agency or franchise. Monthly financial analysis.

Table 1.1 continued

	IT case management	HR and training	Marketing	Finance
March	Make a decision on the case management system and agree terms.	Begin to train staff on the case management system. Advertise, recruit and train staff for estate agency, if it goes ahead. Assess fee earner numbers to determine if releasing some or redeployment is needed.	Launch of marketing campaign. Tactics to include: PR, articles in press, radio interviews, advertising in press and backs of buses, leaflet distribution, direct marketing. Plan launch campaign for estate agency.	Determine cost savings if some fee earners are released and redundancy costs. Evaluate costs against budgets. Monthly financial analysis.

If you follow an operational plan you will:

- break tasks down into their component parts;
- give timescales for each;
- give responsibility to named people;
- identify critical paths and milestones;
- undertake a risk assessment for each part;
- set measurable targets on a weekly or monthly basis;
- have a leader who keeps track of targets and receives reports on time;
- encourage people to highlight problems as soon as they arrive to avoid longer term problems;
- carry out the plan according to the schedule, making adjustments where required;
- evaluate results and act on missed targets.

Financial analysis

Potential costs, revenue and cash flow need to be stated in detail (as far as possible) for year one, and an outline given for years two and three.

The financial analysis part of the operational plans needs to include:

- break-even analysis;
- operating costs;
- cash flow;
- turnover forecasts;

- profit and loss account;
- funding needs;
- capital expenditure;
- balance sheet.

Detailed coverage of financial matters is beyond the scope of this book. For further reading see Otterburn (2003).

Departments' plans

Departments' plans dovetail or feed into the firm's business plan to ensure that each department directly contributes to achieving the firm's overall objectives. The advantage of having separate departmental plans is to assess the profitability and continued viability of each department.

It may be that a corporate decision is made to retain certain departments under the guise of providing a service or for cross-referral purposes, even when they are not particularly profitable.

Individual departments have their own operational plans. The firm's business plan is a summary of the departmental plans. Summarising the plans helps to identify overlaps and gaps.

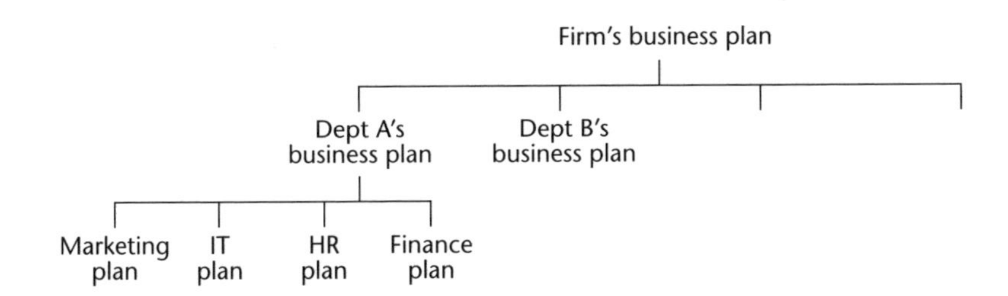

Figure 1.5 A firm's business plan

Practice Rule 15 and business planning

Any changes planned for the practice may have an impact on Practice Rule 15 information supplied to clients.

For compliance purposes, to avoid potential costs of complaints and for prudent commercial reasons, firms need to regularly review their Practice Rule 15 client care letters and terms of business. They may need to be amended to take into account changes in legislation and regulations and to incorporate new sections that include money laundering and charging for completing the Land Transaction Return forms.

This may lead to different Rule 15 information for different departments or types of transactions to avoid any confusion or misunderstandings.

If out-of-date Practice Rule 15 information is sent to clients, this could potentially lead to a series of costly problems consuming time which could otherwise be spent fee earning. There may be complaints by clients arising from lack of relevant cost information, resulting in claims on firms' professional indemnity insurance, Law Society intervention and the Law Society Consumer Complaints Service's involvement.

FURTHER READING

The Bullet Point, sample issue (2000) 'Why change fails'.

Davidson, J.H. (1987) *Offensive Marketing,* Penguin.

Jobber, David (1995) *Principles and Practice of Marketing,* McGraw-Hill.

McDonald, Malcolm H.B. (2003) *Marketing Plans,* Heinemann.

Otterburn, A. (2003) *Profitability and Law Firm Management,* Law Society Publishing.

Stutely, Richard (2002) *The Definitive Business Plan,* FT Prentice Hall.

Wilson, R.M.S., Gilligan, C. and Pearson, D. (1996) *Strategic Marketing Management,* Butterworth Heinemann.

SOURCES OF INFORMATION AND WEBSITES

National statistics (**www.statistics.gov.uk**) 2001 Census information is now available. Includes: the annual abstract of statistics; monthly digest of statistics; social trends; economic trends; census of production; business monitors; and local government economic development units.

Neighbourhood statistics (**www.neighbourhood.statistics.gov.uk**). This site includes data on the population and age, ethnic group and religious breakdown, marital status, employment activity household breakdown, average house prices, and crime rates about specific post code areas or local authority wards.

Land Registry (**www.landreg.gov.uk**).

UpMyStreet (**www.upmystreet.com**) This provides similar information to neighbourhood statistics above.

National and local and financial press. Use the Internet search engines, for example, go to **www.google.co.uk** and type in the name of the publication you want to research.

Organisations that produce business and consumer data, e.g. Financial Times Business Information Service (**www.ft.com**); Reuters (**www.reuters.co.uk**); Extel Group; Mintel; Key Note Reports.

Professional institutions:

- Chartered Institute of Marketing;
- Industrial Marketing Research Association;
- British Institute of Management;
- Institute of Practitioners in Advertising;
- Law Society (**www.research.lawsociety.org.uk**) (includes publications from the Law Society's Strategic Research Unit);
- Royal Institution of Chartered Surveyors (**www.rics.org**) (includes surveys on construction market, lettings market, and housing market).

Specialist libraries

Business school libraries

City Business Library in London

Internal records:

- client comment questionnaires;
- records of enquiries made by potential clients and not gained/followed up;
- database of existing clients;
- turnover by work type and client type.

2

Costs, pricing and product

Michael Debens

KEY POINTS

This chapter will

- provide an overview
- explain available structures
- discuss management issues
- describe key costs and how to minimise them
- review cost and credit control
- show how to maximise margins
- emphasise the importance of marketing
- explain pricing techniques
- offer thought for the future

Overview

Conveyancing is a business like any other. The same considerations apply to success as apply to any business for which you undertake work. Once this is understood, you can start planning to work profitably.

As with any business there are a significant number of ways in which conveyancing services can be delivered and you must set out to find a structure and strategy that works for you, your staff and your customers. Once you have done that you need to construct a model of your vision capable of being understood and shared with your staff and those who are or whom you would wish to be your clients.

A good starting point will be to identify the location, number and type of clients you wish to attract to your business. This will set parameters for the premises, personnel and systems required to fulfil those objectives.

Most readers will, however, not have the benefit of starting with a clean sheet, but will rather be part of an existing firm. While this will provide benefits such as established goodwill, it may equally bring with it problems in terms of premises, personnel, types of work, old fashioned methods and even poor quality clients who may be seen as insurmountable hurdles to the implementation of your model and the achievement of your goals. This may particularly be the case when you are seeking to deal with a conveyancing department in isolation from the remainder of a larger practice, where the objectives and methods of the whole may be quite different from those of your model.

In such a case two basic alternative approaches are available and you will need to decide at an early stage which you are going to adopt.

The first, and the one most people will tend toward, is to accept the limitations imposed by your current circumstances and to modify your model to allow a partial implementation to the extent permitted by those limitations.

The second and more ambitious approach is to determine that the objectives, once set, are paramount and that whatever the difficulties met, you will not hold back from taking the decisions and measures required to overcome them. Such decisions are unlikely to be easy and may, indeed, be widely unpopular, involving relocating offices, bringing in new personnel and even ceasing certain types of work or ceasing working for certain types of client entirely, with the inevitable consequences for those members of staff, including partners, who previously serviced these tasks and clients.

This requires both leadership and management skills. Without leadership, fully supported by the partnership or other power base of the business, there is no guiding light or direction for the project and no driving force behind it. Without management there is no ability to deliver, monitor or improve. However, perhaps the most important skill for the creation of a successful outcome is change management, for you will certainly have to carry others – partners, staff and clients – with you.

Looking at management as the first prerequisite to the successful creation and implementation of a plan for a profitable business, whether legal or any other, we must realise that lawyers, even good lawyers, do not always make good managers. While many lawyers have good ideas about the way law should be practised, few have the time or aptitude to structure and develop those ideas or to carry them through to final implementation. As a result, few such ideas see the light of day and even fewer achieve the level of success they deserve. How many businesses, good businesses, have you seen fail or fail to achieve their potential as the result of bad management?

With your leader, a model and a detailed plan for its implementation you are ready to start creating your business or, as appropriate, developing your existing firm to fulfil your objectives. However, to create a truly profitable business, you need to ensure that each part is developed in harmony with the remainder. There is no point in having good quality clients, if you cannot deliver the level of service they require. There is no point in delivering a high level of service if the cost of doing so is not covered by the fees you are able to charge. Equally, there is no point in delivering invoices which are not paid or are paid so late that the cost of funding the cash shortfall erodes the profit element of the bill. A good service business is a balanced, well oiled machine, with a very human face – in this case, you and your staff.

Structures and products

Historically, solicitors, and conveyancing solicitors in particular, have practised as individuals or small groups, either as High Street firms or as departments of larger firms. They have not been particular users of technology and they have seen little competition from other directions. The future is likely to be very different. There will be greater competition. There will be greater use of technology and it is likely that overheads will have to be cut to maintain margins. How can this be done?

Your vision of practice (assuming it is one for the future) will be defined by the type of work to be done, the type of client to be attracted and the level of service to be delivered, but is likely in broad terms to fit one of the following models:

1. The mass market approach will be aimed at significant levels of work of particular types (such as remortgages or registered freehold sales/purchases) and may well be based heavily on businesses (such as lenders and estate agents) able to refer volume work. This may be done by a larger single firm or a group of smaller firms acting in unison. There are likely to be fewer qualified staff and more junior staff undertaking limited and specific tasks (ratios as high as 40:1 have been achieved by some practices specialising in remortgaging and 12:1 by firms undertaking specific transactional business, in each case using sophisticated case management systems). The firm is likely to be systematised and to have invested heavily in IT. Margins may be small, but profits can be considerable, based on the volume of work undertaken. Like building societies and banks, it may be possible to offer a range of defined services at fixed prices, enabling the development of products which can be advertised like any other in a competitive market.
2. The efficient smaller firm will be aimed at a local market or dependent on Internet marketing. It will have relatively low overheads (based on inexpensive offices or even virtual offices for firms aiming to undertake Internet business). The aims and approach of the firm are likely to be more individualistic and to reflect the personality of the lead partner(s). It is likely to compete on price, local knowledge and connections. Staff may work from home and margins will be

maintained primarily by low overheads. Several firms may work together to compete for volume or referral work. The product offered may be very standard in form, albeit a range of services may not be offered, and in this way the smaller firm may also develop a definable product capable of being marketed in terms of both quality and price.

3. The specialist firm, aimed at a particular sector, will again have low overheads. It is more likely to have invested in technology. It will trade on its level of specialisation and service rather than on price. It will have a high proportion of qualified staff undertaking work (it may take as its example the London commercial firms where ratios of four and even six fee earners to one secretary have been achieved). This may well be the sort of firm that has the requisite technology and will outsource document production to external bureaux, who may be based overseas to reduce cost. Margins will be maintained by the relatively high prices the firm is able to charge combined with low office costs and potentially low support staff costs. In its own way this kind of firm is potentially as much a product as any other, in that it establishes a level of service which can be sold in the marketplace.

BOX 2.1 Direct conveyancing model

Direct conveyancing has been defined as:

> The carrying out of residential conveyancing in volume as a discrete legal service, carried out by people who are carefully selected, trained, managed and motivated, aided by the best of technology and communicating with the customer by whichever means they prefer, but increasingly electronically. Direct conveyancers operate without requiring the customer to attend on them or visa versa.
>
> *Source*: Direct Conveyancing Association

The aim of direct conveyancing is to have a more focused, transparent and hassle free service. The business model focuses on providing a person to person service aided by the best technology to meet clients' growing expectations.

Direct conveyancers differentiate themselves from traditional High Street conveyancers by emphasis on technology aided communication, such as secure web-based updates (as they happen), available to customers 24 hours a day seven days a week. They have fixed, completion only, fees and longer opening hours. However, direct conveyancers understand that this is a people to people basis and all clients have their designated case handler. The technology aids the delivery by people.

The Direct Conveyancing Association's members consist of solicitors and licensed conveyancers of varying sizes and backgrounds. The requirement is that aspiring members have sufficient critical means to provide the service on a discrete, focused basis, with adequate technological systems for volume work. Members are spread throughout the UK.

The objectives of the Association are 'the improvement of the experience for the home moving public, to take a fresh and innovative approach to that process, to drive forward opportunities to raise standards and to co-operate with all others involved in the pursuit of those objectives'. It works with estate agents, lenders, the Land Registry and others in a co-operative and consultative manner.

Direct Conveyancing Association member Goldsmith Williams, based in Liverpool, operates in the intermediary conveyancing and remortgage markets. The firm offers a seven-day service, covering the hours of 9.15 a.m. to 8.00 p.m. Monday to Friday, and 9.30 a.m. to 4.30 p.m. Saturdays and Sundays. Staff work in teams in open plan offices. Unusually for law firms, staff voted to have background music playing during the day throughout the office. A selection of jazz, local radio stations and personal CDs are played on different days. This helps staff to work more effectively.

All staff are expected to have first rate keyboard skills to utilise the case management system, therefore making the need for secretarial staff unnecessary. In addition to technical training, emphasis is placed on training staff to have sound telephone skills to understand clients' anxieties and expectations to be able to deliver a first rate service.

To some extent the choice of model to be adopted may be determined by the style of practice of your firm in other areas. However, is it necessary to conclude that only a single model can be adopted? Firms have started to achieve success by packaging and marketing specific activities, whether conveyancing, personal injury or financial services, under unique brands, but utilising the management structure already available within the firm. This allows the development of styles of practice which may be at variance with the 'core' activities of the firm, without creating a negative impact on those core activities. Such an approach offers considerable flexibility, without increasing the cost of core administration facilities. It also provides an opportunity to explore new ideas, such as the creation of saleable products, within a limited part of the practice; if the ideas are successful they may be taken up by other disciplines.

Management

Any firm must have a management structure appropriate to its commercial objectives. It must furthermore have management personnel and systems capable of providing information regarding the business and the way it operates, in order to analyse adequately how the business is performing and whether those objectives are being met. It is essential to know whether the firm as a whole is profitable, which parts of the business are most and least profitable, and whether changes made increase profitability or not. This will involve both financial management accounting and departmental reporting.

If you are not one of those fortunate lawyers who has good management skills and the time to utilise them and if your firm is not one already able to employ professional managers, you will need to consider ways of acquiring those management skills as a cornerstone of your planning process. Even if you are fortunate enough to have management skills available, you are likely to need additional expert help if you are to achieve success. Modern systems are complex and you will probably need help with management reporting, choice of IT systems, data management, marketing and probably other areas as well.

You will be well advised to involve your managers from the earliest planning stages, particularly if a profitable outcome is your objective. They will provide an alternative perspective, focusing on such 'business' issues as costing, funding, budgets and cost/benefit analysis. They can advise on personnel issues, such as training and motivation, and will most importantly look at the practicality and workability of your ideas and timescales. Systems will undoubtedly form a significant part of your plan and finding the right products to support these may prove critical. They must not only deliver the required performance, but do so within budget if profitability is to be maintained. Your managers, or your external experts, must be able to help you critically define and assess these systems in the context of your particular business and plan.

Most specialist legal software packages for lawyers have the potential to provide extensive management and marketing information. The difficult parts are to persuade users to collect and possibly input the required data accurately and then to extract information in a meaningful manner before it is interpreted and decisions made on how it is to be acted upon.

Without good raw data, you will never be able to make informed management or marketing decisions. You will therefore need to identify what information is needed for your particular purposes, before ensuring that you have the systems to collect it and staff who have been trained and understand the importance of collecting and entering data accurately. In relation to management decisions, time data will be critical, even where charging is not time based. Without accurate data on how people spend their time you will have little idea who is working well and which types of work produce the best results. You need to know what type of work each person is doing. This will be easier where the scope of work is small and strictly controlled by case management software. In other circumstances, you will want a detailed breakdown of work types, identifying whether work is sale/purchase/mortgage/other, whether freehold or leasehold, and whether you are acting for seller/buyer/lender /borrower, and you will also want data on the value of transactions. Having collected this data you will also need a method of manipulating it to provide you with the information about profitability needed for good decision making. Tools such as Crystal Reporting or Impromptu are ideal for this, although both require expertise to provide useful results.

In relation to marketing you will need to collect and maintain accurate data on your existing clients as well as obtaining the information relating to prospective clients. At the very least you need to have accurate names and addresses to allow standardised mail merging. Beyond this you will want information on the type of client to assess what sort of marketing might be appropriate, and personal information may also be valuable when deciding whom to invite to a golf day or a race day or, indeed, any other specific marketing project.

Methods of recording data may vary, but critical to the success will be your ability to convince the only people who have the information, your fee earners, to record it or otherwise provide it to you. This will involve ongoing training, in relation to both the methods and the reasons why completing the task is important. There are always competing demands on time and it is easy for administrative tasks to be postponed or abandoned if completion is not understood to be an important part of each day's normal activity.

Costs

The secret in any business that wishes to trade profitably is to control the cost of producing the product or service. In the context of conveyancing the biggest costs are staff, buildings, professional indemnity premiums, IT, administration and credit control.

Staff – the largest single recurring expense of any professional business

It is vital to get a staff structure appropriate to maximising productivity in the context of your individual 'model', i.e. the right people doing the right job for the right cost.

The balance between partners, qualified solicitors, other qualified staff and a range of support staff is an essential ingredient to profitability. In the mass market approach, this is likely to be a high ratio of support staff to partners and qualified fee earners. For those basing their business on quality of service, it is likely that the proportion of fee earners will be higher. However, even here, where client contact with the fee earner may be seen as a crucial part of the service quality, efforts will have to be made to have the procedural elements of the process handled by less expensive staff. This may be facilitated by computer software systems or merely by allowing specific tasks in relation to each transaction, for instance exchange documentation or post-completion work, to be undertaken by a single person specialising in that task.

Management of change is a key element. Existing staff are likely to resist change, and staff turnover and retention costs are a significant issue in productivity and overhead control. A balance will be needed. Existing staff may be those most resistant to change and, indeed, often not well fitted to work in the ways defined by your model; but they are often more loyal than new staff, there will be limited recruitment costs and they are people who have already been trained by you and may often prove to be the staff who will stay and see the job through. As a result, if you want to retain staff to work within your new model, you will need to prioritise change management. This will involve ensuring that staff understand what you are doing and why, together with what you want from them and how it is to be achieved. You will need to provide extensive training, and if old habits are to be changed and new skills learned, this will need to be monitored and carried out on an ongoing basis over a considerable period of time.

Systems such as case management software may enable fee earners to work in ways which increase productivity or enable less qualified and support staff to undertake a greater proportion of the work at a lower cost. This is likely to be a cornerstone of most plans, and a range of options exist. Various companies supply 'backbone' systems which have the flexibility and power to achieve objectives set by the user, but they require very considerable investment in time, money and expertise in order to construct the plans needed to achieve those objectives. As a result, these products are best suited to the larger firm with in-house IT expertise. Other systems will come with pre-constructed plans or 'starter kits', which should enable you to get up and running much more quickly, but which may to a significant degree define the way you work unless considerable time is spent redesigning the starter packages to fit your current or planned way of working. They also have the disadvantage of requiring updating whenever there are changes in the law or procedure. Yet others will come supported by the supplier. These will often be hosted by an application service provider and be provided on a cost per case basis. They will tend to be relatively sophisticated products and will be updated with changes in the law by the supplier, but they will be inflexible and you will have to be prepared to work within the parameters of the product as defined by others. However, this may suit the smaller firm looking for a sophisticated product, particularly one wishing to work as a marketing group with others, as all the firms could offer a standardised package, with any reporting facilities required by particular referrers of business.

Outsourcing of secretarial services may become increasingly practical. This is likely to utilise digital dictation to facilitate transmission by e-mail. The use of e-mail will mean that distance becomes less significant and the transcription bureaux could be abroad as easily as in other parts of the UK, with consequent savings in costs. This process can already be seen in other industries, where call centres and similar operations have been moved from low cost parts of the UK overseas to maintain quality while gaining the benefit of lower wage levels, and there is no reason to assume that this would not be equally effective in the legal profession. Indeed, there are already examples of larger firms such as Allen & Overy moving document production departments overseas. Such larger practices and the bigger mass market firms may be able to create their own arrangements and others may be able to make use of bureau services as these become more popular.

In the short term secretarial efficiency is likely to be improved by better dictation systems. Digital dictation provides better quality, ease of transmission for transcription where fee earners are working away from the office, and ease of distribution between secretaries, whether they are in the office or working from home. Such systems offer the possibility of breaking the dependence of fee earners on individual secretaries and may reduce the number of secretaries needed. They may also increase efficiency within the group of secretaries employed by maximising utilisation of each secretary's time, thus ensuring some are not overworked while others have spare time; facilitating the redistribution of work. It should also reduce tensions between support staff.

Dependence on secretarial services may in due course be further reduced by voice recognition systems, which will automate the production of documents from digitally dictated material. These already exist and some firms have had considerable success using them. They are bound to improve and at some stage are likely to play a significant role in the efficient lawyer's office.

There may also be opportunities for outsourcing in other areas, such as management functions, IT support, marketing, human resources, etc., further reducing your fixed costs. For smaller firms, the creation of groups may allow cost savings from sharing overhead expenses or, alternatively, you may be able to bring in new skills which no one firm on its own could afford. This may become particularly important in the area of marketing, where firms are in competition with larger firms or legal work is being handled by businesses outside the profession (with the Tesco law concept particularly in mind).

Buildings – often the largest fixed cost of a professional business

What sort of building is appropriate to your business? Those who need high quality offices are likely to decide on grounds of location and cost that these should not be in town centres, but rather located in out of town business parks with good parking. Those who feel that they need to be in the centre of town as part of their marketing strategy are likely either to look for secondary locations or perhaps to have small head office premises in prime locations and secondary offices elsewhere to minimise costs. You may also seek to reduce your dependence on offices by using technology to allow work to be done either from home or by bureaux located elsewhere, possibly outside the country.

Larger firms or groups of firms may decide to utilise more than one building and location to allow for different trading patterns or cost saving. They may have small in-town head offices for client meetings, with out of town processing centres where the work generated can be undertaken more cost-effectively, using staff who can be recruited at a lower cost. Equally, firms that adopt the idea of more than one trading style may be able to use cheaper accommodation for some operations without affecting the style of their core business. Groups of firms may naturally operate in different environments and may be able to exploit this by concentrating certain services in individual members' offices for the benefit of the group as a whole. So one firm in a low cost area might take over secretarial work for the whole group, while another provides city centre meeting facilities and others provides particular specialisations.

Whatever decisions are taken, the effective use of your buildings is an essential element in productivity. Few firms can afford to occupy excessively expensive space or to underutilise the space they do occupy or to pay the cost of expensive offices to carry out relatively unprofitable work.

More flexible working patterns may be an important element in the better use of space. Two shifts per day would double the utilisation of the same space. Investing in technology may allow home-working, which in turn may allow either expansion without increasing fixed overheads or underutilised buildings to be sold off. Similar benefits may also be derived from the use of technology to allow for outsourcing secretarial work to other parts of the country or the world where staff costs are lower. It may even in due course be possible to outsource professional work overseas. In the meantime, offices will become more in the nature of administrative hubs providing core support and communications facilities.

Professional indemnity premiums – a growing issue for most firms

Conveyancing is viewed as a high risk area of practice and premiums are calculated accordingly. When the Solicitors' Indemnity Fund published comparative risk factors in its explanatory notes for firms on renewal, conveyancing was rated at nearly double the next highest risk and more than 5,000 per cent higher than debt collection work. Successful firms will, therefore, be organised to minimise this risk and the financial costs associated with it, in terms of both compensation for errors and the consequential effects on the cost of maintaining insurance cover.

Failure to persuade insurance companies that you can carry out work with a minimum of risk may jeopardise your ability to continue in the business at all. Firms will, therefore, invest in management systems and implement the procedures associated with standards such as Lexcel, with a view to ensuring that risks are identified and dealt with in a pro-active manner. Firms are also likely to invest in training to allow staff to identify and deal with these issues more effectively.

In addition to establishing clear standards to which fee earners are required to work, an important part of any system will be a review procedure, to ensure compliance. This will normally include a regular file review process carried out by a fee earner's peers or superior.

Case management systems, in addition to providing benefits in the form of increased efficiency, also allow a greater degree of control over the way any particular service is delivered and are a method of recording that important steps in any transaction have been actioned at the correct time. They will ensure standardisation of documents and process, allowing anyone in a trained group to pick up and deal with a file quickly and efficiently. They will provide prompts whenever decisions regarding the progress of a matter are or should be made. They can create a record page to show at a glance its current status, assisting fee earners to provide information to clients and third parties quickly. They can automate the distribution of information to clients, agents and others to save valuable time within the fee earning team. When taken together, these can significantly reduce the major factors resulting in client dissatisfaction and claims for negligence.

Case management can address issues of delay, failure to carry out tasks when required and can ensure use of up-to-date forms and precedents. Knowledge management systems are a way to address similar issues in relation to professional education. You cannot afford to have only some of your fee earners fully up to date on the law and procedures relevant to their area of practice. Knowledge management systems help you to identify information relevant to particular groups of fee earners, to distribute it quickly to all relevant fee earners at the same time and then to retain that information in a way that ensures that it can be located whenever it is needed.

IT – another area of major expenditure for most firms today

IT is a complex area that today links to every aspect of our business as conveyancers and will increasingly do so in the future. Many firms' current systems are the result of a series of relatively unconnected decisions made over a period of years and as a result often suffer from a lack of integration. To change this and to get a real return on IT, strategic investment planning is essential and should form an integral element of the work that goes into your business plan.

Always bear in mind the need to future proof your systems, insofar as this is possible. These are big investment decisions and will take time to provide you with a return. This means they need to be able to develop and continue in use, making the most of your training, for a considerable time.

Once you have decided upon your requirements, how do you manage the process of acquisition and maintenance? The Law Society produces helpful material on the range of products available in the marketplace and the principal suppliers. While this is limited in scope it may be a useful starting point. However, there is no substitute for independent expertise when evaluating systems. It is dangerous in the extreme to assume that products will perform in accordance with suppliers' sales pitches, at least without a very considerable element of additional investment from your firm. Again, once you have determined the systems to be adopted and the suppliers to provide those systems, the process of implementation will need expert management to succeed and this will to a large extent be a process of communication and training.

In the context of budgeting for IT investment, do not underestimate the cost of integration and implementation. To achieve a high level of integration will often preclude adoption of the cheapest solution to individual needs. Training is not cheap in terms of time out from fee earning work or provision of trainers, but the failure to provide adequate training is probably one of the biggest reasons for the actual or perceived failure of such systems to deliver the desired rewards in practice.

The true objective of IT investment should be a specific and planned return on that investment. IT for its own sake rarely makes a contribution to profitability. Planning must, therefore, include an assessment of the benefits to be derived and the methods needed to measure the success of acquisition, training and use. The results of such measurements should be reviewed periodically to assess success and, more importantly, to identify areas of weakness which might be addressed to improve the performance of users.

Case management systems are likely to play an increasing role with the introduction of e-conveyancing. Standardisation of communication with the Land Registry systems will create an opportunity best exploited by automated systems in the lawyer's office.

On this issue see also Chapter 3 and Chapter 15.

Administration – an essential part of all organisations

As with IT, your business plan needs to focus on the management team, its structure and the roles and cost of individuals. Good internal management is an essential of success, without necessarily contributing directly to output. A bad plan will seek to reduce the management team simply to save overheads. A good plan will focus on how to get the management skills required for success at the lowest price.

The management team will be critical to the process of change. They will have significant contributions to make to the planning process and they are critical to providing the support needed by those in charge of the personnel involved to facilitate change.

The skills of the management team may be utilised to assist in the evaluation of departments, teams and individuals to highlight and to suggest ways of addressing issues of delay and inefficiency.

Within the management team you will need to ensure that the person management skills needed to assess the requirements for implementation are present, including those required for training. These skills will also be needed to assist in effective implementation of change.

The management team will also play a role in ensuring that systems comply with relevant legislation. This now extends beyond the rules specifically for lawyers, such as the accounts rules, and will need to encompass such issues as compliance with money laundering regulations.

Credit control – the lifeblood of your business

Even work efficiently done is of no value if that work is not correctly billed and those bills paid in a timely fashion.

Everyone quoting for work should be trained to ensure they understand and can explain to potential clients the firm's policy on quality of service and fees.

The firm should have a clear policy on disbursements and the need to obtain funds from clients before third party costs are incurred. This will be particularly important for new clients.

Clients need to be vetted to avoid the firm acting for those who are unlikely to pay or who will always insist on a reduction in the bill which eliminates the profit element of work or for those who will complain or allege negligence, which can be costly in time and money as well as affecting the reputation of the firm. Such clients may change firms regularly; they may have stories of how poorly they regard the standard of service offered by your competitors; they may spend a lot of time on the phone over apparently trivial matters and seem to demand levels of service disproportionate to the fees to be paid. As with quoting fees, it will be important to train the individuals responsible for taking on work to identify and deal with clients potentially falling into this group.

There may be no point in doing work which does not provide a profit at the end of the day, unless for a clear and costed marketing objective, i.e. to keep clients whose other work is valuable or as a loss leader to gain new and otherwise valuable clients.

Margins

In the world of profitability, the two primary issues are volume and margins. Having settled on the type and volume of work to be done, you need to set targets for the profit to be derived from that work, your margin. Without a target, you have no baseline to work from or objective to measure success against. A series of issues are likely to affect your margin:

- the cost of the business – the cost of bringing in new clients from different sources may vary and marketing for new clients may have a higher cost than increasing income from existing clients;
- the level of turnover – the greater the levels, the smaller the margin may be;
- the level of automation and delegation you can achieve in undertaking the work;
- the type of client – some will be willing to pay more than others, based on perceived quality of service. Others may generate repeat business, giving an increased return on the initial investment made;
- some jobs may be much more profitable than others – registered freehold conveyancing may be much more profitable than unregistered work or leasehold work. Do you have the means to measure or a model which allows you to develop profitable work types?
- your ability to recover the time needed to meet new administrative tasks – as an example, will you be able to automate the process of completing the new Stamp Duty Land Tax forms or will you be able to increase your costs to cover the time involved? If not your margins will suffer;
- your risk in relation to abortive work – can you recover the cost of time in such circumstances? Similarly, if it is necessary to prepare a Home Information Pack, what will it cost and will you be able to recover that cost?
- whether you have to pay a third party for the business, by way of referral fee or otherwise;

- whether you have to pay out money on behalf of the client, with its effect on cash flow, and your level of risk in terms of recovery;
- some work may be intrinsically unprofitable and may need to be ceased unless it can be demonstrated that it has an acceptable return in a marketing context.

The majority of these are a function of structure and cost control. Others will be affected by marketing and pricing.

The Centre for InterFirm Comparison enables law firms to compare with others the efficiency of their practice, to identify areas for potential cost saving and to set benchmarks for productivity development. By way of example, Table 2.1 shows for conveyancing, the profitability, charge-out rates, conveyancing staff time by category and additional conveyancing ratios of a selection of firms listed as K–T, in the Midlands, with five equity partners. If some of the figures of firm S are compared to the median figures, the following are apparent:

- Revenue per conveyancing staff member is above the median and cost per conveyancing staff member is below, leading to higher gross profit per member than the median.
- Revenue per fee earner is below the median. Firm S's commercial conveyancing is only 3 per cent of total revenue compared to the median of 17 per cent.
- Domestic conveyancing contributes 23 per cent of total revenue compared to 16 per cent for the median.
- There are no details for growth in revenue. The median is 10 per cent growth. The gross profit from conveyancing for firm S is 56 per cent. This is marginally above the median of 54 per cent.

Care must be taken when comparing figures for firms, and median figures may be deceptive. Many factors relating to individual firms or the way in which figures are recorded or calculated may not be apparent from a simple table, and in reality figures vary considerably from the median. For example, gross profit from conveyancing is shown as varying from 28 per cent to 61 per cent and revenue growth varies from minus 3 per cent to plus 31 per cent.

If used carefully, and notwithstanding the difficulties of interpretation, such figures do form a useful basis, enabling a firm to benchmark itself against other similar firms in its region, and thus they provide a valuable basis of comparison.

Table 2.1 Interfirm comparison table – conveyancing

Midlands Firms		K	L	M	N	O	P	Q	R	S	T	FIRMS K – T 2ND HIGH	MEDIAN	2ND LOW
Profitability														
A1 Revenue per conveyancing staff member	£000	45.9	88.4		67.1	61.3	46.2	45.0	35.2	52.0	42.9	67.1	46.2	42.9
A2 Cost per conveyancing staff member	£000	21.2	35.2		26.2	27.9	23.2	27.5	25.4	23.1	21.5	27.9	25.4	21.5
A3 Gross profit per conveyancing staff member	£000	24.6	53.2		41.0	33.4	23.0	17.4	9.8	28.9	21.4	41.0	24.6	17.4
A4 less share of administration staff cost	£000	2.2	8.1		1.6	3.6	2.6	4.6	4.4	2.7	4.1	4.6	3.6	2.2
A5 Contribution per member of the conveyancing department	£000	22.4	45.2		39.4	29.8	20.4	12.8	5.4	26.2	17.3	39.4	22.4	12.8
Charge-out rates per hour														
A6 a. Partners	£	-	185		-	180	120	-	-	155	150	180	155	150
b. Assistant Solicitors	£	-	150		-	150	100	113	-	145	140	150	143	113
c. Legal executives	£	-	70		-	100	100	85	78	125	135	125	100	78
d. Trainee Solicitors	£	-	70		-	75	75	-	85	-	80	80	75	75
Conveyancing staff time by staff category														
A7 a. Partners	%	13	12		23	11	12	-	-	12	12	13	12	-
b. Assistant Solicitors	%	13	29		12	21	15	60	-	12	12	29	13	12
c. Legal executives	%	-	6		23	21	15	20	70	29	12	29	20	6
d. Trainee Solicitors	%	-	6		-	5	9	-	15	-	3	9	3	-
e. Typists	%	74	47		42	42	48	20	15	47	61	61	47	20
Total	%	100	100		100	100	100	100	100	100	100	100	100	100

Midlands Firms		K	L	M	N	O	P	Q	R	S	T	FIRMS K – T 2ND HIGH	FIRMS K – T MEDIAN	FIRMS K – T 2ND LOW
Additional Conveyancing Ratios														
A8 Revenue per fee earner in the conveyancing department	£000	177.7	167.0		115.5	105.8	89.4	56.2	41.5	98.3	108.8	167.0	105.8	56.2
A9 a. Commercial conveyancing as % of total revenue	%	-	41		3	25	9	10	na	3	1	25	17	1
b. Domestic conveyancing as % of total revenue	%	67	-		85	8	37	9	7	23	18	67	16	7
(See note below)														
A10 Revenue growth	%	(3)	8		14	4	31	(2)	20	-	(2)	20	10	(2)
A11 Gross profit from conveyancing	%	54	60		61	54	50	39	28	56	50	60	54	39
A12 Contribution from conveyancing	%	49	51		59	49	44	29	15	50	40	51	49	29
A13 Conveyancing dept. handle commercial conveyancing?		Yes	Yes		Yes	Yes	Yes	Yes	No	Yes	Yes			

N.B. Where A13 is 'No' only the costs and revenue of domestic conveyancing are included in this appendix. Ratios A9 and A10 are weighted averages

Marketing

How you present yourself to the marketplace will play a vital role in whether your model succeeds or not. Part of presentation is the standard of service and client care received by those who have reason to have contact with your business (whether as a result of advertising, visiting your offices or contact with your personnel). Another element is the way you present or package the services you offer. Here there are a number of considerations:

- your clients along with your staff are your greatest assets – the retention of those clients should be a top priority. Client care and relationship management are key to this;
- it is axiomatic, but it is always easier to market additional services to existing clients than to acquire new clients. The development, improvement and use of an accurate database is fundamental to success in this area;
- what is the place of traditional marketing (information distribution/seminars/seller packs/etc.)? Can you develop databases or other information sources to support or otherwise help clients, adding value to your service? Can you make use of specialist packages to support marketing initiatives, such as client relationship software?
- use of IT (particularly case management) to package the way services are provided may allow services to be targeted at particular parts of the market – the price conscious, first-time buyers, those remortgaging – at a fixed price or on price terms which are attractive;
- the ability to generate referral work;
- offering added benefits to make the process easier, perhaps by extending the scope of your service, say, by preparing Home Information Packs, or making the process safer, perhaps offering 'no sale no fee' as part of a packaged price. Alternatively, you might seek to add indirect benefit by allowing clients to undertake tasks themselves or to answer questions without incurring the cost of speaking to fee earners, along the lines of the Blue Flag Internet site offered by Linklaters.

Pricing

Both existing and potential customers for legal services are becoming increasingly willing to review the marketplace rather than relying on loyalty. Many will still regard a perceived level of quality in the service offered as a determining factor in choosing an adviser, but increasingly customers are willing to accept that a range of providers are able to offer an acceptable level of service, and the determining factor between those providers is thus the price of the service on offer.

Pricing structure and transparency of pricing will therefore be fundamental to success. The most common approach is, and is likely to remain, fixed fee quotes and this trend may be reinforced by further steps to ensure that the purchaser of the service knows what it is going to cost from inception. This may be achieved by:

- packaging of services, so that the purchaser buys a level of service that can be delivered for that price. This would leave the parties to discuss the cost of additional services should the need for them arise;
- no move, no fee, removing from the client the risk of abortive costs;
- contracts with referrers who will provide volume business of agreed types at an agreed fee, with the volume acting in effect as insurance to balance the difficult cases with the easier;
- considering the ability of title insurance to fix the cost of the transaction for the client.

If the client is not obliged to meet abortive costs, then the cost of that abortive work will have to be addressed in your pricing strategy. In practice, the fees charged to all will have to include an element to contribute to those cases where work is abortive – in effect, all clients will pay an insurance premium to exclude that risk. This might be part of your standard fee or it could be a separate element, with clients perhaps being offered the choice of whether they want to pay the extra for the benefit of this protection.

The principal alternative will be a fee based on the amount of work done, and this traditionally has been measured by the number of hours spent on the particular transaction. While fair to both parties on a case by case basis, most potential customers are wary because they have no way of knowing in advance what they will have to pay, and there is no insurance element, should they be unlucky enough to have a particularly difficult and time-consuming transaction. This fee basis is perhaps more common today where conveyancing is not a core service, but is offered as an addition to other services charged to the same client on a time basis. Clients' fears can be addressed by:

- fixing hourly rates, perhaps linked to the type or value of the transaction, so that registered freeholds are charged at a lower rate (or assumed to be dealt with by a different level of fee earner) than, say, leaseholds;
- parameter pricing, with an agreed minimum and maximum, with a basis of calculation within those parameters based on the degree of difficulty or time spent.

All pricing structures are open to modification to cover such issues as:

- client discrimination – those who are able to pay more are asked to do so;
- variation dependent on the required level of service;
- competition – this would vary price over time to keep in line with local competitors;
- seasonal variations – the level of work at some periods of the year may allow higher prices to be charged, because securing enough work is not an issue.

The future

The one certainty of commercial life today appears to be that the environment in which solicitors trade will continue to change, and change at an increasingly fast pace.

To deal with this it is not enough to wait and see. You must be proactive in your planning and preparation, whether dealing with change in the substantive law, in procedures or in market conditions. Change offers opportunity to those who see it coming and are able to effectively adapt to take advantage. This requires a high level of planning within your management structure.

Think ahead. Be aware of probable changes and position your firm to deal with them effectively. Look at the ways other professional firms are developing, whether practising in the area of law or otherwise. Keep an eye on new competitors who would like to enter your marketplace. Be prepared for the changes in technology which may give you the competitive edge or which may be needed to comply with the requirements of either clients or introducers. Keep abreast of developments in your industry, whether it be the requirement for new forms and procedures, Home Information Packs, online search facilities, e-conveyancing opportunities or otherwise.

Those who find the right solutions first will always have an edge on others. This involves medium-term planning, in the context of managing both the affected department and the firm as a whole. This may best be dealt with at specific cross-group meetings, where a variety of different views and skills can be brought together, with the necessary time allocated to pay attention to the day-to-day needs of the business.

Take action. We have all heard those who talk a good tale; but what value is the best insight into the future, if nothing is done to equip a firm to deal with it or exploit it? This will require the involvement of all those affected. Form working groups responsible for the development of the idea and its implementation, fully coordinated with decision makers and managers. Make sure you have the support of those who need to put the ideas into practice and that they are fully supported and trained in that process.

3

Using IT to improve profitability

Malcolm Price

KEY POINTS

This chapter will provide a brief overview of available technology and explain the possible benefits and drawbacks of systems for:

- case management
- practice management
- document production
- document management
- client relationship management

Assumptions

It is assumed that anyone currently involved in residential conveyancing will at least have some basic technology (fax, PCs, printers, accounts software and Internet access) and that most will be using e-mail; that a lot of firms have at least basic practice management software; and that many medium-sized firms will have some experience of case management (CM) software (although it may be outdated and, with a few exceptions, is unlikely to have been developed to its full capability).

Brief description of available IT

Basics

It is necessary to be able to produce documents and management information and to communicate within your own firm and with the outside world. Nowadays this presupposes the use of word processing and modern telephone systems but also includes for almost all practitioners some use of e-mail. Many firms also now use the Internet, not only to receive information but to send it to clients and referrers or, at least, make it available to them.

Thus, to go with your PCs and telephones you will have printers, servers, modems, fax machines and, perhaps, scanners. At the bottom end of the scale you have the obligatory (at least for now) photocopiers and the franking machine. Advice on the acquisition of any of these items is simple – if you do not know enough about it to make an informed judgement yourself find somebody to advise you, who does not have a vested interest in the sale. There are a number of reputable independent legal IT consultants about. Seek a couple of recommendations from other firms like yours.

Do not feel obliged to discard old equipment just because you have had it a while and it looks worn out. Do so only when it is worn out or is obviously missing functions which you (and not the salesperson for new equipment) perceive to be essential.

With every purchase of basic equipment, ask yourself two questions:

- Do I need it (i.e. can I see clearly how it will pay for itself by increasing productivity or reducing cost elsewhere)?
- If it has functionality I am unlikely to use, is there a simpler and cheaper version?

Case management (CM)

A CM system is not a substitute for a conveyancer. However, it may help the conveyancer to be more productive by carrying out some tasks in an automated manner and allowing a number of other tasks to be carried out safely by less experienced members of the conveyancer's team. A well-written system will maintain a consistently good level of letter and other document presentation in a concise and (most importantly) understandable form. But it is in the realm of risk management and limitation that a fully developed system will be of greatest value – something of which professional indemnity insurers are increasingly aware. Not all conveyancers will want to learn new CM techniques but management may find itself having to insist.

Briefly, CM systems run a process which links information held on databases with a library of forms, precedent letters and other documents in a chronological or 'action on demand' basis. In the past customers had to 'develop' their own system from a very basic platform provided by a legal IT provider or, in the case of large firms, on a platform which they had developed themselves. More recently, 'fully developed' conveyancing CM systems have become available which have the advantage of saving hundreds (some claim thousands) of hours of development time but have the disadvantage of requiring conveyancers to use someone else's style in their letters and documents.

An effective, fully developed CM application may offer conveyancers the following benefits:

- the potential for increasing profitability without prejudicing client satisfaction (basically increasing the bills delivered/staff cost ratio);
- the quality of letter and other document production referred to earlier;
- the possibility for smaller firms to compete with the bigger players on a more level playing field;
- the reduction in risk of negligence claims and accounting errors; and
- an improvement in the ability to report to referrers and clients.

People and 'buy-in'

It should be remembered that CM is only a tool and that people remain the most important component in the process. The systems rely on accurate information, both at inception and during the gestation of the sale or purchase. Well-developed systems will produce prompts, reminders and guidance, but these can frequently be overridden. Systems also have to be aimed at a particular level of expertise so that, to keep experienced practitioners from climbing the wall, a certain degree of knowledge and training will always have to be presumed. Thus the system will only assist in improving client satisfaction if the people using it are up to the task.

Problems may arise when persuading more experienced practitioners to 'buy in' to a system which does not permit them to tailor every letter to the particular client or requires them to accept a format for the completion statement which, despite being guaranteed to pick up every disbursement automatically and never let them miss a second charge, may not be quite the layout with which they are most familiar.

If you are prudent with what you spend on all other cost components of your profit and loss account then the key element in improving profitability is the staff cost to bills delivered ratio ('the golden ratio'). A CM application properly chosen, commissioned and used should enable each fee earner or team to complete more cases in any given period, but the benefits will inevitably take time to filter through.

Development

Remember that most CM systems, particularly those provided by companies which major in practice management software, are only basic platforms and need a great deal of effort and time to customise and develop (which most users fail to do adequately).

Once you have committed to a particular application you will come to rely on the system and its stability. Down time must be kept below 0.05 per cent. Thus a robust network managed by knowledgeable and reliable IT people will be essential. It may be that you have those skills (many practitioners – including sole practitioners – do have the necessary knowledge and enthusiasm). You may, however, outsource your IT support. There are no rights or wrongs here – it is simply a matter of choosing the arrangement with which you are most comfortable.

Training

There is absolutely no point in investing heavily in other aspects of CM if you do not give training top priority. In time your best conveyancers and other team members are likely to be those you have 'grown' yourselves.

Cost

Whichever route you choose to take, the cost is not insignificant. If you want to go it alone the up-front cost in terms of hardware and software will be a five- or six-figure sum (some of the largest operators have spent millions). Added to that will be the cost, in terms of time and delay, in having to add your own letters and documents. For those firms that go for a fully developed application running on their own network, the likely method of charging is on a per case basis (something between £15 and £25 at the date of publication).

Firms choosing the application service provider (ASP) route will have little to outlay in capital costs, but the per case cost is greater. This is an Internet hosted service. In other words, someone else owns, pays for and maintains the servers running the application to which you have subscribed, and provides 'bug fixes' and updates the application. All you need is a PC and access to the Internet. You pay, in one form or another, a fee for this service.

Imperatives

Return on investment is a crucial issue and adequate volumes of cases need to be available to justify the investment. To profit from CM you will need to:

- plan – the principles of business planning in general are dealt with in Chapter 1 and IT planning comes later in this chapter;
- manage client and referrer expectations (see Chapter 12);
- develop the system (unless you have acquired a fully developed system);
- commit to and strictly enforce the necessary training (initial and ongoing);
- ensure 'buy-in' at all levels and effective implementation;
- police the use of the system. Left to their own devices most practi-

tioners will revert to their old ways and your investment will finish up being used as a glorified (or, from a risk management viewpoint, inglorious) word processing system.

The following mantra is worth remembering: no system is ever finished; no system is infallible.

Benefits

The following benefits may accrue from the successful implementation of a CM system:

1. Examining your business processes will reveal things which you can change for the better.
2. Your firm will be better placed to adapt to the changes planned for the implementation of e-conveyancing.
3. Clients will be better informed by post, e-mail or online status reports. Any delay in keeping clients and referrers up to date inevitably results in chasing phone calls which slow down the process and lead to a downward spiral of inefficiency.
4. A well-written system will prompt and guide the operator at every stage, resulting in fewer errors. It may be that your fee earners have never failed to pick up a disbursement and that you are 100 per cent confident that there is no risk of someone in your firm accounting to a client for the balance proceeds of a sale without retaining the amount required to repay the second charge. However, as the number and quality of experienced conveyancers decreases and the drive to improve the 'golden ratio' of staff costs to billing becomes more pressing, the risks increase. CM will not necessarily save you from the unscrupulous or totally reckless employee but it should materially reduce your overall risk.
5. You will be able to market to volume providers and local referrers because:
   - you will be able to build real-time automated reporting into the system;
   - you will demonstrate that you are progressive.
6. Increased effectiveness of teams (including the basic conveyancer and secretary model) enables you to ensure that expensive people do not do simple repetitive tasks.
7. Tasks such as requesting Land Registry searches will be automated. Fully developed systems will produce virtually everything you need, including draft contract, pre-contract report to client and a completion statement which picks up all paid and anticipated disbursements and the amounts required to repay all charges.

8. There will be reduced reliance on the paper file – for example, with an up-to-date case history and a forward diary available immediately on screen, the person picking up the phone can field a large proportion of enquiries, but beware the effect on customer satisfaction of stressed clients not getting the comfort of a familiar voice.
9. Savings will result from fewer errors, in terms of fewer claims and cheaper professional indemnity insurance.
10. You will be able to produce management reports on such issues as:
    - number of live files (it is not sufficient to know how many files have been incepted. In the case of sales you will also want to know how many of them have a purchaser as most will be incepted at or soon after the agent receives instructions to put the property on the market);
    - allocation of those files;
    - ageing of files;
    - which cases have reached designated stages or milestones;
    - abortives as a percentage of inceptions (vital for cash forecasting);
    - comparative performance of teams and individuals;
    - average turn round times, fees, etc.

Practice management (PM)

Legal PM systems have developed out of the early basic accounting software. Their main purpose is to provide financial information to a range of people within the organisation. Typically a system will provide:

- a Solicitors' Accounts Rules (SAR) compliant accounting function for posting of transactions and procedures from which are derived those reports which the SAR require (such as month end reconcilations);
- management reports on such matters as bills delivered, time recorded, aged debtors and disbursements, and nominal bank balances;
- VAT information;
- draft profit and loss and balance sheet;
- a 'fee earner desktop' which enables time posting and ledger viewing;
- archiving information.

The Law Society publishes an annual guide to PM software, *Software Solutions* (see **www.lawsociety.org.uk/productsandservices/services/usingtechnology/softwaresolutions.law**). The systems of those included in the guide are put through a rigorous process of evaluation. While most of the major providers are there it must be remembered that only those who volunteer their products for scrutiny (and pay the fee) are included. Do not be surprised if your preferred CM provider does not appear. At the time of writing the guide only deals with PM systems.

Using a PM system for financial management

If you do not have a PM system or, as part of your IT planning, are thinking of changing the one you have, it is worth considering why you might want to have one. The answer is that the more information you have about your business the better the chance of making the right decisions at the right time. A quick response to changes in the market or to your firm's performance is difficult but can make the difference between success and mere survival.

Management accounts

Reviewing your financial performance will provide one of the indicators of what you might expect for the future. Most firms will have accounts staff and all but the smallest will have someone capable of producing management accounts. This can be a laborious and time consuming process and it may be weeks before they are published. You can be half way through a quarter before you know how you fared in the quarter before. That is no way to run a business. Any decent PM system will have the capability of producing a balance sheet and profit and loss account at the push of a button.

Unfortunately it is not quite as simple as that because, as with basic CM systems, you need to put a considerable amount of time and effort into setting the system up, otherwise the figures which you produce will be meaningless.

Benchmarking and key ratios

A PM system can and should be used to produce reports for the managers of the business on key areas of performance. Some key areas are explained below.

Staff costs to turnover – 'the golden ratio'

This is the single most important issue in determining profitability, and probably the most difficult to control within an operation of some size. You have to know what this figure is historically and be able to work out what it is likely to be. Relatively small percentage improvements can have a dramatic effect on net profit. Because of continuing pressure from staff for increases in salary you will need to be proactive in continually improving productivity. All pretty basic stuff – but impossible without accurate and up-to-date financial information. Running reports in relation to teams (even one fee earner plus one secretary is a 'team') enables you to benchmark teams' performance against each other. Using the information to benchmark against competitors is more difficult, although those accountants who target law firms tend to produce benchmark surveys and these can be useful, if only to check that your figures are not too far adrift from the rest of the pack.

There is a risk to client satisfaction and of exposure to claims in driving the staff cost base too low. Salaries and conditions need to be attractive to people with the right levels of expertise and intelligence to perform the tasks you require well. Too few people and the good ones you have may well leave or simply be too stressed to work. It does happen. This is where a properly developed and used CM system can be of value.

Establishment costs to turnover

A PM system will enable management to monitor expenditure against budget quite simply. If you do not monitor and actively look to control costs, they will increase at a faster rate than turnover. There is hardly a firm that has not had this experience in some part of its business in recent years.

Profit to turnover

It is absolutely pointless pursuing turnover for its own sake – it must be profitable turnover and the level of profit must reflect the effort and risk. You cannot judge whether the offer of work from a referrer who asks you to work to a particular scale of fees will make an adequate profit unless you have accurate and detailed financial information of the type available from a good PM system properly used.

Periodic comparisons

It is possible to place too much reliance on comparisons with the past, particularly as circumstances change. The fact that a particular team has turned over £5,000 more in this quarter than last is not to be regarded as 'a good thing' if at the end of the last quarter you added an additional member to the team whose salary and National Insurance contributions amount to £2,000 per month (although that person might only just be getting into his or her stride and justify your decision by helping to produce a £10,000 increase in the next quarter). Some of the comparisons available are:

- actual to budget for any items for any period;
- this month with last month;
- this month with the same month last year;
- year to date with same period last year.

Cash management

Your PM system will help you to produce your cash flow forecasts, which you need not only for your own purposes but also for your bankers. It will also enable management to monitor on a daily basis your actual cash resource/requirement. The overnight use of the money market can materially improve the amount of interest earned on client money and the PM system will assist with this. Credit control should not be such an issue for residential conveyancers as it is in other disciplines because funds will be in place to cover your fees at or before completion. If you do complete without being paid en route then the PM system should enable you to report on your debtors and facilitate rigorous pursuit of what is due.

Performance

We have made passing reference above to performance monitoring. You need to know how your conveyancers and their teams are performing, and the good ones will want you to know.

The fee earner will tend to concentrate on only two figures, what is billed and what he or she earns. Management and the fee earner know that the total cost of earning those fees is as important as the gross fees billed and that the fee earner's salary is only one component. The ability to produce, say, monthly figures which accurately reflect individual and team performance enables the manager to encourage and reward those who are doing well and to tackle promptly those who are not.

Performance monitoring should not, of course, be limited to the financial aspects as other areas which you should be monitoring will have their impact on profitability. Although a fully developed and used CM system will usually be the better tool for reporting on these other areas, a good PM system can also be used to report on:

- the number of current files and the current value thereof – it is a moot point whether or not time recording in residential conveyancing transactions is cost effective. Some would say that it is the only way to judge if you are charging enough. The writer is not persuaded, as profitability can be calculated by other means;
- the number of files incepted in a given period (in the writer's firm the teams monitor them daily and a weekly report is produced to the management board);
- the number of files which have exchanged (both in total and within a given period);
- how much cash will be generated by the exchanged matters and when;
- how much in disbursements the conveyancers have failed to recover (in theory this should be zero but it does happen);

- the individual and average times from inception to exchange and from inception to payment.

Use of this information can be both predictive and retrospective – retrospective in the sense of spotting that a problem has occurred and promptly taking the appropriate remedial action, predictive, for instance, in the use of inception figures to estimate income three months hence (or whatever your average turn round time may be).

Interpreting inception figures is not straightforward:

1. The system will need to have been running for a while before you can get usable average times.
2. A slow down in the market may have a material effect on the time it takes for a sale file incepted at the time the seller put the property on the market to become 'live' and the period it takes both sales and purchases to exchange.
3. The final component in forecasting is to examine the average ratio of abortives to inceptions; but this takes time and can fluctuate with the state of the market.

PM system costs

Trying to give cost guides in a publication such as this is dangerous as the information may quickly be out of date. We will not attempt to do so often, but we can say that the licence cost per seat of a decent PM system might be somewhere between £850 and £1,250 per annum with initial training costs at £500 to £850 for a full day. Other costs depend on whether or not you need more hardware and, in particular, the capacity and specification of your existing network.

Compatibility

The provider of the PM system best suited to your needs may not have the best CM system and vice versa. Some of the best CM providers do not actually produce their own PM system and integrate with only certain PM systems produced by others. Ideally you want the systems to talk to each other. This can give rise to problems in a variety of scenarios:

1. For those acquiring both PM and CM for the first time, which should take precedence in making your choice? Charles Christian suggests that the decision depends on whether or not the CM system is 'mission critical' ([2004] *Gazette*, 25 September). For firms specialising in residential conveyancing, the choice of CM product is likely to be the most important, with PM being chosen from compatible options.

2. For those who already have an up-to-date and user friendly PM system from providers who offer CM as well, the likely solution will be to take that CM product. But if you are looking for a 'fully developed' system make sure that they genuinely have one.
3. If you regard CM as mission critical but the best CM system for your needs does not integrate with an ageing PM system, consider changing the latter.

Document production

Word processing

Every conveyancing firm uses some IT for document production, even if it is the version of Word included in the Microsoft Office suite pre-installed on the receptionist's PC. It will also have a printer and a photocopier. Basic word processing systems can be made more effective with the use of the facility for producing macros and by subscribing to precedent forms on CD or online.

Networks

It was not long ago that even medium to large firms used stand-alone PCs for word processing, but networks became essential once internal e-mail became the norm. A network functions by running systems on servers which are accessed by users either local to the servers (via a local area network (LAN)) or remote from them (via a wide area network (WAN)). Local network connection may be wireless or by cable. With wireless there can be speed and capacity (or 'bandwidth') issues. Cabling can be expensive, restrictive and disfiguring but is still the choice of most firms. The production of documentation via the Internet is increasing and may become the norm.

Case management

CM systems produce their documents from a library of forms (which in some instances you may have had to draft) and whose fields (blank spaces) are populated (filled in) from the information entered at inception or later in the transaction. Some of the forms used (searches, etc.) are protected by copyright and are therefore only available by payment of a licence fee which is usually based on some criteria for measuring usage, such as number of partners. Most subscriptions offer an updating service. These forms can be used independently of a CM system, but when they are used with such a system, the fields are populated directly and automatically from the database.

Printers

It may only be the writer's experience but printing seems to cause the greatest number of niggling problems and frustration. Sharing printers across the greatest number of operators implies a greater return on investment, but this may be illusory. A reasonably priced machine (provided it has at least three trays), exclusive to and placed within easy reach of each team will usually be more efficient and cause less grief than a centrally located state of the art printer.

Digital dictation and voice recognition

Reports and non-standard letters will need to be typed, and for many dictation is probably the most efficient route. There may be a use for conventional or digital dictation, even for those with fully developed CM when home-working is a possibility. There is a repository of relatively untapped conveyancing expertise among people who may be unable or unwilling to work full time, but who would be willing to take on work at home. These people could be your salvation if you are more successful in garnering work than you are in recruiting or retaining conveyancers to do it. You could install a full remote access connection to your network for these people, but this may not be cost effective. Alternatively, you could, at investigation of title or report stage, batch up paper files and send them off site for a night. The files come back the next morning. In the case of conventional dictation they are accompanied by tapes: if the digital option is used the dictation is sent in to you using basic e-mail technology.

If your conveyancers no longer dictate, their secretaries/typists may have more time for other tasks. In any case, typing was only ever part of their job. Secretaries have always done a whole raft of other tasks and, using CM systems, they will be able to do them more quickly and efficiently. They can train more junior members of what now becomes a larger 'team' and their jobs may become less stressful and more fulfilling.

Voice recognition technology continues to improve, but at the time of writing there is little to suggest that it will become a common adjunct to CM systems. It can be used to replace traditional dictation and some who have taken the trouble to learn how to use it swear by it. It does not, however, appear to be an essential tool for improving productivity in a process-driven residential conveyancing environment.

Document management

Scanning

Large law firms have highly sophisticated and costly systems for managing incoming documents and those produced internally. Smaller single-site firms are unlikely to be able to justify (at least for the time being) investment in a system which sees all incoming documents scanned and electronically dispatched to their intended recipients, but firms with a number of branches might be able to get a return on investment from doing so.

Archiving is one area in which the use of powerful, high volume, hopper-fed scanners with associated word-search software should be cost effective. Despite the cost of this technology and the cost of those required to operate it, you should be able to make material savings by ridding yourself of the cost of storage of recently completed files at a stroke and of already archived paper files over a period.

Quite simply, you scan the file and shred it. Scanned copies of shredded documents are admissible to the same extent as the original provided that you can produce evidence of destruction. Electronic data storage is cheap and, because of your back up procedures, safe. (Anyone who does not back up everything at least daily and send the back up off site deserves whatever comes their way – do not shred the file until this has happened.) Once you are up to speed and are comfortably shredding all of your recently completed files you can get to work on your files already in store and eventually (probably after your death) the project will be complete.

The really smart thing about this scenario is retrieval. The search software available is so powerful that by putting together a few key words you will be able, from your desk, to access any file and specific documents within it in seconds.

Here are a couple of tips:

1. Do not ask fee earners to 'fillet' files before archiving. People are expensive but, as mentioned, the electronic storage is cheap.
2. Do try to encourage everyone using the paper file to avoid the use of staples, treasury tags, etc., as these need to be removed before the file goes into the scanner for digestion.

Client relationship management (CRM)

The vital importance of CRM (remembering that for 'client' you can also read 'referrer') is dealt with in Chapter 6, 'Relationship management and building brands'.

There are simple and inexpensive software tools which assist with CRM. There is also much more expensive and sophisticated software but this is is only likely to show a return on investment to the largest and best managed firms that have already inculcated their staff with the theory of CRM and have actually managed to get them to perform the relatively simple and repetitive tasks which make it work so effectively.

For instance, those who have Microsoft Office can use the tools within the calendar for many of the basics such as setting regular reminders to contact key referrers. The contacts facility can be used not only for keeping and retrieving the communication information but also for making more extensive notes (while making sure that the information is not used in breach of data protection legislation).

Moving up the scale but at no great cost there are 'shrink wrapped' products which can be purchased off the shelf and which work with products such as those within the Microsoft Office suite to enhance their CRM capability.

Finally there are those top-end products which are expensive to acquire and have substantial annual licence fees per user. While these can be very powerful tools in the hands of an experienced marketing team working in a large full-service firm with highly motivated lawyers, they are never likely to show a return on investment for the average residential conveyancing outfit.

Other tools and services

National Land Information Service (NLIS)

The NLIS is a massive project of unprecedented proportions. It is basically a hub through which licensed operators (NLIS Searchflow, TM NLIS Search, and Transaction Online) submit local searches and other property information enquiries. Various bodies provide information to the system, including local authorities. At the time of writing all 370+ local authorities in England and Wales process, at various levels of sophistication, local authority searches submitted through the NLIS network:

1. Level 1 authorities receive their NLIS searches in paper form and deal with them by such means as their internal processes permit. They then return the completed paper search using the DX system.
2. Level 2 authorities receive their search requests electronically and process them via a mix of manual and computerised systems. They sometimes, but not always, return completed searches electronically.
3. Level 3 authorities deal with searches wholly electronically, in terms of receipt, processing and return.

A decent CM system will have been designed to interact with the NLIS provider of choice, by providing 'fast button' access to the provider's website and then automatically populating the necessary fields from the CM database. The CM system then diarises the anticipated date of receipt of the result and records the fees so that they appear later in the completion statement.

Online defective title and restrictive covenant indemnity cover

Some insurers provide a service, already widely used by conveyancing firms dealing with large volumes of transactions, to produce defective title and restrictive covenant indemnity policies using an online system accessed via modem or the Internet. Selection of the risks required to be covered and provision of information using a simple question and answer routine enables an immediate quotation and draft policy to be issued. Once it has been agreed between the buyer and seller who is to pay, the quotation is accepted and the firm is able to print out a policy in return for being debited with the premium. Premiums tend to be very competitive.

Portals

A number of services on offer on the Internet combine some of the features of a CM system with the ability to access various other service providers, such as the NLIS licensees. These tend to charge on a per case basis. With the advent of fully developed CM systems available via an ASP these services may, in time, be materially extended to provide all of the features of a complete system.

Writing an IT plan

The theory

Your IT plan needs to form an integral part of the firm's overall business plan and must be put together with the strategic objectives of the business firmly in mind. For instance, if your strategy is to groom the business to be taken over by a larger suitor there is very little point in investing large sums on a new bespoke network. Someone in the firm has to have ownership of the plan, taking responsibility not only for getting it written but also for monitoring its implementation (see Chapter 1 for detailed information on business planning).

Finance

It is pointless devising a plan which the firm cannot afford to implement. Your IT spend affects your balance sheet and profit and loss account, the former in terms of capital expenditure and the latter by virtue of depreciation, licence fees, equipment maintenance and salaries. So you need to be writing your plan annually in advance of the firm's budgeting process. Do not be too distracted by benchmark figures for IT spend as a proportion of turnover. Just because another firm spends a sizeable proportion of its turnover (5 per cent is not uncommon for larger firms) this does not mean that the money is being spent wisely. Huge amounts have been spent by some firms on intranet or knowledge management projects which have never produced an adequate return.

Planning

Get together everyone who is involved in the IT planning process (which may include outsourcing providers) and remind yourselves of the firm's strategy. Then come up with a wish list. Apportion costs to the implementation of the items on the list and narrow the list to what you believe you can afford to spend, giving priority to 'mission critical' issues. Then produce an action plan which can be a simple chart with the headings: 'what', 'by whom', 'by when' and 'how verified'.

Review

Revisit the plan at regular intervals – say quarterly – to see how you are progressing. Take the reviews seriously. If something has not happened, or is taking longer than specified, find out why. Perhaps you simply got it wrong or perhaps someone is not performing. You can learn a great deal from implementation failures about the quality and quantity of your IT resources and you need to act early to address such problems.

Summary

It is possible for good people to produce reasonable results using simple tools but even the best IT will not increase profitability in the hands of poorly managed, trained or motivated staff.

Failure to give consideration as to whether a CM system will suit your business may have a profound effect on:

- the cost of your professional indemnity cover or, worse still, your ability to get cover;
- your ability to attract work from agents;
- your ability to be competitive.

If you do have a CM system:

- Have you fully developed it? If not, what risks are you exposing yourselves to?
- Are you using your CM system efficiently? Careless/incomplete entry of information or the failure to keep the diary up to date can render the system virtually useless. Good line management and policing are essential.

If you have a PM system are you making proper use of it? Unless you put the effort into extracting the information which it is capable of providing, you are not getting an adequate return on your investment.

The High Street is where the majority of the existing conveyancers choose to work and, equipped with the right tools, they will be able to compete. Even in a market which comes to be dominated by large chains of estate agents or utility companies, small firms with the right technology can offer their services to panel managers either within those organisations or retained by them. Firms can continue to act for those clients who prefer to come to them direct or be referred by local independent agents while augmenting and, perhaps, eventually replacing that work with panelled work.

The balance between prudence and daring, cost control and investment, quality and quantity has never been so important. Those who make the right decisions on the choice of what IT to use and who use it properly will have a head start.

CASE STUDY **Recognise any of this?**

In the late 1980s the firm which is now BPE had a small residential conveyancing department which commanded a material share of its local market.

It decided to install a case management system called 'Mover'. The department head championed the initiative. The champion, however, moved to another department before the end of the initiative and the fee earners were left to make such use of the system as they chose and it became a word processing system, functioning at less than 30 per cent of its capability.

In 1996 a large mortgage lender offering 'free legals' asked BPE to join its panel. The firm borrowed an additional six-figure sum to provide the space and other infrastructure to take up the challenge. Time was at a premium and the suppliers of the firm's existing CM system were unable to move quickly. Every conveyancing partner was pressed into working long hours to produce the library of letters and other documents which even a simple 'lender only' remortgage CM system required.

Then came the second blow. It became apparent that the new CM supplier was not as 'user friendly' as the firm's other provider and it introduced a Windows-based version of its CM system materially more slowly. The prospect of another change of system was unwelcome but the partners rallied and the firm ditched its remortgage system in favour of that offered by its original supplier. That system is still in use and has produced a formidable return on investment.

In the late 1990s BPE took the opportunity to take volume referrals from institutionally owned estate agents. Once this work commenced (and remember, never take on new volume instructions without at least a three-month pilot) BPE put together a new residential CM system based on the platform provided by the supplier of their existing remortgage platform.

The decision was taken at the end of the 1990s to build on the residential platform to provide a 'fully developed CM system'. The firm's senior partner had taken an interest in the technology and the firm had recruited a team member within remortgages who was familiar with the platform and interested in software development. The partnership persuaded the two of them to give up fee earning and devote their time almost exclusively to the project.

The senior partner's commitment to his remortgage CRM role had to take precedence and his colleague was, at the time, the only developer within the firm capable of 'tweaking' other CM systems in use. Additionally the whole task proved much more complex than originally envisaged. Deadlines were missed and the delay caused a detrimental effect on management within the volume residential operation, in terms of both morale and attempts to improve working practices. Profitability stalled because the staff had to continue using a wholly inadequate system. Just when it seemed ready, along came the 2002 Act and all the forms had to be rewritten.

Once the rewriting and testing had been completed the training could begin. BPE's residential department is divided into teams dedicated to particular work referrers and, to cause least disruption, the teams were trained separately. The system was written with request prompts, guidance and instructions to the operator, which allowed for a short training period of four days maximum per team and member. The training revealed some minor faults for correction by the developers. BPE opted for more rather than less guidance because of the need to use the system, insofar as it is ever possible, to eliminate risk and to enable as many tasks as possible to be carried out by the least experienced people. Later versions will enable conveyancers with proven experience to 'switch off' the lower end instructions.

4

Direct marketing to gain and retain clients

KEY POINTS

This chapter will

- explain what is involved in direct marketing
- enable you to segment clients and referrers
- inform where to rent or buy lists of similar types of target clients
- explain what to include on the firm's direct marketing database
- advise which Acts and Regulations apply
- show you how to manage a direct marketing campaign

Definition

Direct marketing is defined as:

> The planned recording, analysis and tracking of individual customers' responses and transactions for the purpose of developing and prolonging mutually profitable customer relationships.
>
> Institute of Direct Marketing, **www.theidm.com**, 2004

Direct marketing is a way of encouraging people to buy legal services from a firm by contacting them using individuals' records on a database.

It requires a database made up of contact details and further information regarding the individuals such as their age and occupation. The database is used for two reasons. One is to separate clients into groups of seemingly similar people, called segments. The second is to be able to differentiate the offers according to the likely needs of individuals and segments. The more a firm knows about a client, the more it can tailor its offer or message in a way that will be of interest to that client.

Direct mail is sending offers or information by post to individuals where there is a strong possibility they will want to take up the offer or will find the information beneficial.

Direct marketing works best when it is used in conjunction with a number of marketing activities where each supports the others. The response to direct marketing campaigns tends to be fairly low. Where direct marketing is used to remind clients of a firm and to offer something that is of benefit to clients, for example warning of a change in the law that will directly affect them, it helps to create good feelings towards the firm. It encourages clients to use the firm again.

Client segmentation

Cost-effective marketing is attracting clients at minimum or acceptable acquisition cost. Firms need to decide what kind of clients they want to concentrate on. A profile of clients will help the firm identify similar ones. An example of a profile is: clients aged 25 to 35, with a household income under £30,000 living in properties valued under £150,000 within 15 miles of the main office or in specified postcode areas.

Once the firm has decided what kind of clients it wants to service, the next step is to find those clients. The most cost-effective clients are generally existing ones.

Client or customer segmentation is separating clients into groups of people with similar needs who respond in a similar way. This enables you to market your services to selected target segments in a cost-effective manner. Segmentation can be done by profiles of individuals or businesses or by behaviour, e.g. what they have bought and how many times. It is often helpful to give a name to the different segments, since this makes it easier to identify them.

Client segments will be treated differently in terms of cross-selling or cross-referring. Clients may not stay in the same segment. A 'high potential' client, may become a 'high value' client. A 'cost-conscious' client may turn out to be a 'reservation' client. Clients need to be reviewed periodically to assess whether they now fall into another segment.

BOX 4.1 Client segmentation by behaviour

First-time clients

This could be the name given to people who approach you for legal services and who have never used a solicitor before. These people will need to be treated in a different way from people who are used to using legal services.

They will probably need more time spent on them to explain legal issues, procedures and timescales. The time may be seen as well spent, because it is also used to develop the relationship with them, to make them feel comfortable and at ease. This means they are likely to use your services again and recommend you to their friends who may be going through the same life stage of buying a first home, and this will bring in more fee income. They may not be very profitable as fee income may be low.

Cost-conscious clients

These clients will have bought one or two services from you, but you think they have only bought on price and are unlikely to buy more – unless the price is right. In marketing terms, these people are often called 'promiscuous buyers' as they will be attracted to the best deal, wherever it is. You will probably only want to spend a lot of time and effort on this group if your services are sold predominantly on cost.

High potential clients

This name could be given to a segment of clients who have bought some services from you, but who you think may have bought from other firms too. The profile might be clients who are running their own business, with household income over £55,000, married or living with a partner, with children, and home-owners aged 35–55 years old. The clients may have used you to organise their employment contracts and for agreeing a lease arrangement, but not for buying their home. These clients may be of high potential and it is worth investing effort in them to encourage them to buy other services from you as time goes by.

High value clients

These clients would typically have bought three or more services and see you or the firm as 'our solicitors' or 'our family solicitors'. They are loyal and are unlikely to go to another firm. They need to be treated with respect and given contact, probably once a year. These are bread and butter clients who are likely to recommend the practice to others. They are likely to be less price conscious and are therefore more profitable. The key issue here is not to take them for granted.

Reservation clients

You may choose to place in this segment clients for whom you do not want to act again for whatever reason. Perhaps you think they have cost the firm rather than been profitable. You have reservations about wanting to do further work for them.

In the course of their work for clients, solicitors will to a degree get to know them and be able to make a judgement about the segment into which they fall.

Segmentation by profile is based on a combination of an individual's age, gender, occupation, income, life stage (e.g. whether single, half of a couple, with young children, older children, with children who have left home, no children, retired), house value and location.

Behaviour and profile segmentation

A firm segmenting by behaviour can then segment by profile, for example: 65 per cent of high value clients are over 50 years old, in professions, middle or higher management or with their own businesses. They have annual household incomes over £55,000 and live in detached houses worth over £250,000 within 14 miles of the branch which they have used.

Law firms tend to segment by product category alone, e.g. a conveyancing client, a personal injury or family client. Segmenting clients by which services they buy can result in pigeon-holing clients and not seeing them as having other legal needs which the firm can provide with a little prompting (see Chapter 6 on relationship management and building brands).

Referrers' segment

A separate segment is needed for referrers of business. These people or businesses will be treated differently from clients.

The difference between a customer and a consumer is that the customer buys the product or service, but the consumer consumes or uses it. In relationships with referrers, referrers are the customers and the clients they pass to the law firm are the consumers. Different messages need to be given to customers and consumers.

BOX 4.2 Segmentation of referrers

Where a practice relies heavily on business from referrers, segmentation of referrers is likely to be by:

- business type:
  - estate agents;
  - mortgage brokers;
  - independent financial advisers;
  - banks;
  - secondary financial loan institutions;
  - building societies;
  - surveyors;
  - developers: local, regional and national;
  - panel managers;
  - other solicitors who do not do conveyancing;
  - local government authorities;
- location – local, county, regional, national, international;
- status – independent, regional or part of a national chain;
- size – number of branches
- volume of business referred (number or value in pounds);
- whether the firm is on the referrer's panel of solicitors formally or informally and dates for review;
- regularity of passing referrals, value and quality of referrals.

Referral fees

The segmenting of referral clients becomes increasingly important with the payment of referral fees (subject to review). Firms may want to form agreements with selected referrers, the value of which will depend on the frequency, volume and quality of the referrals. A database which measures such data is essential in referral negotiations and management.

Building selected client relationships

One of the key purposes of segmentation is to identify those clients who are more and less likely to buy from the firm again. It is not financially worthwhile trying to develop ongoing relationships with all the firms' clients.

Not all clients will want a relationship and some approaches will fall on deaf ears. Some clients will simply be more important than others. In some firms which do bulk remortgaging, for example, relationships with referrers will be more important financially than those with the individual clients for whom they are providing the legal services.

Direct marketing is most cost effective where particular clients or contacts are identified as those most likely to buy from the firm again or provide regular quality referrals.

Renting or buying lists of potential clients

If you are going to target existing clients, it takes little extra work to send the same messages to similar potential clients. This requires the firm to decide which segments to target and then to profile or describe those clients in general terms. You can buy or rent lists of contact details of similar profile clients from businesses who compile the lists, called list brokers. Use your local telephone directory or go to **www.google.co.uk** and search for 'list brokers' to provide a number of suppliers. You can tell the list broker the details of the potential clients you want to contact. These may be the contact details of:

- couples in age bands 35–55 home owners, with a household income of £45,000 to £65,000 living in ABC postcode areas; or
- people living in private rented accommodation earning over £23,000 a year in postcode areas XYZ (who may be looking to buy a property).

The list broker will be able provide a database of people or businesses that match most or all the profile details supplied.

A charge is made based on per thousand contact details, subject to a minimum value. The lowest fee will be for renting a list for once-only use. A higher fee will be for renting the list for unlimited contact within a set time period, e.g. a year. The highest fee is paid to purchase the list.

When a list is rented, the agreement will be for one or a certain number of uses. If the agreement is for a once-only use and it is used further times, you will be invoiced as the list will probably contain dummy addresses to check whether the list is used more than the agreed number of times.

Only rent from businesses that are registered with the Direct Marketing Association and who clean their lists against the relevant preferencing services (see Appendix B). Check how often they clean/update their lists as with people moving and changing circumstances lists become out of date very quickly.

If you decide to purchase a list, it can be used multiple times. It will go out of date, though, and someone in the office will need to be responsible for cleaning/updating it, with 'gone aways' returned, and for checking it against the preferencing service lists.

As you probably do not want to send marketing material more than twice a year, it may be better to rent lists of external potential clients.

The Privacy and Electronic Communications (EC Directive) Regulations 2003 (SI 2003/2426 (Privacy Regulations)) regulate direct marketing activities by electronic means of e-mail, telephone SMS (short message service for mobile devices, commonly called 'texts') and fax. If you are renting or buying a list for electronic direct marketing purposes, given the rules on having to gain people's prior permission, it is sensible to ask the list broker for a warranty that the names were compiled lawfully and that none of the names has decided to opt out.

Information sources

List brokers compile data on people based on information available to the public or that the person has provided. The UK government through the Office for National Statistics (ONS) collects information every ten years when a census is carried out. The last one was in 2001. Information based on census data becomes increasingly unreliable as time elapses.

Leading firms that provide geo-demographic data (based on geography/location and demographic data) include CACI which produces ACORN (A Classification Of Residential Neighbourhoods), and Experian, which owns MOSAIC. Firms take the census data, then add additional data sources which may include the electoral roll, county court judgments, credit-referencing data, mail-order data and market research information.

ACORN groups and types

ACORN is a geo-demographic tool used by businesses to improve their understanding of clients and target markets. ACORN categorises all 1.9 million postcodes using 125 demographic statistics and 287 lifestyle variables. The result is 56 categories of household.

Table 4.1 Selected ACORN classification categories

Category	Group	Type
Wealthy achievers	Wealthy executives	01 Affluent mature professionals, large houses
		02 Affluent working families with mortgages
		03 Villages with wealthy commuters
		04 Well-off managers, larger houses
	Affluent greys	05 Older affluent professionals
		06 Farming communities
		07 Old people, detached houses
		08 Mature couples, smaller detached houses
	Flourishing families	09 Larger families, prosperous suburbs
		10 Well-off working families with mortgages
		11 Well-off managers, detached houses
		12 Large families and houses in rural areas
Urban prosperity	Prosperous professionals	13 Well-off professionals, larger houses and converted flats
		14 Older professionals in detached houses and apartments
	Educated urbanites	15 Affluent urban professionals, flats
		16 Prosperous young professionals, flats
		17 Young educated workers, flats
		18 Multi-ethnic young, converted flats
		19 Suburban privately renting professionals
	Aspiring singles	20 Student flats and cosmopolitan sharers
		21 Singles and sharers, multi-ethnic areas
		22 Low income singles, small rented flats
		23 Student Terraces

If a law firm wanted to target clients moving to larger properties, the firm might target 'prosperous professionals' and 'flourishing families' (see **www.caci.co.uk/acorn.acornmap.asp**). By using a database of people who are more likely to become clients, it avoids wasting money sending information to people who are less likely to use the firm or be profitable to it.

Components of a database

To be able to act on life triggers for cross-referring purposes and so encourage existing clients to use the firm for their next legal matter, an effective, usable database is required.

A survey of 155 conveyancing solicitors by Progressive Legal Training found that only 63 per cent had a client database ([2004] *Gazette*, 4 March, 11).

A good database will have certain components:

- **identification details:**
  - name, address, telephone and mobile numbers, e-mail address, date of birth of self, spouse, children and their names (money laundering requirements could be included here – what forms of identification have been given?);
  - date the information was gathered and when it was last cleaned/checked – is it still correct?
- **services purchased and dates:**
  - services purchased;
  - services updated;
  - trigger dates (e.g. wills – contact the person every five years; new house purchase – contact the person in 18–24 months' time);
- **propensity to buy certain services identified:**
  - regular house mover?
  - family with young children?
  - growing business?
  - job changer?
- **contact notes:**
  - when did the person last receive information?
  - what was the information?
  - what was their reaction to the information?
  - subsequent actions?
- **segmentation:**
  - which segment is the client in?
  - is it still valid or has it changed?
  - is this a high potential client who has moved into a high value segment?

Gathering information

In terms of gathering information about clients, formal as well as informal conversations that staff have with clients provide opportunities to understand individual clients better in order to give an enhanced service.

Information about clients that extends beyond the obvious factual information, to their attitudes to risk, their need for security, their fears and concerns, will help to target information that they want and need.

A database which allows for the inclusion of the information required will be the foundation of successful direct marketing and cross-selling. When new clients come to the firm, they can be invited to complete an application form or a terms of engagement form. Alternatively, the solicitor or secretary can complete the form by asking questions of the client. Not all the questions may be asked initially, but as the solicitor gets to know clients better, further information can be added to the database.

Data protection

Be aware that the principles of the Data Protection Act 1998 state that data must not be excessive and not kept for longer than is necessary.

Individuals have the right to object at any time to the processing of their personal data for marketing purposes by whatever means, including mail, e-mail, fax, telephone and SMS (s.11 Data Protection Act 1998). Go to **www.informationcommissioner.gov.uk** for further information.

Engagement form

The engagement form can include the following contact details:

- what the client wants to be called: in letters (Dear . . .); on envelopes (Mr and Mrs . . .); on the telephone; and in person;
- date of birth;
- what methods of communication the client happy is to accept (post, fax, e-mail, text, telephone);
- how the client wants to be treated – how he/she wants to interact with the firm (is the client happy to receive information from the firm that could benefit the client?).

Further useful information includes:

- spouse/partner/family names/dependants and dates of birth;
- second family;
- home ownership/rental;
- mortgage – remortgage;
- how long owned;
- occupation and position;
- products already purchased: conveyancing, wills, enduring powers of attorney, etc.;
- solicitor already used;
- type of legal service required;
- solicitor providing assistance;

- billing arrangement – frequency or when an amount has been reached;
- other side's advisers and contact details (for personal injury and family matters);
- court and public funding details;
- file checks: conflict;
- checked by;
- form completed by;
- date last updated.

Client relationship management (CRM)

CRM has been the buzz word for a number of years. CRM is about managing the relationship with clients, one person at a time. It involves getting to know clients and so knowing what matters to them individually so as to be able to provide the information or services that they are likely to want. Direct marketing is used to develop relationships with target clients. Software has been developed that aids the client relationship through setting up a usable database. It enables the management and analysis of clients' data to establish target client segments and individuals for marketing purposes.

CRM is labour intensive in that it needs the efforts of individuals within the firm to identify key clients, to get to know people or businesses better, to develop the relationship and to encourage them to use the firm for other services. Networking and direct marketing are the main marketing methods used in CRM. For further information see Chapter 6, 'Relationship management and building brands'.

Regulation of data management

The collation and use of data for marketing purposes is regulated under the following:

- Data Protection Act 1998;
- Privacy and Electronic Communications (EC Directive) Regulations 2003;
- preference schemes;
- advertising and marketing codes;
- Electronic Commerce (EC Directive) Regulations 2002;
- Consumer Protection (Distance Selling) Regulations 2000.

It is beyond the scope of this book to cover all of these in detail. It is recommended that each of these is checked before undertaking direct marketing activities. See Appendix B for a brief summary of marketing-related legislation and rules, and the list at the end of the chapter for useful websites.

Direct marketing campaigns

Direct marketing involves contacting existing and potential clients to provide information that encourages them to use your services. The more direct marketing is targeted to people or businesses who are most likely to want to buy your services, the better the response is likely to be. Direct marketing can use the media of the telephone, post, fax, e-mail and text messaging.

When deciding on a direct marketing campaign, consider these questions:

1. What are your objectives for the campaign?
2. Who are you going to send information to?
3. What are you going to send to them and how?
4. How often?
5. Who is going to organise it?
6. Who is going to send it out?
7. How will you evaluate the results?

Objectives for the direct marketing campaign

The clearer you are about what you want to achieve, the more likely the planning and execution will achieve the stated results. This applies whether you do it in-house or use an external marketing consultant to assist you.

Objectives can be written using SMART, meaning that they need to be specific, measurable, achievable, relevant and set in a timescale. By using a timescale and a measurable target, a method of evaluation is automatically incorporated into the objectives. A direct marketing objective could be phrased as follows:

> 'To increase conveyancing fee income by 6 per cent from clients in XYZ post-code areas by 31 December 200X. To assess whether the objective is on track to be achieved, at the end of May and September, 200X, fee income should have increased by 2 per cent and 4 per cent respectively. If it has not, then additional action should be taken.'

Who are you going to send the information to?

Your most profitable clients in the future will probably be your existing ones. They already know you and are therefore 'warm' to receiving an approach from you – less convincing or reassuring will need to be done. These may be clients from other departments, not just the conveyancing department.

By segmenting your clients, you will be able to target those clients who match the description of clients identified in your objective and who are likely to be most profitable to you.

A firm-wide database set up to identify clients by postcodes, which indicate the value of property, and hence conveyancing fees, can be applied to your target client segments.

For example, you may select clients from the 'first time' segment of clients. These are people who have bought their first home and so are likely to move again a few years after their first purchase. Although the home value may be moderate, and so may the conveyancing fee, a high number of clients in this segment are likely to move and so increase turnover by higher volume. Alternatively, you may target your 'high potential' segment, accepting that although these clients may be at a life stage when they are less likely to move as frequently as the first time segment, the value of their homes is likely to be higher and hence the conveyancing fee income increases in value rather than volume.

Consider renting or buying a list of people with a similar profile to your internal client segment. For example, target people in the age band 26–35, earning over £24,000 annually living in postcode areas XYZ.

What are you going to send them and how?

Send different specific messages that will be relevant to particular groups.

The information needs to be of value to readers. If it is not, it will have no relevance and risk causing annoyance. For this reason, consider sending a single page two-sided newsletter with four or five short articles on a variety of relevant topics, together with an advertisement of the benefits of the firm's services and/or an offer which will lead into further work – with an expiry date to take up the offer.

The advantage of an expiry date is that it encourages people to take action and contact the firm. The disadvantage is that it makes the newsletter go out of date and left-over copies have to be destroyed.

EXAMPLE **Newsletter**

Content: a newsletter with articles on:

- buying your home – a conveyancing service which gives you access to progress via the Internet 24/7;
- buy to let – how to get your tenants to pay for your pension, highlights and pitfalls;
- 'But I thought I'd get half!' – your rights on divorce;
- remarried? Have you disinherited your kids?
- how to be generous to the government – don't write a will!

Offer: Writing or updating a single will for £95 plus VAT before a specific date

Do not be tempted to tell clients about new people who have joined, internal promotions or other internal issues, e.g. a new case management system. Clients are rarely interested and this is more likely to be a turn off. Use photographs, but avoid people shaking hands and pictures of your office building. A good graphic designer will suggest professional library photographs to 'lift' the newsletter to gain attention (see Chapter 7 on brochures, flyers and newsletters).

Small A5 flyers can be sent out in a blanket non-targeted format at low cost to every household in specified areas. They can be delivered on their own, at higher cost and generally higher impact because they are not 'fighting' for attention from other flyers. Alternatively, they can be delivered with other media, such as other mailings and local free papers at lower cost and impact. Contact distribution networks through local telephone directories and local newspapers that generally distribute flyers at an economic cost.

Flyers or leaflets are used to inform and remind potential clients of the firm. Take care not to negatively affect the perception clients may have of the firm. If the practice has positioned itself upmarket, sending out flyers could cause more damage than good to target clients' perceptions. If it is a typical High Street firm providing a range of services, it is more acceptable to do this.

If you are targeting your own clients, send the newsletter with existing (appropriate) correspondence, or send it separately by post or e-mail (where you have the client's permission).

Personal letters informing clients of one issue that is likely to affect them may have a higher impact than an impersonal newsletter. Letters sent with the solicitor's name printed on the envelope will almost certainly get opened and read.

Contact the Royal Mail to enquire about discounts off postage rates where many letters are sent which are already sorted by postcode.

Permission marketing

Where contacts' permission has to be gained before they can be contacted by electronic means, this is referred to as permission marketing (see above for the laws and regulations relating to direct and electronic marketing). Permission marketing includes SMS text, e-mail, fax and telephone use.

Text marketing

SMS text marketing is still in its infancy. Messages need to be kept brief. As the use of text spelling becomes more widely used, some firms may consider using it with younger target clients to show that they are up to date with use of the medium.

E-mail marketing

E-mail can be used to send newsletters and individual messages, with the necessary communications-to-cease clauses. 'Spam', which is the sending of unsolicited e-mail messages, is becoming an increasing problem, hence the introduction of ever more restrictive regulations.

In the author's opinion, solicitors have an advantage where the word 'solicitor' is used as part of their e-mail address or in the message title. People are more likely to open and read the e-mail than if it is from another type of business.

Experian ContactMail has over 2,000,000 e-mail addresses collected by online and offline collection methods. It has 150,000 MOSAIC high income families and 130,000 addresses of people who have bought online. All have given their permission for their details to be used for marketing purposes. If a firm is concentrating on building its client base with high income families, a refined version of this type of database enables it to undertake a direct e-mail marketing campaign, often in a fraction of the time it takes to do a 'print and deliver' one.

If a firm sells or wants to sell more of its conveyancing services online, it would make sense to use a database of people who have already purchased online. These people are more likely to have a greater propensity to buy other services online than a person who has never bought online (see **www.experiancontactmail.com**).

Telephone marketing

The Solicitors' Publicity Code 2001 prevents solicitors from telephoning a member of the public unsolicited (see Appendix C). A member of the public does not include a current or former client, another lawyer, an existing or potential professional or business connection or a commercial organisation or public body.

How often will you send out direct marketing information?

Check the terms of engagement form to see what the client has agreed. Send direct marketing messages no more than twice a year for domestic clients and three times a year for commercial clients.

Who is going to organise it?

Consider appointing a business development or account manager to manage direct marketing campaigns. This person will be responsible for:

- developing the database and managing it;
- identifying client segments;
- developing direct marketing and in-office cross-referring opportunities;
- producing newsletters and other materials;
- organising for them to be sent out; and
- monitoring and evaluating the returns.

In a smaller firm, the practice manager may be able to incorporate the role. Firms that do not have the marketing skills in house can use an external marketing consultant with specialist knowledge of legal marketing to organise the direct marketing campaign. This person will be able to suggest articles, write the articles and organise the design and printing of the newsletters and subsequent distribution to existing clients and potential ones through renting lists.

Articles for the newsletter can be written in house, if a fee earner has the time and can write for the layman. It is a good idea to ask an experienced copywriter to edit or rewrite it to ensure that it is written in layman's terms. The final article must be checked by a partner. Avoid legal jargon and emphasise that it is an outline and does not cover every eventuality. At the end of each article, write: 'For further information contact XYZ in the firm on [direct telephone number].'

Who is going to send out direct marketing information?

Newsletters can be sent out by post by staff in your firm. This can take considerable time and effort.

There are businesses that provide direct marketing services from printing letters and newsletters, printing envelopes, folding and inserting materials and posting them using Royal Mail postage discounts available for bulk mailings with quality addresses. They are called 'fulfilment houses'. They can also accept postal enquiries for forwarding to the law firm. If the practice does not have spare capacity to undertake direct marketing activities, the use of a fulfilment house should be considered. Find them in the local telephone directory or on the web.

As an example of costs, for 2,000 items:

- to send out a newsletter, insert it into an envelope, supply and print the envelope with contacts' addresses: £234.00;
- to send out a newsletter, laser print a personalised letter, insert the letter and newsletter into window envelopes: £308.00.

The newsletter and postage costs are in addition (figures supplied by Trapeze Mailing Services Ltd).

How will you evaluate the results?

One of the advantages of direct marketing over traditional marketing is that it is easier to assess the level of response and hence the return on the investment. Direct marketing can be used in isolation, but is better used as a supporting marketing activity.

The advantage solicitors have when sending direct mailshots is that their name on the envelope virtually ensures that it will be opened.

To monitor the response for direct mail campaigns:

1. Ask respondents to mailshots to quote a code when they contact the firm. Monitor response levels of people quoting the code.
2. Set up a separate code for people who become clients or who give extra work as a result of the mailshots and put it on your database.
3. Evaluate the value of the work and the potential long-term value of each new client. Clients may give a small item of work before they feel comfortable to discuss other issues.
4. Cost out the returns over a 12-month rolling period to avoid any seasonal highs and lows.
5. Assess the returns against taking out advertisements in the local paper and compare the response.
6. Always ask people how they heard about the firm, in order to assess marketing activities to know what to use in the future, to amend or abandon.

The Law Society Solicitors' Publicity Code 2001

The Code does not prevent solicitors writing to potential clients/members of the public unsolicited, but does not allow them to be telephoned or visited unsolicited. This means that solicitors are free to rent or buy lists of potential target clients and to write to them offering legal services. The full text of the Code is reproduced in Appendix C.

Further reading

Adam, L. (2002) *Marketing Your Law Firm,* Law Society Publishing.

Adler, M. (1990) *Clarity for Lawyers,* Law Society Publishing.

Bown-Wilson, D. and Courtney, G. (2002) *Marketing, Management and Motivation,* Law Society Publishing.

Carey, P. (ed.) (2004) *Data Protection Handbook,* Law Society Publishing.

The Law Society (2004) *The Client Care Guide to Keeping Clients* (only available online at www.clientcare.lawsociety.org.uk).

Trapp, A. (2001) *Principles of Direct and Database Marketing,* Pearson Education.

Webb, N. (2003) *Internet Marketing,* Law Society Publishing.

Useful websites

Committee of Advertising Practice **www.cap.org.uk**

Data Protection Information **www.dataprotection.gov.uk**

Direct Marketing Association **www.dma.org.uk**

Information Commissioner **www.informationcommissioner.gov.uk**

Law (of marketing) links **www.marketinglaw.co.uk**

Law Society's *Gazette* **www.lawgazette.co.uk**

Law Society's client care pages **www.clientcare.lawsociety.org.uk**

Royal Mail **www.royalmail.com**

Trapeze Mailing Services Ltd **www.trapezemailingservices.co.uk**

5

How to save money on advertising

KEY POINTS

This chapter will

- explain how to set objectives for advertising
- demonstrate the difference between good design and advertisements that sell
- give suggestions on how to write advertisements and where to place them
- explain how to use advertising agencies

Introduction

Media advertising is controlled by the Advertising Standards Authority (**www.asa.org.uk**), which acts to ensure compliance with the British Codes of Advertising and Sales Promotion. Advertisements must be legal, decent, honest and truthful and be prepared with a sense of responsibility to consumers and society at large. Solicitors are further controlled by the Solicitors' Publicity Code 2001 (see Appendix C).

Solicitors have been free to advertise for nearly twenty years, yet outside of advertising in Yellow Pages, comparatively little is done.

Objectives of advertising

The first step in considering whether to advertise is to decide what you want to achieve from it. Reasons for advertising include:

- to build awareness of the firm, service or brand;
- to change people's perceptions of the firm;
- to remind;
- to persuade;
- to sell the services.

The more defined the objectives, the easier it is to determine the best marketing tactics to use to achieve the results wanted.

Is advertising the best way to get these messages across to potential and existing clients? Yes and no. It is a supporting tactic that helps the effectiveness of other marketing activities. For example, it is easier when networking or doing direct marketing, if the potential client or referrer has already heard of the firm. If a firm has been recommended, people may feel more comfortable using the practice if they have seen an advertisement beforehand. It helps to build awareness of the practice, which is the first step in developing trust.

Advertising goals might include:

- to increase the number of people telephoning for quotes by 8 per cent during the time frame of the advertising plus one month;
- to increase conversion rates of people asking for quotes by 12 per cent by the end of a specified month;
- to increase turnover by 13 per cent by the end of the year;
- to gain 85 instructions for properties over the value of £650,000 by the end of . . .

The more the objectives are quantifiable and set within a time period as shown above, the easier it is to assess the results.

Advertising can be an expensive luxury. It is often difficult to evaluate the returns and judge which is more productive when several marketing tactics are used at once. A firm can only really assess the value of the business gained from advertising when:

- the firm has just set up and does no other form of promotion;
- advertisements are placed in a new geographical location some distance from the firm's established client base.

The more precise the objectives are, the better. If the type of clients you want to attract are also described when setting the objectives, it makes it easier to pinpoint which media to use. Successfully gaining the desired increase in the number of people wanting quotes may be satisfying, but if the quotes are unlikely to convert into business, then the achievement is hollow.

Advertising is often used to build awareness of the firm's corporate brand. Corporate image development aims to get the firm's name across to target clients and to build and encourage positive perceptions of the practice. The messages in the advertising, the quality and where they appear all help to develop a picture of the firm in clients' minds. They need to be in harmony with the image the firm aims to develop or reinforce. An advertisement placed in inappropriate media will send mixed and confusing messages to core and potential clients.

Budget setting

According to research carried out by Wheeler Associates and McCallum Layton, firms spend 2.8 per cent of their revenue on marketing (*Marketing the Advisers II*, 1999). Methods of allocating a budget include:

1. Last year's budget plus a percentage increase. This ignores the appropriateness of last year's budget and whether it achieved the results required. It also assumes that last year's objectives are this year's goals too.
2. What the competition are spending. This is based on reactionary or defensive advertising. A competitor is advertising heavily in the area, so other firms also advertise. A 'keeping up with the Jones's' mentality of advertising assumes that your firm has the same objectives as the competition.
3. A percentage of turnover – or what the firm can afford. This ignores what is actually needed to achieve the marketing objectives.
4. Whatever is needed to achieve the marketing objectives. This method considers what combination of activities are needed to gain the required results, then costs them. At this point, the firm can decide what it can and cannot afford to do.

Selecting types of advertising

There are many different types of advertising. New innovative 'opportunities' become available at an alarming rate.

As with all forms of marketing, the type of advertising selected has to be what is right for the firm and the clients' perception of it. A simple rule should be applied: if it could adversely affect clients' opinion of the practice, do not do it.

If the firm serves a predominantly upper middle market, it would be inappropriate to send out leaflets with the local free newspaper, which is more down market. Where advertisements are seen, as well as what is in them, affects people's perceptions of the advertiser and their products or services.

Promotion

Promotional signs are not advertising in the truest sense, but they raise awareness of the firm.

Office name sign

The sign outside the office premises is a form of advertising. It needs to be easy to read at a glance and lit up at night, where local authority permission allows. Signs at eye level are always going to be seen more and have a bigger impact than those where a person has to look up or search for them.

Window signs

Window signs stating the range of services the firm offers are good, provided window panes allow for them to be easily read. Small Georgian glass panes look better without signage. Use white vinyl lettering rather than darker colours on windows. Windows often appear to be dark from the outside so white vinyl lettering is more prominent than dark colours or gold.

Consider carefully whether you want to have the range of small window signs telling passersby that you are members of various panels: they are likely to mean little to the 'man in the street'. They may simply clutter up the windows and distract from the key messages you want people to gain.

Call waiting advertising

Call waiting advertising uses the brief time clients are kept waiting on the telephone to tell or remind callers of the other services the firm provides, and the benefits of using the firm.

When callers are waiting, they are a captive audience and so potentially more receptive to subtle messages. Providing the call waiting advertising is done well, it should be effective. It makes better use of the contact time when people are on hold than music or bleeps.

A-boards

An A-board is two pieces of wood or other material which form the two sides of an 'A'. A piece of rope or hook holds them together. You often see them on wider pavements to draw attention to a business. They need to be located with care to avoid causing an obstruction.

Ideally they have a white background with black or dark print. Avoid the use of block capitals. Use lower case, which is easier to read. Keep the message simple and do not put too much information on it. Think of what gives you a competitive advantage and include it. Examples are 'Appointments not always necessary – call in now' or 'open Saturday mornings' and 'we keep you informed'.

Include your telephone number and an arrow telling people where to go. Use a simple logo or graphic to emphasise what the service is. A-boards are most suited to High Street firms catering for the 'man and woman on the street'. They are not appropriate for largely commercial practices or firms targeting the upper end of the market.

Banners

Banners can be very effective when used occasionally or for a special promotion. A 10 metre by 1 metre vinyl banner hung once a week across the building's first floor windows or tied to railings outside the office will be eye catching. Use simple wording such as the name of the firm, 'conveyancing service' and the telephone number e.g. 'Bloggs & Co. conveyancing service, tel. XXXX XXXXXX'.

For easiest reading, use a white background with black or dark print and avoid block capitals.

Banners gain attention only when they are used occasionally. If they are up all the time they become like background wallpaper. They should appear then go, so that they stay fresh and eye catching.

Print advertising channels

Buses

A number of High Street firms use backs of buses as a way to increase awareness. As buses are on the move, they have less tendency to become 'wallpaper'. Firms can decide on which routes they want the advertisements to appear, although this will not be guaranteed. There is some control, though, over the broad geographical area where you want the advertisements to be seen by potential clients.

Keep the advertisements simple with messages that are easy to read on the move. For example:

'XYZ Conveyancing Lawyers To Make You Smile
Call for a quote
Tel XXXXXXX'

'For a moving experience
Call XYZ Conveyancing Services for a quote now
Tel XXXXXXX'

'Buying or selling your home?
Call XYZ for a quote
We are quick, efficient & friendly
Tel XXXXXXX'

'XYZ Conveyancing Solicitors
We help to take the stress/hassle out of moving
Tel XXXXXXX'

'XYZ Conveyancing Lawyers
We help to make your dream home come true
Tel XXXXXXX'

Billboards and posters

Outdoor billboards in prominent positions, e.g. where traffic has to queue, on bus stops and at railway stations, can be effective, depending on where the target market is likely to see it. Use large print and keep the message simple and brief.

Indoor posters

Advertising posters displayed within a firm's premises aid cross-selling and remind clients of the range of services on offer (see Chapter 6 on relationship management and building brands for more on cross-selling opportunities).

Newspaper advertising

There is a choice of where the advertisements can be placed within a publication. If they are put in the classified sections, they are likely to be missed by readers who rarely look at those sections (however, see the example below).

Advertisements placed 'run of paper' (ROP), in the main body of the publication, next to articles, are likely to be seen by more people as they are reading articles in the publication.

Advertisements placed on the right-hand side and preferably near to where the thumb holds the newspaper are in a good position. Newspapers usually charge more for guaranteed places for an advertisement.

For many practices, there is a limited choice of local publications in which to advertise. However, one solicitor told me that he regularly places lineage advertisements in the classified sections. He puts in a famous quote or a few words of wisdom. He said clients often referred to seeing his quotes and looked forward to reading them. He thought it helped to bring in clients. This is a different and innovative approach to building awareness.

National advertising is probably only worthwhile if the firm has branches across the country or provides a nationwide service. British Gas advertised under the slogan of 'Find a solicitor who won't leave you in the dark when you move. Visit **www.house.co.uk/solicitor**' – a very simple advertisement placed in national newspapers offering an apparent competitive advantage and a benefit all in one sentence. Clever. It is worth visiting their website for the simplicity of it.

Telephone directories

The main national printed telephone directories are Yellow Pages and the Thomson Local Directory. Many areas also have local directories. If the clients you are serving tend to be within a 10–15 mile radius, it is worth having a listing in the local directories, providing they are well supported by local businesses. This is particularly the case where the main regional directory is substantial.

Do your own straw poll research regarding usage of directories before you commit to advertising in your local one. Ask everyone in the office which directory they turn to first if they want to find a restaurant, an estate agent, a surveyor, a solicitor and a plumber. Crude as this is as a research method, it may give an indication of the most popular directories locally.

Before placing an advertisement in a telephone directory consider the following points:

- potential clients are looking for a firm for a specific purpose;
- your competitors' details sit alongside your own details;
- details included or excluded from the advertisement may be used to select or eliminate the firm from the client's potential shopping list of firms to call;
- clients may simply use the directory to find your number again;
- the advertisement helps to remind them of other services you provide;
- once the advertisement is placed, it cannot be changed until the following year.

Be cautious about advertising in the local council's directory of its services. Advertising space is generally sold to local businesses to help pay for the production of the publication which is to the benefit of the council. In the author's opinion, your advertising budget is better invested elsewhere.

If you advertise in a number of telephone directories, test the return of the advertisements by changing the message and style of the advertisement in different publications. If you want to target particular types of clients, make the messages appeal to the target group. One conveyancing practice set up and the only promotion it did was advertising in Yellow Pages in a number of geographical regions. Within two years, nine people were employed on the back of it. It probably helped that the firm's name began with a B and so was near the front of the list of solicitors. Had it begun with a Y this method possibly would not have been as successful.

Other advertising channels

Radio

Contact your local commercial radio station and ask for their rate card. It will usually include details of the geographical coverage of the station and the number of listeners by gender and age band at different times of the day. Various cost packages will be offered in terms of the number of times an advertisement will be broadcast in a day, when and for how many seconds. The most expensive times are in the mornings before 9.00 a.m. and the evenings when people are travelling home.

Ask the radio station for the names of solicitors who advertise on their stations in different parts of the country other than in your own area. Contact the firms and ask what level of response they have had and if they are planning to repeat the advertising.

If you use radio advertising, keep messages simple and repeat them often. Have several advertisements made by the station at relatively low cost and use a variety to stop them from becoming stale. If the firm is near the centre of the broadcast area, or it has branches that cover the broadcast area, radio advertising may be worthwhile, if a reasonable cost is negotiated.

The radio station's style of programmes and advertising needs to be compatible with the firm's target market. For example, if the firm is aiming to attract people with high value properties, it could adversely affect its image if its advertisements are broadcast before or after an advertisement for cut-price double glazing.

Television

For the majority of firms, the cost of a television commercial will be prohibitive. Television advertising is therefore beyond the scope of this book.

Internet

The use of the Internet by conveyancing firms is discussed in Chapter 15.

Cinema advertising

Cinemas tend to attract younger age groups. If they are your target market, consider cinema advertising. The style of advertising needs to reflect the expectations of the target market. An advertisement which focuses on the firm having solid/staid, old fashioned values is unlikely to appeal to the 18–30 market who tend to look for leading edge, fast moving, cool talking, hi-tech products and services to which they can relate.

Flower bed advertising

Many councils allow firms to put advertising signs on a flower bed at a roundabout to say who has sponsored it. Given the often limited size of the advertising panel, these are generally used to raise awareness of the firm rather than to market a specific service.

Taxis

Advertising can be on the side of and inside taxis. Contact the local taxi company to assess the cost. Consider the quality and cleanliness of the taxis. Do they reflect the image you want potential clients to have of the firm?

Painted vehicles

Put an advertising message on the side of the firm's van, if it has one. Attention-grabbing, brightly designed messages will probably appeal to a younger audience, useful where first time buyers are a prime target. A lower key approach is using bumper or window stickers.

Sports grounds banners

Advertising at the local football team's grounds, costs permitting, will predominantly target local younger potential clients.

Village, parish and church newsletters

Many villages, parishes and churches produce their own newsletter distributed free of charge to all the households in their catchment area. If the profile of many of the households closely matches the type of potential clients you want to attract, ask to place an advertisement in the newsletters. The cost is often very low.

School activities

Some private and state schools allow firms to sponsor school activities in return for advertising in the school's publication or event programme, where these will be seen by the parents of children whom your firm wants to attract. The cost can be reasonable.

Theatre and concert programmes

Local theatres and concert organisers may be able to supply data on the type and age of people who attend productions or type of productions. If this fits the profile of target clients, then consider advertising in the programme for particular productions.

Rates and wastage

Rate cards

Each publication and broadcaster produces media rate cards which will give you data on the number of copies sold, readership, or listeners/viewers, their socio-economic breakdown and what geographical area is covered. It may tell you the editor's philosophy for the medium and at whom it is aimed. This information will help you decide whether sufficient people who see or hear the advertisement are the same as the target clients you aim to reach.

Contact the medium you are considering advertising in and ask for their rate card. This will tell you the cost of advertising in various parts of the publication or at different times of the day for the broadcast media. Many publications will also place the advertisement on their website at no extra cost.

Rates tend to be negotiable, subject to the number of times an advertisement appears. An advertising agency may be able to get better rates as they are sold the space at a discount and may be willing to pass some of the discount on to the client.

Wastage

For every advertisement, there is an element of wastage. Wastage is the number of people who potentially see or hear the advertisement who are unlikely ever to be clients. Wastage cost is measured by the total cost of advertising divided by the sum of the maximum number of people who are likely to come into contact with the advertisement, divided by the number of those who are most unlikely ever to become clients. An example of wastage would be a local newspaper covering a wide geographical area, when clients of the firm generally came from within a ten-mile radius.

What are you selling?

Developers and estate agents sell dreams, aspirations, happiness and fulfilment when they sell homes. Happy smiling faces, children laughing and parents arm in arm feature alongside photographs of new homes. They sell excitement, a better lifestyle and a better future.

Solicitors sell words: 'competitive', 'efficient', 'professional', 'fixed price'.

Yet solicitors are part of the dream package. They help the dreams come true. Their role is similar in some ways to that of a travel agent. They should help buyers make the right choice, manage their expectations and support their enthusiasm.

Enthusiasm tends to be in short supply when giving quotes for legal work. A typical client care letter, informing clients of costs and their rights if they are not happy, is hardly a welcoming letter to a happy forthcoming relationship. However, solicitors are not restricted to this letter and providing it need not exclude dream building in advertising and promotion.

Conveyancing services:

- help people to move on in their lives;
- help growing families move into better homes;
- help first time buyers have that amazing experience of owning their own home;
- help people change their lifestyle by releasing capital in their homes.

Conveyancers are the link to making this happen and advertising needs to reflect it.

Take a cursory glance at Yellow Pages advertising for conveyancing services. They tend to reveal the following generalities:

- the name of the firm is at the top of the advertisements;
- many repeat the same words: professional, competitive, fixed price, fast, efficient, conveyancing;
- few offer any real benefits;
- few name their target market;
- few use pictures or graphics to attract attention other than their logo;
- few try to distinguish themselves from their 'me too' competitors;
- virtually none build dreams.

To take an example, Benussi & Co. Solicitors is a firm specialising in family matters. The interesting feature of its website (**www.benussilaw.co.uk**) is the use of scenes of a tropical beach and palm trees in its photographs that evoke feelings of freedom, dreams of a better life, happy holidays and release. Rather than the doom and gloom of a divorce, the pictures give the impression of a brighter future which the firm will help its clients achieve.

Designing effective advertisements

Do not try to design an advertisement yourself unless you are a qualified or experienced designer. For all but the simplest messages, use a designer, but be aware that a lot of money can be wasted on a well-designed advertisement that does not fulfil its objectives. It may win a design award, but will it win clients?

An amateur designed advertisement looks just that – but do not assume that a 'designer' at a newspaper is any more qualified than you to design an advertisement.

The problem with designs for advertisements is that many of us think we know a good design when we see it, because it appeals to us. If you are not typical of the target market you aim to attract though, it could be that you liking it is an indication that it will not appeal to the target market. If you are aiming to attract first time buyers aged 25–34 and you are aged 50 plus, you may not be the best judge of the advertisement's appeal.

The purpose of this section is to offer guidelines as to what makes one advertisement better than another. It will help you to judge the selection of layouts which designers put forward.

Advertisements take readers on a journey in a very short period of time:

- the first mission is to attract readers' attention;
- once gained, that interest must be retained;
- the final stage is to motivate readers to take the desired action.

It has been said that people are beings of the familiar. We tend to feel more comfortable with an idea or a concept once we have seen it a few times. If advertising is used, there needs to be some consistency over a period of time so that people gain familiarity with the idea. That is not to say that it should not change, but the style needs to be consistent to gain recognition.

Features versus benefits

Businesses often sell the features of their products or services. This means that customers have to translate these into the benefits to themselves to decide whether or not to buy. The danger is that customers may not see how the features have value to them. Features are the knobs and whistles.

Benefits are what the knobs and whistles will do for the buyer. Firms should promote the benefits rather than the features. This applies whether in print, conversation or broadcast.

The concerns that many clients have revolve around time and money. If you can promote your service to relate to those issues, clients are more likely to look favourably at the firm.

Table 5.1 Features and benefits

Features		Benefits
We have conveyancing specialists	which means that . . .	our conveyancing specialists have the experience to see through problems quickly, saving you time and money.
Open five days a week	which means that . . .	you don't have to take time off work, we will open early and stay late if you can't make appointments in office hours.
We use the latest technology	which means that . . .	you have access to a secure area on the Internet, so that you can keep track of what is happening 24/7.
We keep you informed	which means that . . .	you won't have to spend time chasing us.

Using Ogilvy's guidelines in conveyancing

The following guidelines for writing advertisements that sell are provided in the late David Ogilvy's book *Ogilvy on Advertising* (Pan Books 1983). His guidelines stand the test of time and are invaluable for lay people to use to assess advertising layouts put forward by designers.

Layout

The eye first goes to the illustration, then the headline and if it gets that far, the body copy, so use that order in advertisements:

1. illustration;
2. headline;
3. body copy.

Illustrations

Use colour photographs rather than drawings.

Have a caption under the photograph which includes a benefit to the reader and the brand name.

Have photographs of people readers can identify with. A photograph of a woman will attract women's attention. On this basis, if women tend to telephone for quotes use photographs of women in advertising. If you want to attract people with young families, have a photo of happy smiling people with young families. Use the photograph to emphasise who it is you want to appeal to.

Headlines

The majority of people do not read the body copy, so the headline has to attract attention. Include a promise or a benefit in the headline and the brand name. If it includes a news item, that is a bonus. For example:

> 'New Complete Control Conveyancing
> puts you in control when buying a home
> with Bloggs & Co. Property Lawyers'

If the headline is just the firm's name, money is probably being wasted on placing the advertisement.

Use the name of the client type in the heading if you are appealing to a narrow range of buyers, to attract their attention.

> 'First time buyers . . . Freehold property buyers . . . Women under 30 buying a home . . . Buyers over 50 . . .'

> *When you put your headline in quotes, you increase recall by an average of 28%.*
>
> Ogilvy on Advertising

> 'We promise to help make your home move as hassle free as possible.'

Body copy

People will only read the body copy if they are interested in the service. Write the body copy as if you were writing to just one person. Use short sentences and simple everyday words. Tell readers specifically what the service will do for them individually.

Testimonials make the copy more believable. The words of another client praising your service are more credible than those of the advertiser. Put the testimonials in quotation marks to increase their eye appeal and gain attention.

Ogilvy recommended including the price in advertisements, but this is not commonly done in conveyancing advertising. Perhaps there is an argument for including the cost of legal work (see the Solicitors' Publicity Code 2001 reproduced in Appendix C). The cost of products is usually included in advertisements. It is likely to be the first item a person looks at to see whether it is worth reading on. If you quote on a fixed cost basis according to the value of the property, then including the cost of the conveyancing saves people telephoning to find out the fee for property in a particular price band. It may be less than or in line with what readers expect. A deadline date can be included after which prices may change. This could be particularly useful to attract additional work in the short term. 'From £x for August only.'

If the advertisement has a long shelf-life, i.e. a telephone directory will last for a year or longer, take care to ensure that the advertising wording will still be relevant at the end of the advertisement's life.

In Ogilvy's experience as an advertising guru, long copy sold more than short copy. The copy must be written well and grab attention from the first paragraph onwards. Include facts to give weight and avoid superlatives; use sub-headings; start the body copy with a drop-initial; and use short lines of 35 to 45 characters wide rather than long lines, which are difficult to read.

Set the type black on a white background rather than reverse which is harder to read. If you do use reverse print, white on black, only use it for 'star bursts' with one or two words in it, e.g. '10% OFF', and use a sans serif font (without lines at the top and bottom of letters – like this example).

In the normal text use lower case in a serif typeface (as in this book) as this is easier to read than sans serif. Newspapers, magazines and books tend to be written in a serif typeface.

Avoid the excessive use of block capitals, which are often almost impossible to read.

Use bullet points to draw attention, or number a list of facts.

Avoid mixing font styles. Two are just acceptable, but avoid more than that. Use bold to emphasise points rather than changing the font style.

BOX 5.1 Persuasive advertising

According to K. Johnson, there are fifteen most persuasive words to evoke positive feelings towards a product or service:

1. ***Discover***: this implies the promise of something better.
2. ***Good***: good does not over promise. It is a solid word that implies stability and reliability.
3. ***Money***: it takes a long while to earn it and we don't want to spend more than we have to for the service we are given.
4. ***Easy***: moving home is complicated enough. Simplicity appeals.
5. ***Guaranteed***: we don't want to make the wrong decision. Anything that has a guarantee with it minimises the downside of risk. It helps to reassure.
6. ***Health***: moving home is stressful. It can adversely affect our health. A service that takes the worry and anxiety out of handling difficult situations will appeal.
7. ***Love***: love comes in many forms. 'Friendly, approachable people.'
8. ***New***: it must be better, if it is new. It must be cutting edge and up to date, if it is new.
9. ***Proven***: if it's proven, it gives reassurance that it works. It implies experience.
10. ***Results***: we pay to get results. We want to know what results we will get for the payment made.
11. ***Safe***: if we know the file is in safe hands, it is reassuring.
12. ***Save***: the thinking here is that saving is better than spending. If the firm can save the client money and time, that must be good.
13. ***Own***: owning implies possession and is better than spending. Refer to owning their home, rather than buying it.
14. ***Free***: while we might believe that you can't get something for nothing, the thought of getting something for free still appeals. Whatever is free though, has to have a value. Offering to give a free quote fools no one, as people expect quotes to be free.
15. ***Best***: if you can quote why your service is the best (won awards, e.g. Lexcel quality award; 98 per cent of clients are satisfied or very satisfied with the service; top 10 in the country/region) then it encourages people to use it.

Adapted from Johnson, K. (2003) *Selling with NLP*, Nicholas Brealey Publishing

Call to action

Tell readers what to do next:

- Telephone for a fixed quote.
- Go to www. . .. . for an online quote.
- Telephone (name) for a friendly no commitment chat to discuss your home purchase or sale . . .

Include the firm's name, the word 'solicitors', address and telephone number. Where the advertisement is in a telephone directory, people will use the directory to find out location and telephone numbers. Make both large and easy to read.

Be aware of the print and paper quality of the medium you are using to advertise in and check how it will look on similar quality materials. An excellent advertisement on high quality paper may look completely different and disappointing when reproduced in a local free newspaper.

From the author's painful experience, insist on seeing the advertisement before you give approval to print. Do not trust the member of staff who tells you he has checked it and it is fine.

The conveyancing advertisement example shown in Figure 5.1 is strong in the following ways:

- It is particularly eye-catching in colour with the unusual use of the cheetah implying speed (but reproduced here in black and white).
- The cheetah looks into the advertisement drawing the reader's eye to the wording.
- It has shape in the form of the semicircle.
- It uses bullet points to draw the eye down the page.
- With the headline of 'Moving Home?', it speaks in layman's language.
- It avoids the use of the jargon word 'conveyancing'.
- It uses black print on a white background for the key buying points.
- It gives the firm credibility by stating that 72 per cent (a believable figure) clients return or are recommended.
- It offers further help of appointing an estate agent and obtaining a mortgage.
- It provides a benefit with the simple words 'More speed less stress'.
- It includes 'cause marketing' to generate good feelings by stating that the new animal hospital is supported by Gard and Co. Solicitors.

Figure 5.1 Gard & Co. advertisement

By kind permission of Gard & Co. Designed by Bryn Davies of DDA Design Works in collaboration with Steven Hudson of Gard & Co.

Briefing an advertising or design agency

If you plan to use an advertising agency, aim to see two or three before you make your decision. First ask to see a number of advertisements the agency has designed for similar service clients. The purpose of the advertisements is to achieve an objective, so whether you like the advertisement or not, in some ways is immaterial. What matters is: whether it achieved its objective and how this was assessed.

Discuss the advertisements the agency has already done and ask:

- what the objective of the advertisement was;
- how the response was measured;
- for the name of the person in the client's office to find out how successful it was;
- what the agency's fees are;
- where the agency would recommend advertising, when and how frequently;
- what discounts it can get from the rate card (list of charges) of the selected medium.

Be prepared to give the agency the specific objectives you want to achieve from the advertising. If you are not clear about these, wait until you are sure what you want. Substantial money can be wasted on advertising that does not have a clear purpose. Think how you will measure the results of the advertising to assess its worth and take advice from the advertising agency.

Tell the agency:

- the target clients you want to attract: age, gender, socio-economic background;
- the type of property purchase or sale;
- the geographical area;
- the timescale;
- the budget;
- the ethos;
- the benefits of using the firm, your competitive advantage, what makes you stand out;
- the key messages or perceptions you want clients to have about the firm;
- the facts and background to conveyancing;
- the testimonials that clients have said about you.

When the agency shows you the rough layouts of advertisements, show them to people in the office who are representative of the people you aim to attract. Their comments are often more relevant than your own. Do get someone to check the accuracy of the wording and spelling of the final layout of the advertisment.

FURTHER READING

Hahn, Fred E. *et al.* (2003) *Do-it-yourself Advertising and Promotion,* John Wiley and Sons.

Johnson, K.L. (2003) *Selling with NLP,* Nicholas Brealey Publishing.

Ogilvy, David (1983) *Ogilvy on Advertising,* Pan Books.

6

Relationship management and building brands

KEY POINTS

This chapter will

- recommend how to manage existing clients to generate fee income
- explain the components of retaining clients
- provide the path to gaining recommendations
- suggest ideas to encourage staff to cross-refer clients
- show you how to develop brands to reassure clients

Managing existing clients

When people become clients

Do you know how much it costs your firm to bring in a new client? It costs considerably more than it does to retain an existing one, yet many firms place greater emphasis on gaining new clients and pay insufficient attention to retaining their existing ones.

The acquisition costs of new clients include the marketing expenditure, the time it takes to encourage clients to give instructions, such as giving quotes over the telephone and following up with letters and literature, time to get to know clients and their situation and the set up costs of money laundering regulations. With existing clients, many of these costs will have already been absorbed which, together with goodwill, makes these clients potentially more profitable.

The results of a survey of 61 leading law firms recommended that less than 40 per cent of the marketing budget should be spent on gaining new clients, leaving more than 60 per cent for retaining existing ones (Wheeler Associates and McCallum Layton (2000) 'Marketing the Advisers 1999', *The Lawyer*, 7 February).

In some firms lawyers are recognised and rewarded for gaining new clients and less attention is given to those who generate fee income from existing clients. New clients may be given higher levels of attention to develop the relationship. Once the work has been completed they become 'existing clients' and attention levels drop as the focus is on attracting new ones.

The first issue, therefore, is to decide whether the necessary effort will be put into retaining existing clients.

When writing an article for a Law Society magazine on client care, I worked out that I had used six different firms of solicitors in the previous sixteen years. They all gave me a good service. There was only one I probably would not use again, but I would have been happy to use any of the others again, except that none of them ever really tried to keep me as a client. Only one of them ever contacted me again. They were not interested in me after the initial legal task was completed.

To encourage clients to return to the firm, consider the points made in Figure 6.1.

Figure 6.1 Keeping clients

Product or client orientation

Product orientation is a method of classifying clients according to the products (services) they buy from the firm. Are they conveyancing clients, family clients, personal injury clients, commercial clients – or are they classified from the perspective of need? If clients are pigeon-holed by the service they use, they are likely also to pigeon-hole the firm, as a conveyancing practice, for example, and not to use it for other services.

There is a tendency for firms to work almost as a collection of individual businesses consisting of departments, where clients are considered the 'property' of a particular department. A survey in 2004 found that just 5 per cent of law firm respondents strongly agreed with the statement that 'Their firm's customer relationship management initiatives ensures that the firm delivers excellent service to its key clients in a seamless, proactive and cost-effective manner' (*One for all, and all for one?*, a report by Wheeler Associates and McCallum Layton, 2004; see **Kevin.Wheeler@wheelerassociates.co.uk**).

Client orientation is an attitude of mind as well as a business process. It revolves around seeing a client as a whole person with a range of different needs. It is not about classification but about seeing clients as human beings with commercial and non-commercial legal requirements over a period of time.

It is about being responsive to the clients' needs as age and life events progress. The advantages are that if you are responsive to clients' needs, by tuning in to what they want, they are more likely to use you again, and they are more likely to recommend you to others.

Proactive to clients' needs: life triggers

By taking a client-orientation rather than a product-orientation approach, typical life triggers can be identified when the clients are likely to need particular services. Contacting clients when you think they need to be alerted to changes in the law likely to affect them and when they may have other legal needs, is taking a proactive approach to looking after them. It is going the extra mile and helps your firm stand out from its competitors.

EXAMPLE **Life triggers**

A couple in their mid to late 60s, married with children and grandchildren, and two parents, one from each spouse, are likely to need legal services for:

- conveyancing;
- enduring powers of attorney for themselves;
- enduring powers of attorney for parents;
- updating wills;
- trust set up for grandchildren;
- welfare advice for themselves/parents;
- mental health advice for themselves and parents;
- landlord/tenant advice;
- employment disputes;
- sex discrimination advice;
- criminal and matrimonial advice;
- driving offences.

It is easy to see people as stereotypes and therefore not consider their wider potential legal service needs (see Chapter 4, 'Direct marketing' on gaining and retaining clients, for client segmentation and setting up a database; also see Chapter 3 explaining how a customer relationship management (CRM) system may help).

Recommendations

How much of your business comes to you through recommendations? Is it 60 per cent, 70 per cent, 75 per cent or more of your fee income?

Why do people recommend you? Giving a good service is not a sufficient reason to risk giving a recommendation. Think why you are willing to recommend a restaurant or a garage to someone. It has to be something more than the business simply doing what it says it will. It is something extra. It has to be enough to make you willing to risk your own reputation to a degree by making a recommendation. After all, if the person to whom you make the recommendation has a bad meal or poor service, that person will not think much of you, the recommender.

To recommend your firm to others, clients have to have a commitment to you and your firm. They need to feel that they can trust you to give a consistently good service to the person they are recommending you to. They want to feel that the recommendation won't backfire on them. How is this sense of commitment developed? It is partly done by showing that you genuinely value people as individuals and are looking out for them. That you want to provide a service over and above what they expect. One way of doing that is by seeing the client as a person with changing requirements.

The other aspect is that clients need to be informed that you do provide other services, so their awareness needs to be raised.

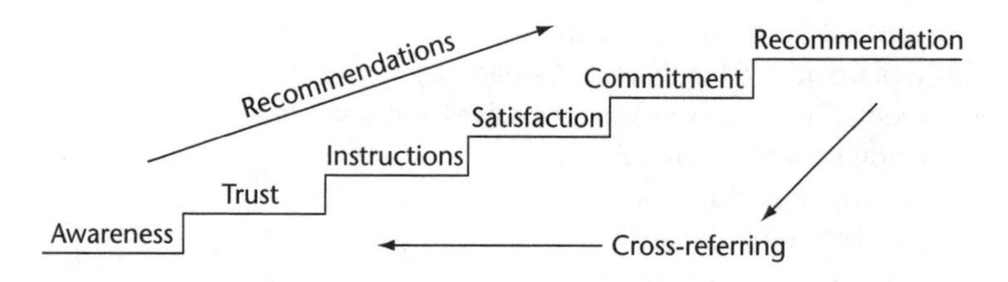

Figure 6.2 The path to gaining recommendations

Cross-referrals

Cross-referring or cross-selling is identifying clients' additional legal needs and informing them of other legal services the firm provides to meet these needs. Colleagues in appropriate departments are informed of the client's requirements; they then are introduced to or contact the client to assist them.

Who is involved?

First look at who is involved in cross-selling or cross-referring and then lead into how the information is gathered. Everyone in the practice should be involved. Everyone from the receptionist to the senior partner has a part to play in helping the client feel appreciated. Every contact clients have with the firm will contribute to making them feel valued or taken for granted.

Staff need to understand the values of the firm so that they can project them in everything they do. Does the firm see clients as the most important people? Does it want to make each individual person feel welcome? Does it emphasise to clients that the firm is there to look after them and to take the worry of dealing with legal issues off their shoulders?

Dealing with resistance to cross-referring

In many firms there may be resistance to cross-referring clients to colleagues in other departments even though generating fee income from existing clients is generally more profitable than from new clients. If there is resistance to sharing clients, the blockage needs to be removed or minimised so that proactive cross-referring of clients can become a reality.

The reasons why there may be resistance to cross-referring clients include:

- time pressures;
- laziness and apathy;
- ignorance of other services available;
- possessiveness of clients to achieve targets;
- lack of awareness of other fee earners' roles and expertise;
- insufficient contact between fee earners in other departments or branches;
- concern that if the client is not treated well by the fee earner in another department, it may damage the client's relationship with the original fee earner;

- forgetfulness; and
- not knowing the client well enough.

Solutions to breaking down these barriers include:

- taking a client-orientated proactive approach;
- developing a culture that a person is the firm's client, not the fee earner's client;
- leading by example, with partners as role models and mentors;
- emphasising that everyone in the firm is involved;
- getting to know clients better (relationship development);
- introducing cross-referring as a part of staff job descriptions and appraisals;
- improving internal marketing so that everyone knows the range of services available;
- having regular team meetings and cross-team presentations;
- using a procedure to ensure that referrals are acted upon;
- appointing a client champion (commonly called a key account manager in other industries) to look after specific clients.

Client culture and role models

The partners play a significant role in changing attitudes and cultures within firms. Fee earners and support staff will look to the partners to see what they do and how they treat clients. They will assess how well partners identify cross-selling opportunities and look for evidence that they have introduced the client to another specialist within the firm. If the senior people in the firm are not committed to cross-referring and prefer to keep clients to themselves, others will tend to do likewise.

Partners need to be role models and mentors. They need to encourage, praise and reward cross-referring activities to emphasise the desire and drive to achieve results from it. Other staff will look at the partners and will do as they do. Actions speak louder than words.

When new staff join the firm, they need to be told of their role in cross-referring. During team meetings and internal training, ways that people can help with cross-referring can be discussed. Culture is developed over time. To change it, there needs to be a consistency of messages and actions over a period of time.

Get to know clients better

The more individuals know and understand clients, the more they can identify when they are likely to need further legal services. While it is not practical to know sufficient about all the firm's clients to give a personalised proactive service, through segmentation (see Chapter 4 on direct marketing) it is possible to identify target clients who are likely to want a number of services and so be more profitable to the firm.

Appraisal system

To stress the importance of cross-selling, part of the appraisal system can be dedicated to achieving it. Fee earners can have target figures, whether to do with the number of clients they have introduced to other specialist fee earners, or a target fee income figure the other fee earner achieved.

Part of staff training and development requirements can include how to identify cross-referring opportunities, brainstorming clients' needs, developing further and deeper relationships with identified clients, and introducing them to other key people in the firm.

There are two attitudes towards giving incentives for successful cross-referrals. One is that only if people are motivated by incentives, will it encourage them to work harder to identify opportunities. The other view is that cross-referring should be part of people's roles and that they should take it as seriously as any other part of the job for which they are paid.

Cross-departmental meetings and presentations

One of the reasons given for not cross-referring clients is that people in other departments may not be familiar with the other services the firm provides and the people who provide them. In larger firms, staff may not know colleagues in other departments and so not have full confidence in them. This is an internal marketing issue.

The more people are familiar with other departments, the more they should be willing to cross-refer clients. Arrange to have people from different departments give short lunchtime presentations to cross-departmental teams about what they do. This will aid understanding and knowledge. It will give an opportunity to get to know other staff and partners better. Informal social events and interdepartmental in-house training where people sit with others from different departments will also assist.

Consider having interdepartmental team meetings. Before the meeting, each fee earner will earmark a handful of clients to whom they think a better service can be given by identifying their other legal needs and arranging to introduce them to fee earners in other departments.

Develop formal procedures

Opportunities to pass on referrals to people in other departments may slip through the net in the absence of formal procedures. These allow the person who gave the referral to see what happened to it and to follow it up if necessary.

People will be reluctant to forward referrals if the person who receives them does nothing with them. This can damage the relationship with a client who has been told to expect a call from a colleague in another department that subsequently never materialises.

Consider using a simple form which can be sent by e-mail to a colleague in another department who has been given the referral details. A copy can be sent to the person responsible for marketing the firm and developing client relations and to the client champion (see below) to monitor and analyse the results (see Figure 6.3).

Client champions

For certain clients, consider appointing a person who will act as their 'personal account manager'. This person can be called a client champion and focus on one-to-one client relationship management. The client champion will identify potential future legal needs, coordinate colleagues and approach clients, showing that the firm takes a proactive approach to looking after them.

The client champion's role is to identify changes in the law that are likely to affect clients of which they may not be aware. It is to act in a business or personal advisory role, not just to do what clients have asked for, but to get to know them and their business, where relevant, and to identify areas where clients would benefit from legal protection from the myriad of new laws and regulations.

This person will manage the contact and ensure there is no duplication in targeting clients. They will also be the person clients contact if they have a problem or if they want to discuss additional legal services.

In-office cross-selling

When clients first come to see you, it will be about a particular issue that needs addressing. You may give them a copy of your brochure, but it is unlikely that clients will give it more than a passing reference and scan read it. Even if it has the range of services that the firm provides in it, clients are unlikely to remember them without further reminders.

Reminders

In the reception and waiting room, on the wall facing where clients sit, have a framed A2 poster of the range of services which the firm provides.

In the interview rooms and in solicitors' offices, behind and to the side of where the solicitor sits, place the framed poster so what when

Referral form

Name of client: Reference details:

Name they prefer to be called face to face or on the telephone:
(Mr, Mrs, Miss, Ms, first name, other)

Telephone number: Address:

Best time to telephone:

Originating department and branch:

Name of person referring the client: Telephone number:

Destination/referred department and branch:

Name of person referral information given to:

Brief background of the client and potential services required:

Brief details of any ongoing matter including the department and name of the fee earner dealing with it:

Date referral given: Date followed up:

Actions taken:

Fee income generated: £
Date referrer advised of the follow-up outcome:

Date form passed to XXX for analysis:

Figure 6.3 Referral form

clients are not looking at the solicitor, they will see the poster and be reminded of the services.

On any advertising or Yellow Pages advertisement, to form the border, have in small print, the list of services the firm provides.

Letter-headed sheets of paper are potentially the most powerful sales aid to help you cross-refer services.

If they are not already listed, include in small print down the right-hand margin the range of services provided. You can decide for each letter whether you will have the list printed on it or not as it can be inserted when the letter is printed as a template.

Membership/business card

Use your business card as an opportunity to remind or advise clients of other services. Consider having on the back of the card the range of services and a photograph of the solicitor named on the front to show or remind people of what he or she looks like.

Have space for the appointment time and to write down the password to gain access to a secure area on the website to check the progress on the file for a conveyancing matter.

Conveyancing

For couples buying a home together, emphasise the importance of their need to write a will, particularly if they are not married.

If clients have bought a new house, make a diary note two years later to contact them in case they are thinking of moving again and want conveyancing services. Offer to give them a discount and emphasise that it will be more convenient and easier for them if you do the sale of the property as you have all the papers to hand.

EXAMPLE **Cross-referring opportunities: wants and needs**

Clients will know what their wants are, but may not be aware of what their needs are.

A client may come to your firm to do the conveyancing on a property. If a client is buying or selling a property worth more than £250,000, there may be a need to mitigate inheritance tax and write a (new) will. It should be automatic, therefore, to raise these needs of which clients may not be aware to give an enhanced service.

Identification of clients' needs and sales training for all fee earners may help to maximise cross-referring opportunities – and fee income. A procedure in the firm to ensure that all target clients are assessed for their legal needs will emphasise the importance the partners attach to it.

Wills

Consider areas of legal work where other people may be involved. With wills, for example, you will have the names and addresses of executors.

Write a simple guide to an executor's role and duties and offer to send it to the executors with the client's agreement. Invite the executors to come in to discuss their role and ask them if they have written a will or whether they have updated it in the last five years.

Divorce

Remind people of the need to rewrite their wills on separation or divorce and on remarriage. Pass their details to the conveyancing department where a home sale and purchase is likely.

Commercial

See clients as people rather than as company representatives. Offer them personal, family and residential conveyancing legal services. Occasionally send them a domestic newsletter as well as a commercial one.

Professional contacts

Consider what opportunities there are to cross-sell to other professional contacts' clients. An accountant, surveyor or estate agent may be happy to let you take space with a relevant article in their newsletter in return for taking space in yours. This gives an opportunity to reach a wider market, but with the added credibility of the other professional's business name.

Events

With professional contacts, consider putting on joint events for clients. These may be 6.00 p.m. seminars or talks where selected clients are personally invited. This provides an opportunity to have your name placed in front of the joint host's clients in the form of the invitation and to be introduced to and meet potential clients face to face.

All the key staff should be invited to attend, but consider giving them training on how to get the best out of networking to avoid them huddling together and not speaking to clients and developing contacts (see Chapter 8 on networking and Chapter 9 on profile-raising activities).

Entertaining clients is one way to subtly cross-sell, simply by introducing clients to solicitors who work in different legal areas.

'Clients . . . deem corporate entertainment an important factor in assessing their relationships with law firms, according to a survey carried out by London commercial firm Campbell Hooper' ([2001] *Gazette*, 30 November). In the same study, '78% wanted to be updated on legal issues with newsletters, and 71% wished to attend legal seminars'.

Brand building

We are all familiar with the power of brands as consumers. We tend to select certain brands because we trust them to give a consistent service and no surprises in quality. We tend to have an emotional response to a brand. This is shown when people want to be associated with the brand by being willing to wear the brand's name on clothing, for example.

Brand stretching is where the same brand is used across a range of products and services. A typical example is Virgin. It started out as a music retailer and through innovation, stretched the brand to include soft drinks, hotels, train and air travel and financial services, to name a few. Where people trust the brand to give them quality, they are more likely to be willing to try other products or services with the same brand name.

A service brand embodies the values of the firm and the expectations developed by clients of the level and quality of service they will receive. The development of brands helps firms to give an element of tangibility to their service offering. Everyone in the firm needs to be familiar with what the brand represents and be constantly working to show that they are part of the brand and help to enhance it. The brand is also used to differentiate the firm from competitors in clients' minds.

One way to manage and meet clients' expectations is to establish clear brand values in clients' minds by promotional activities and, most importantly, by the behaviour of everyone in the firm towards clients. Behaviour is firm evidence of the brand in action.

The brand is developed through:

- interactions of the firm's people with people outside the firm, both clients and non-clients;
- the physical representation of it through the logo, letter-headed paper, brochures and pamphlets, signage and even colour coding of interior decorations;
- perceptions of people outside the firm if it is compared to competitors.

Building a brand

Every time a person within the firm interacts with others, this will contribute towards their perception of the firm. The first stage in developing a brand is deciding the values of the firm and how it wants to distinguish itself from competitors. Research to assess clients' perceptions of the firm will indicate whether there is a need to change their perceptions or build on them.

The values that a conveyancing firm may want its clients to identify with the practice are, for example, that it puts its clients at the centre of the action, keeps them informed, is straight-talking and efficient.

Next, the values have to be translated into staff's behaviour and attitudes before they can ever be communicated to clients. A good public relations campaign to announce to the world, or even to the local area, that the firm's brand values are speed of response times and efficiency, immediately lose credibility if clients have difficulty getting telephone calls returned.

EXAMPLE **Actions to support values**

In response to a telephone banking enquiry in the middle of a working day, a High Street bank answered with an automated voice message. An enthusiastic female voice announced in a delighted tone that 24-hour telephone banking was now available seven days a week for customers' convenience. At the end of the message, another automated message informed the caller that as all the staff were busy on other calls, the caller might like to call back later.

To develop a brand requires levels of consistency across the firm in terms of how clients are treated. When there is consistency of behaviour towards clients, the next two stages of developing the brand can progress: deciding the physical presentation and informing clients and referrers.

The physical representation of the firm includes the external impression the buildings give, the internal environment, the reception décor, the type of chairs and even the floor covering. The quality of the paper of its letter-heads, the feel and quality of its brochures and the impression given by advertising also provide the physical representation, in addition to the logo and any slogan used. These are designed with the expectations of the target clients in mind. There needs to be harmony in meeting these expectations. For example, a firm aiming for the upper middle and upper end of the market would damage its brand image if it subsequently had flyers stuffed through households' doors together with the local free newspaper.

The physical representations of the brand are used to inform clients of the brand's values either implicitly or explicitly. A series of press announcements, newsletters, articles in journals, seminars, advertisements and everyday client contact is used to inform clients of the brand values.

Firms have a brand whether they are consciously aware of it or not. The pertinent question is if and how well it is managed.

Some firms have brands that have a clearly defined personality that would not benefit from stretching. If a firm is known as a leading commercial practice, but it also has a residential conveyancing department, for example, the firm could benefit from establishing a separate brand for its conveyancing services. This is to develop a perception in clients' minds of that service, which does not water down or affect the perception core clients have of the main firm.

For example, Bath firm Withy King established a separate brand called 'Complete' for its residential department. It set up in a retail shop just off the main shopping area and fitted it out with modern wooden flooring and airy interior design to establish its brand profile and attract and service passing trade in addition to its core clients. Withy King Solicitors also created a brand called 'Accrue', for its investment and stock-broking clients. This has a completely separate brand image, livery colours and also uses a retail premises for its clients.

Through its fresh innovative approach and leverage of its assets, Withy King won the the Wiltshire Business of the Year award.

The growth of personal injury marketing cooperatives among law firms is an example of innovation and leveraging the marketing budget. The cooperatives use a single brand name for all the firms taking part. Rather than taking a competitive approach, cooperative marketing using an umbrella brand can harness the buying power that bulk purchase of media advertising space can bring. This helps to cut costs and gives firms access to forms of mass media, such as television, which would otherwise be out of reach. The brand name is used to establish perceptions in clients' and potential clients' minds of what to expect.

The conveyancing sector is ripe for the development of marketing cooperatives to challenge the increased influence estate agents will have over clients with the introduction of Home Information Packs.

The Home Information Pack Action Group (HIPAG) is in the fledgeling stages of development. It plans, through a marketing cooperative of conveyancing firms across the country, to introduce an umbrella brand, HIPPO (Home Information Packs Prepared to Order), to offer an alternative to clients wanting to sell their homes, rather than going to an estate agent to have a pack made.

Further reading

Adam, L. (2002) *Marketing Your Law Firm,* Law Society Publishing.

Adler, M. (1990) *Clarity for Lawyers,* Law Society Publishing.

Bown-Wilson, D. and Courtney, G. (2002) *Marketing, Management and Motivation,* Law Society Publishing.

Carey, P. (ed.) (2004) *Data Protection Handbook,* Law Society Publishing.

Law Society (2004) *The Client Care Guide to Keeping Clients* (only available online at www.clientcare.lawsociety.org.uk).

Webb, N. (2003) *Internet Marketing,* Law Society Publishing.

Useful websites

Committee of Advertising Practice **www.cap.org.uk**

Direct Marketing Association **www.dma.org.uk**

Home Information Pack Action Group **www.hipag.co.uk**

Information Commissioner **www.informationcommissioner.gov.uk**

Law Society's *Gazette* **www.lawgazette.co.uk**

Law Society's client care pages **www.clientcare.lawsociety.org.uk**

Royal Mail **www.royalmail.com**

7

Brochures, flyers and newsletters

KEY POINTS

This chapter will

- provide guidelines for producing brochures, flyers and newsletters
- recommend what to do when appointing a design agency and how to use it efficiently
- suggest tips on how to save costs in design, printing and distribution
- advise how to write a newsletter that will attract attention and fulfil its purpose

Brochure and flyer/leaflet differences

A flyer is a single sheet of paper and a brochure is in a booklet or folder format. A flyer tends to be used for short-term messages and simple calls to action.

If business is in a quiet patch, a flyer may be produced to tell potential clients of a special reduced offer for conveyancing before a certain date. This would then be distributed to households within a selected geographical area or, better still, sent to referrers to pass on as a benefit to their clients.

A brochure tends to have a longer life and is of higher quality. It is used to give confidence to potential clients and to reassure them of the quality of service and advice they can expect from the firm. It is the firm's window display. It gives an impression of what the client can expect when instructing the practice. It may be sent out to clients when a quote is given, an appointment made to see a legal adviser or given when instructions are gained. It helps to set and manage clients' expectations.

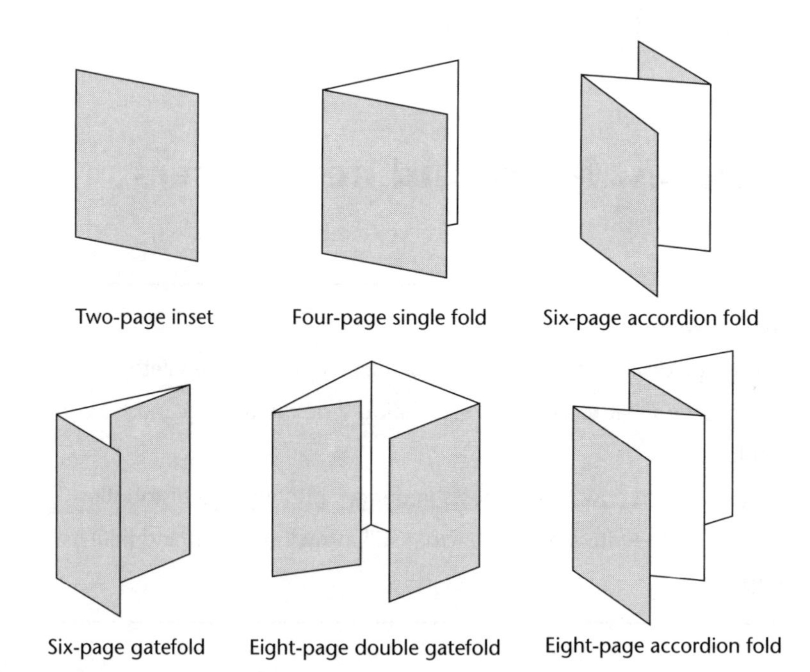

Figure 7.1 Leaflet flat plans

Guidelines for producing brochures, flyers and newsletters

Consider:

- What do you want it for?
- What is the budget?
- What is the time frame?
- Who will produce it?
- How will it be distributed?

What do you want it for?

First of all, be clear about the reasons for wanting the literature:

- Is it to update a previous brochure?
- Have your competitors updated theirs and so you think you need to do the same?
- Is it to give a certain message, e.g. the fact that you have moved/are moving premises?
- Do you have new services available and new people to deliver them?

- Is there something new that will give an added benefit to clients using you?
- Do you want to develop the brand?
- Do you want to change perceptions clients have of the firm from a traditional, 'High Street' practice with a range of services to one that is predominantly commercial, business solutions orientated, leading edge, modern and stocked with 'vampire' solicitors?
- Is it to target a specific type of potential clients, for example, people with properties worth over £350,000 or under £120,000?

Consider which would be the best medium to use to get the message across. If it is for a short, sharp message, you may not need a brochure. It will probably be better for short messages to use flyers, letters or newsletters rather than a brochure. You may choose to use a combination of an introductory letter followed by a flyer or a newsletter. Whichever is selected, always include a call to action and easy ways of contacting the firm. Tell readers what they need to do next and make it easy for them to do it.

A brochure and a series of newsletters are best used when the message is longer term and requires a slow and steady build time. For example, to change people's perceptions of the firm or to develop the brand in terms of recognition and what it stands for, a brochure and a series of newsletters would be better than a leaflet.

For most firms, the brochure route involves a corporate brochure rather than a stand-alone one for just the conveyancing department. A stand-alone brochure is particularly used when the firm wants to establish a separate brand from the firm's core brand. It may have decided to target an alternative client type to be given different messages from those given to the firm's traditional clients. With the intention of not watering down or damaging the core brand, a separate brochure for the new brand is generally used.

What is the budget?

There are two ways to approach deciding the budget. The first is the results orientated approach. Decide what is needed, then get it costed to see if the firm is happy to spend that amount. The second is the budget approach. Fix a maximum amount the firm is willing to invest and stick to it. There are three elements of costs: the designer's cost, the printing cost and the distribution cost.

What is the time frame?

Leaflets can be produced fairly quickly, within two weeks or sometimes less, but it is rare for all the steps to be taken in that time frame, and for the firm to be happy with the outcome. Always overestimate how long it will take. Add on extra time when more than three people are involved in the decision-making process. A period of a month to six weeks is fairly common to produce a simple brochure or leaflet.

One client approached three local designers for quotes. Two came to see her. One produced a quote in a week and the other took six weeks. Both were excessive in their charges compared to a third quote from a long-established company, which was less than half the amount of the other two and arrived within 24 hours of the request.

Who will produce it?

Do not be tempted to design publicity material yourself unless you are a skilled designer. The documents are too important to risk giving the wrong impression of the department or the firm. Potential clients may receive a brochure or pamphlet following a quote over the telephone and use it to form an impression of the practice. If you do decide to design the leaflet yourself or to have it designed by someone within the firm, it would help to follow the guidelines for writing an advertisement provided in Chapter 5, on how to save money on advertising. They can also be used to assess the layouts suggested by the design agency.

How will it be distributed?

Distribution can be by post, e-mail, included in other correspondence to clients, included with a local free newspaper distribution or other individual mailings delivered door to door.

How publicity material is distributed sends a message to the receiver regarding the importance of the publication. A leaflet distributed by the local free newspaper together with other leaflets for double glazing, etc., is less likely to be given close attention than a personally addressed and signed letter with a brochure or leaflet in the post. However, the former is likely to be substantially cheaper to distribute than the latter.

Post, generally the most expensive method, can be the most effective in terms of the material being seen. If the postal route is selected plan to use second class post to keep costs contained. Check that the mailing list is up to date, that addresses are correct, e.g. if the communication is to a previous conveyancing client, check that the address is to the new home rather than the old home address. Check whether clients have said that they do not want to receive any marketing materials from the firm.

Check with the probate department that the client is still 'above ground'. Marketing campaigns designed to generate further business can cause clients to turn against the firm if names and addresses are not correct.

As a final check, assess the first impression which the leaflet or brochure presents. Does it use the firm's colours so that the corporate image is carried through? What is the size, shape and colour? If an address label is used, is it put on straight? A brown envelope is offputting. Is the firm's name and logo given on the envelope, possibly by the franking machine? If people know it is from their solicitor this will encourage them to open it.

When receivers open the envelope, do they see their name correctly spelt and the firm's name? Does the covering letter look attractive to read? Does it start off telling the client about the firm (a turn-off) or does it relate immediately to the client's situation? Is the leaflet or brochure visually appealing? Does it encourage the reader to want to open it and read it?

Using a design agency

There are two types of brief for design agencies. One is where the law firm says 'This is what we want – now do it'. The second is where the firm says 'This is what we think we need, what do you think we need?' and uses the design agency for their experience and skills.

Turn-offs from the agency's point of view are:

- not getting to speak to the decision maker;
- when the decision will be made by a committee of more than three people who all feel they are not fulfilling their role unless they change the design (something about horses designed by committees ending up looking like camels, comes to mind);
- there is no clear brief.

Stages of production

1. The clients define the target set of people the publicity will reach. They describe the perceptions they want their clients to have of the firm or the department. For example, 'To target 35 to 55-year-olds living in rural properties. The firm wants clients to see the conveyancing department as giving a high level of personal service where their solicitor will deal with every part of the conveyance. By instructing the firm, they will be using a safe pair of hands.'
2. The clients are clear about the budget, using either method above, and tell the design agency so that it knows which approach is being taken.
3. The clients have a feel for what they want the final newsletter, brochure or flyer to look like. It can help to look at competitors' publicity materials or other businesses' literature to see what they like and don't like. It may be that they want the feel to be leading edge

and ultra-modern or prefer a reassuring, traditional style. Once the clients decide they want a certain style, with the perfect brief, they do not change their minds radically,

4. Clients have an idea of the numbers of newsletters, brochures or leaflets needed.
5. Clients decide how the publicity materials will be distributed. If it is to be by post, the weight of paper chosen can make a significant difference to the distribution costs. If the brochure or leaflets are to be put into a display case in the reception, for example, the designers are informed. This will enable them to design the cover so that the title can be seen when in the display unit.
6. The clients, or ideally their marketing person, produce the legal-jargon-free wording to be used, if it is to be distributed to non-legal people. This will show the designers the approximate number of words and the sections of copy (wording).
7. The design agency will then work up some rough ideas.
8. It will then present and talk through the ideas and the thinking behind each one.
9. The client then has time to think about the ideas and discuss them with others.
10. The client goes back to the designer, possibly with some modifications.
11. The selected rough or draft is then modified, proof-read copy inserted and worked up to artwork. The costs for printing are firmed up.

BOX 7.1 Multiples of four pages in bound brochures

At the end of a book, you will sometimes find blank pages that seem to be there by mistake. This will be because the copy does not fit neatly into a multiple of four pages, leaving some apparently unnecessary empty pages.

Brochures and books are produced in multiples of four pages. A single sheet of paper is bound into the brochure in the middle. This produces four sides or pages. If the firm produces copy to fill say sixteen pages, then decides it wants one page extra, this is not possible. It can have sixteen or twenty pages. If it wants just seventeen pages, three pages will be bare.

The use of photographs helps to lift publicity materials. They make them look more attractive. Library photographs cost little extra to include.

Library pictures are supplied by photographic library businesses at a modest cost for use in publications. The cost of a library photograph is a fraction of the amount paid to a photographer to take specific shots.

Where library photographs rather than specially commissioned ones are used, they will substantially reduce the cost of producing the printed materials.

After this point, any changes made will involve additional charges to the client. It is vital that the copy is exactly what is wanted, as changes at this stage can increase the costs of the overall publication substantially.

12. The client proof reads the final artwork. Get a person who has not seen it before to proof-read it. Do not rush the proof-reading. Mistakes can be embarrassing and costly. Do not rely on a computer's spell checking facility to get it right. A person was once described as a 'Manger' in a corporate brochure.
13. The client signs off the final artwork to go to print.
14. The printed literature is delivered.
15. The brochures or leaflets are then distributed.

BOX 7.2 Pitfalls of poor proof-reading

In an advertisement for a shirt-maker that appeared on the front page of a large regional newspaper, the letter 'r' was missing from the word shirt.

A glossy promotional brochure from a county council to encourage new businesses to locate in the area, included details of the shopping centres, libraries, schools and 'pubic' gardens.

A mock up of a Yellow Pages advertisement included an 0800 number as an example. It was not changed to the actual number and went to print. It turned out to belong to a High Street bank.

A drawing of an engine was printed upside down in a book with a print run of 50,000 copies.

A telephone number was put on the back of a brochure and was printed. Unfortunately, the STD code had two numbers the wrong way round and every brochure had to be reprinted.

It is interesting to ponder how many out-of-date brochures reside on the shelves in cupboards in solicitors' offices and other businesses and the cost of the wasted investment that is gradually gathering dust. If this has happened in your firm, do one of two things. Either order an additional 500 copies at marginal extra cost and put them in the cupboard 'just in case they are needed' and distribute the rest. Alternatively, vow to distribute all the copies you have to maximise the use of the investment and order more when the stocks get low, if further ones are needed.

Newsletter articles

Keep newsletters short. A single sheet with three or four brief articles per side together with different advertisements of the firm on the front and back will be more likely to be read than one of several pages. Use photographs to lighten it, add colour and interest.

Where the newsletter is to be distributed to private clients, have a variety of topics to appeal to a cross-section of people. The slant may be towards conveyancing on the front, but include, for example, family, personal injury and employment issues to broaden the appeal.

Resist the temptation to place any article regarding the firm on the front except on rare occasions. If the senior partner is retiring, and she is well known in the area and has been Mayoress, Chairwoman of the Chamber of Commerce and a local councillor for years, then an article on the front is acceptable. Otherwise, if the firm definitely wants an article about itself or its personnel, place it on the back and keep it brief. People are more interested in themselves, than in the activities of a law firm.

Articles which are relevant to the life of the 'man in the street' are more likely to appeal (see Chapter 5 on how to save money on advertising and Chapter 9 on profile-raising activities).

Barnsley Legal News (reproduced in black and white as Figure 7.2) is a good example of a full colour single two-sided A4 newsletter distributed to clients and to households by a Barnsley law firm, Heseltine Bray and Welsh. It has a neutral title rather than the firm's name, and so is likely to attract more attention from readers. It uses the town's name where the firm is based to emphasise that it is specifically for local people.

There are five brief articles on the front with provocative titles to attract attention. There are no articles specifically about the firm. Although it is referred to in two articles, general advice to contact your solicitor is given in the other three. The two-colour advertisement states the range of services available from the firm and offers a free half-hour interview.

On the reverse (not shown), there are three articles, one entitled 'How to keep your marriage together', another on 'Rights for unmarried fathers' and a further one on what to do if you have an accident. A different advertisement for the firm on the back focuses on its separate brand, Accident and Injury Solicitors (part of Heseltine Bray and Welsh Solicitors) for clients with injuries.

The use of full colour (library) photographs makes the newsletter look appealing and attractive. Three photographs of people on the reverse show happy smiling people of different ages and origins.

Issue 002 2004

BARNSLEY *legal* NEWS

Squatters' Rights Become Owners' Rights

The new Land Registration Act 2002 which came into force on 13 October 2003 allows squatters to legally own the land they occupy, sooner. Any person who has been in possession of registered land for more than ten years without challenge, can apply for registration of that land. Previously possession of land in this way could only be obtained after twelve years.

Solicitor Alistair Heseltine, said *"If you've parked your car on land not owned by you or have used a piece of land at the bottom of your garden for a period of more than ten years without the owner trying to stop you using it, for example, you may apply for registration of that land to become its rightful owner. It's worth speaking to a solicitor at Heseltine Bray and Welsh to see if you can own the land without paying for it."*

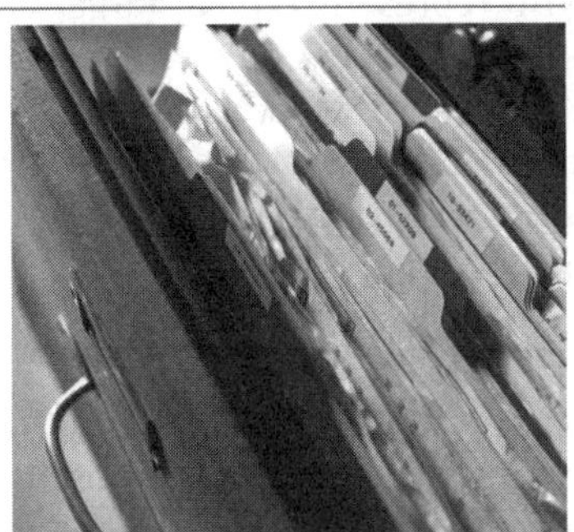

"I don't know where my property deeds are"

Since October 2003, property deeds have been abolished and no longer have any legal importance. Ownership of land is now based on computer records held at the Land Registry. Many banks and building societies already ignore deeds and deeds storage as they do not need to be stored anymore, anywhere.

If you want to retain your old deeds or have any queries, contact your solicitor.

Snooper's Charter

It is now quite simple to find out who owns a piece of land. You can ask the Land Registry who owns virtually any piece of land anywhere so long as it is registered. Contact your solicitor for more information.

A New Tax

When you buy a property, there is in effect, a new personal tax to pay. From 1st December 2003 Stamp Duty changed from being a tax on conveyancing documents to a personal tax with different obligations.

There are now automatic fines and penalties for late submission and payments plus interest. You also have to sign the tax form personally. The tax will normally be dealt with by your solicitors. If there are any doubts, contact them.

BOUNDARY DISPUTES?

A new 'determined boundary' procedure enables an owner to have an exact boundary shown on the Land Register under a new Act of Parliament. Where boundaries are unclear, the procedure can be used to eliminate future boundary disputes that may effect the sale of a property.
Contact Alistair Heseltine at Heseltine Bray and Welsh solicitors to discuss registering your property boundaries.

Figure 7.2 Barnsley Legal News

Analyse your publicity

Try this experiment. Look at your own brochures or leaflets. What is the first impression you get from the cover? Does it look attractive, punchy, quietly confident or dull? Do the colours appeal? Does the front encourage you to pick it up and then open it? Does it preserve the corporate identity?

Flick through the pages. What do you remember from it? Did the headings make you want to read the paragraphs? Did pictures or diagrams attract your attention?

Brochures

On the front of the brochure, consider having a photograph of a montage of happy looking people who represent typical target clients. They need to appeal to readers so that they associate with the firm. Depending on who the firm is targeting, the subjects need to be older, or younger, people, ethnic groups, families and possibly people dressed in identifiable occupational clothes. Photographs of similar people tell the potential client that 'this is a firm for people like me'.

Have simple messages which include the benefits to clients of using the firm.

Have a clear space after the photograph. The first message tells the reader that it is a conveyancing brochure or a corporate one. The second message is the information clients need to know. Part of this section includes the legal details.

Incorporate a simple diagram starting off with 'you are here'. By using bullet points, show the process of what the firm does and what the client needs to do at different stages (see Figure 12.1, Conveyancing UK's residential property purchase step-by-step flow chart in Chapter 12).

It is an educational process of 'This is what happens. This is how we help you. This is what you do.'

Credibility and testimonials

The third message is who does the conveyancing. Have a small section on the firm's credibility. To lengthen the life of the brochure, do not mention specific staff, just the service.

To enhance the firm's credibility, use testimonials of what clients have said about the firm and its service. These may be taken from people's letters or verbal thanks or from client comment questionnaires and used with their permission. Testimonials help to give reassurance to readers that other people think the firm is reliable.

A brochure needs to give a good overview of what the firm does. For a corporate brochure, have no more than half a page of print for each department. People tend not to read more. They will telephone the firm if they want further information.

The brochure should mirror the impression the firm wants to portray. It needs to reflect its corporate image. Dark colours can be sombre. Cheerful colours say that you are selling something upbeat.

With folder brochures (with pockets to insert single pages), have no more than three or four inserts. People tend not to read them and they do not allow the brochure to sit flat. If the folder brochure requires a gusset, it probably means too much information is put inside it.

Folder brochures can help to keep production costs down where the inserts relate to issues which are likely to change within the firm, such as staff. It is cheaper to have new single sheet inserts made up rather than whole new brochures.

Production costs can also be kept down by collation on demand. This means that the law firm decides which inserts are collated and inserted by its own staff. Higher costs are incurred where hand working is done, for example, where the printer has to collate and put in the inserts. Where a special cut to the brochure is wanted such as a window or a curved cut, higher costs are incurred.

Leaflets

Leaflets or flyers are used for short-term messages. Use spot headings to attract attention, but keep the text below it brief, as people tend not to read the text. Include a call to action, for example, 'instruct us by a certain date to get a special offer'.

Paper choice

The quality of the paper used for the leaflet sends messages to the readers. The minimum paper weight is 90 gram paper, photocopy quality; 135 gram paper is cheap and cheerful and typically used for posting volume numbers to keep the costs of postage down. Standard quality paper is 150 gram and 170 gram says 'we are high quality'.

The cost of postage is significant with mass mailings. Before deciding which paper weight to choose, have a dummy made of the envelope, letter, leaflet, staples and any other inserts. Weigh it and find out the cost. Just 5 grams can make a significant difference to the total cost of postal distribution of leaflets.

If the leaflet or brochure is of a non-standard size, it will require envelopes to be made especially, which adds to the costs.

A C4 envelope contains an A4 brochure. The 'C' refers to 'contains'. A DL envelope is A4 folded twice and is also a standard size.

Printing costs

Always shop around to get the best print prices. They can vary widely. It is generally better not to use a designer's suggestion for a printer as the cost is likely to include a 'management mark-up'. Do not necessarily go for the cheapest quote. Ask to see some examples of work to assess quality.

Many firms may own printers (machines not people) that have the capacity to produce high quality leaflets. If you plan to print the leaflets inhouse, tell your designer right at the beginning to make sure the leaflet is designed using software that your printer and computer can read.

FURTHER READING

Hahn, Fred E. *et al.* (2003) *Do-it-yourself Advertising and Promotion*, John Wiley and Sons.

INFORMATION SOURCE

Bath Design Centre, 9 Edward Street, Bath BA2 4DU (fiona@bathdesigncentre.com)

8

Networking

KEY POINTS

Reading this chapter will

- give you an understanding of why networking is important
- identify networking opportunities
- review networking skills
- show you how to prepare for an event
- suggest conversation ice-breakers
- provide ideas to create interest in you
- help you to remember people's names
- indicate how to circulate and leave the bore (gracefully)
- give you follow-up tips

The importance of networking

To get on in the conveyancing world, the old adage 'It's not what you know, it's who you know' is likely to become increasingly true with the changes affecting the conveyancing marketplace.

With the introduction of Home Information Packs supplied by vendors, estate agents will be in a position of increasing power to influence sellers to use particular solicitors. Estate agents can offer to arrange for the contents of the Home Information Packs to be drawn up as an extra service. Many estate agents already have and others will increasingly have panels of solicitors they will use, which means that High Street practices could see a substantial cut in their conveyancing turnover.

The emerging use of e-conveyancing is likely to lead to practices being selected for the panels partly on the criterion of who can offer an efficient service, where the software used enables the cross-interrogation of files between the parties, where there is personal compatibility and the payment of referral fees.

A good relationship with the local branch of estate agents is not going to be sufficient to ensure that a practice is selected to be on the panels. Networking and building contacts and relationships at the highest levels within chains of estate agents will become increasingly imperative for High Street practices.

Networking with professionals for referral business has been standard practice for firms over the years. Some people take to it more than others. Some may consider that it is the responsibility of the more senior partners to network to bring in the business, yet everyone in a practice has a part to play. The head of the firm is its visible representation, yet everyone in the practice is its human face.

'Networking is being able to help or benefit from individuals you directly have a relationship with to achieve life's ends' – Paul Drolson.

The benefits to the firm of networking are that it is used to gain business, cement relationships, pass on and be given leads. It helps to oil the wheels of business and personal relationships. It makes it easier to do business with people and often helps to get things done more quickly to the benefit of clients.

Networking benefits individuals by raising their profile and giving them good visibility, both inside and outside the firm. It means they become better known and meet potentially influential people. It helps to boost their business. They meet different people and find out interesting things. It can be fun and stimulating. It gives them confidence. It is often more comfortable to deal with someone you have already met.

Networking opportunities

Every single person in the practice networks without thinking of it. However, some network more effectively than others. Every contact that a person makes is a form of networking. Some practices recognise the value and importance of networking more than others.

Network at organised business events with other professionals related to your area of work, where appropriate, for example estate agents, panel managers, independent financial advisers, surveyors, bank managers and staff, developers, council staff and potential clients or people who could give referrals.

BOX 8.1 Networking seminars

Business Link organise evening seminars for local business people. They provide an opportunity to hear a good speaker, to network and to have a buffet – all for free. Seventy to eighty business people attend the seminars in Gloucestershire, but I have yet to see a solicitor there. Are there no hungry (in both meanings of the word) solicitors in the area? They are missing a great opportunity to meet potential commercial and private clients that is not being used.

Join associations within and outside the profession and become actively involved on the committees. The organisations do not have to be directly linked to your work to be of benefit. Consider, though, whether you will be meeting potential clients or referrers before deciding which activities to do. We all have limited time, so networking effort will gain the best results the more it involves mixing with target potential client groups or professional contacts.

CASE STUDY **A networking firm**

At BPE Solicitors in Cheltenham, the partners recognise that the future of the firm depends on building contacts with people and businesses.

The firm offers to pay the membership fees for its fee earners to join a hobby or sports club regardless of whether the club is related to work or not. It is considered likely that a number of the people more junior staff members meet at clubs will be at a similar career level within their own businesses. Many of them will become the decision makers of the future. They will ultimately be in a position to appoint solicitors.

By doing the groundwork of building relationships, often years ahead of when they are likely to see a return, the firm is investing in its future prosperity.

The best networking opportunities are often those that seem to happen effortlessly. They could be:

- meetings at the school gates;
- in the pub;
- playing in a sports team;
- children-related activities, such as parent–teacher associations, school governors meetings, raising funds for school activities, watching children play sports, etc.;
- hobby related, whether attending meetings or chatting with fellow enthusiasts;
- leisure activities;
- reunions;
- charity fund raising and voluntary work;
- church and other religious group activities;
- social committees;
- business, occupational or professional committees or attending breakfast or evening meetings;
- conferences, lectures and training seminars attended;
- by chance.

EXAMPLE **Chance meeting**

A gentleman I met at a professional speakers' conference told me about the time he was on his way home from a holiday in Italy. He was transferring from the aeroplane to the bus to take the passengers back to the airport terminal. During the short journey, he met the sales director from a leading jeans manufacturer. He told him briefly what he did and gave him his business card.

Eighteen months later, he got a call from the sales director asking if he would give a talk to their staff. That brief contact resulted in business.

The target market of a conveyancing department could be first time buyers and parents with growing families who are likely to move home more often. With these target markets, it would help to encourage partners and staff to get involved with local sports clubs, activity-based hobby groups, school and related social activities and charities raising funds for special baby care units.

If the target market is older people with higher asset value properties, activities to get involved with may include theatre groups, civic and historical societies, tennis clubs, bridge clubs, church and other religious groups, neighbourhood groups, residents' associations and local business associations such as business luncheon clubs and the Federation of Small Businesses.

Networking levels

It is easy to assume that you should aim to develop relationships just with contacts at the top of a hierarchy. While this is important, great harm can be done and potential future business lost by not networking at different levels within a firm.

Think about networking at all levels. The junior people now will in time become senior. The impact you can have on a more junior person is substantially more than you can often have on a person at the same or higher level than yourself. The impact will be greatest, the more senior you are to them. If a junior person is snubbed, it can have a significant impact when the firm aims to gain business from the person when they become more senior.

EXAMPLE **How not to network**

A chartered surveyor, before he was qualified and when he was quite junior, was rudely snubbed by a senior man in another business. As the surveyor progressed in his career, the day came when he was in a position to give business to the man who had been rude to him. He said, 'I hadn't forgotten it. It gave me some satisfaction to know that I was not going to give a contract to the man or his firm as a result.'

Networking skills

Dr Daniel Goleman, in his book *Emotional Intelligence: Why It Can Matter More than IQ*, argues that a high score in emotional intelligence is said to be a better indicator of how well we are going to do in life than getting a high score in intelligence tests. Emotional intelligence is having the drive to get things done. It is our cooperativeness, our willingness and our open-mindedness towards new ideas. It is our ambition, our sense of hopefulness, our social skills and how well we get on with other people.

Working in a law firm requires both intellectual intelligence and high levels of emotional intelligence. It is not just about how well someone does their job. It is about how well people get on with others, how well they are able to put others at ease, to develop the rapport and trust that will encourage them to want to use the firm and to recommend the practice to others.

The key skills and attributes of good networkers are to:

- be self-confident;
- be good listeners;
- like people;
- be interested in others;
- be approachable;
- smile easily;
- be conversationalists;
- have good questioning skills;
- be easygoing;
- have a good sense of humour;
- not be a stuffed shirt;
- be able to laugh at themselves;
- be warm;
- be eager to meet new people;
- be welcoming;
- be knowledgeable;
- be a good communicator.

Confidence

Many networking skills are related to having strong levels of confidence. To boost confidence, write down your good attributes and read them before you go to an event.

Most people feel an element of trepidation just before they walk into a room full of people. Play brain games to help you succeed. Negative thinking can affect the mind and body. It increases the gloom and depression a person may feel. Alexander Pope wrote: 'All seems infected that the infected spy/As all looks yellow to the jaundic'd eye'. The answer is: do not think negative thoughts. Think positive things. Do the actors' trick and say to yourself that everyone in the room will really like you and want to speak to you and that you will shine. Smile to yourself, then walk in.

Keep a file or book, an 'honours book', in which you store the letters from clients which praise you or give you particular thanks for what you have done. When positive comments have been given to you verbally, write them down and put them in your honours book. Write down three good things you have done each day. By the end of the year, you will have over a thousand achievements in your honours book. Read your honours book just before you do anything that requires you to show healthy confidence or where it would help your performance.

Goal setting

Part of increasing motivation is to set goals or objectives for yourself. They often give us the incentive to achieve what we set out to do. For example:

- the number of new people you want to meet;
- the number of business cards you want to collect;
- specific people with whom you want to renew acquaintance;
- a particular person with whom you want to discuss an issue.

Communication skills

Face to face communication is made up of a combination of the words used, the tone of voice and the accompanying body language. Each is important and has to support the other two. Body language is said to be substantially more important than words and tone put together, with words having the least importance – but that statement has to be kept in context. If the body language is good and the tone just right, but the words are poorly chosen, then the whole message will be received badly.

Body language includes facial expressions, eye contact, hand gestures, arm and body movements and posture. These combine to convey a breadth of emotion, from interest to indifference, concern, anger, hatred and happiness.

Body language is used to help build rapport. It conveys non-verbal messages which could be uncomfortable to say, but are easy to communicate using body language. It tells the person that you like them, have respect for them, are interested in what they have to say, that you consider them important, that you value them and enjoy talking to them. It can also display indifference, boredom, dislike and lack of interest. The message will come across loud and clear to the receiver.

To show respect and warmth to another:

1. Make immediate warm eye contact. Look at the person's face rather than just at the eyes, which can be disconcerting if held for a long period of time.
2. Smile – it generally results in a smile back. Greet the person by name if you know it.
3. Stand slightly to one side rather than face to face. When you meet a person for the first time, it is natural to stand directly opposite. When two people have known each other for some time, though, they tend to stand slightly to the side of one another. Weight falls more on to the foot closest to the other person and this brings you into closer proximity. The message it sends is: 'I am here to support you, I'm on your side, I like and trust you.' To develop rapport and trust more quickly with a person you meet, consider not standing directly opposite.
4. Avoid any physical barriers between you if you can.
5. Use natural hand gestures to emphasise a point using an open hand displayed palm upwards. Lean forward slightly to listen. This helps to reduce the distance between you and shows active listening and empathy.

Gender differences

Two women talking together will tend to look at each other's faces for nearly the whole of the conversation. Two men talking together tend to make less eye contact. Men tend to look away more when speaking.

When a man and a woman are talking, the woman will often aim to make almost constant eye contact or look at his face, while the man will occasionally look away. This can cause annoyance. She wants to know why he is not looking at her to show trust and he may feel that she is staring at him all the time.

When two women are talking together, one will generally wait for the other to finish and leave a space or a gap to signal for the other to speak. This signal does not tend to exist in male conversation. The result can be that the women say less than men, because no space is given in the conversation for them to begin. This is particularly apparent in a mixed group of people. Once men start talking, they tend to dominate the conversation.

The result can be that the men think the women have little to contribute or nothing worthwhile to say and the women think the men are poor conversationalists and are only interested in themselves.

Tone of voice

Consider what message your tone of voice may convey to others. The tone used can tell someone how you are feeling. Aim to have a happy and welcoming tone to put people at ease and to encourage them to want to talk to you. One top salesman recommended always taking the lift before meeting a new potential client. He advised waiting until the lift was empty, then on the way up giving yourself a good shake like a dog coming out of a river. This makes you laugh at yourself and relaxes and loosens the whole body, so that when you walk into the client's premises, you feel confident and agile.

Never tell anyone your problems through your tone of voice. People can often quickly tell how you are feeling from your tone.

EXAMPLE **Up and down**

I took a client to lunch on one occasion when I felt unusually down. Our conversation was only about dismal topics. It created a dire atmosphere. Rather than encouraging the client to give my firm more business, I thought I would lose a client if I let things carry on as they were. I excused myself and went to the ladies. I gave myself a pep talk, jumped up and down to get some energy back and returned to the luncheon table. I was determined to lift the atmosphere and make the client start to smile and feel happier before I left. I lifted my tone of voice and changed the conversation to happier topics. The strategy worked.

For further information on tone of voice, see Chapter 11, 'Converting telephone callers into clients'.

Preparation for an event

Find out who may be attending beforehand to analyse the list and mark out the people you want to meet. If you cannot discover who is attending beforehand, get to the event early and go through the guest list then.

Where you (think you) know who will be attending beforehand:

- make a list of the people you want to meet;
- decide an objective that you want to achieve with each person;

- find out what interests people so that you can bring it into the conversation (some firms put biographies on their web page and include leisure activities);
- find out what is happening in other people's firms – press releases are often given on web pages;
- check how the industry sector is performing and any news items affecting it. Go to trade association web pages or use a search engine to find out about issues.

Read the newspapers that day and listen to the news so that you can discuss prominent and especially humorous events.

Agree to minimise the time spent with other solicitors, unless it is for a distinct purpose.

It is always useful to chat to the people at the reception desk, if there is one. They may be able to tell you if certain people are attending and to point them out to you if you do not know them. Ask them to point out the speakers (if relevant). By being chatty to the reception staff at the beginning, you create a friendly port of call if you are having a bad networking event.

Your name:

Direct telephone number:

Event:

Date:

Host:

Name of person who invited you:

Names and contact details of people you invited:

Your objective for the event:

Date a 'thank you' letter was sent:

Details of people you plan to meet and met:

Name and position	Contact details: address, telephone number	Follow-up action	Add to database	Information to send them: newsletter	Christmas card	Invite to seminars

Figure 8.1 Brief and debrief form

If you are attending an event with a colleague, agree not to stay together. Use each other as a diving board to bounce off on to other people – and act as a rescue centre. Introduce each other to new people, but do not stay together after the initial introduction.

Brief and debrief form

Use a brief and debrief form to record who you want to meet and what you want to achieve from the event. The debrief aspect is to note the names of the people you met, anything you promised to do for them and interesting information about them that will remind you what to talk about the next time you meet. Follow-up activities can also be recorded and the dates when the follow-up actions were completed and the subsequent outcomes.

Conversation

The most difficult time at an event can be when you first walk in. The danger of attending with a colleague is that you stick to each other like glue and reduce by half the number of people you could have met had you split up. The next downside of an event is that if you see someone you know, you are drawn to them like a magnet – then remain together for the rest of the event.

A bee flies around and spreads pollen. The bee strategy is the one to adopt when you know you just have a short time before people sit down to a meal or to hear a speaker. The value of the event is compressed so you have to make the most of the before and after the meal times. Try to get to the event early to have as long as possible for executing the bee strategy.

The bee strategy before the event is briefly to say hello to as many people as possible. It is showing your face, saying a friendly word ('Good to see you.' 'You're looking well.' 'Had a good holiday?') and to tell the people you want to speak to in more depth that you really want to have a chat with them after the talk or meal.

Opening lines

When you do not know someone and have not been introduced, opening lines can include:

- I hardly know anyone here, so it would be good to talk to you. What's your name?
- How do you know our host/hostess?
- Haven't we met before?

- I recognise you, but I can't quite place you . . .
- What a beautiful painting. Do you think it's an original?
- Wonderful weather we're having. Have you heard the forecast for the weekend?
- I'm just about to get a drink. Can I get one for you too?

Ice breakers can be used:

- in the queue to get in;
- in the queue for drinks;
- signing in at the reception;
- walking through to a reception room or leaving it;
- in the loo!
- standing/sitting next to someone;
- anywhere!

Some people are more naturally inclined to mix with people than others. They are often referred to as 'people persons'. They take a genuine pleasure in meeting new people and finding out about them. They are the sort of people who are easy to talk to. Conversation flows naturally. They seem to smile more and have a welcoming look in their eyes. They encourage you to talk about yourself and ask open questions. They are comfortable to be with and warm in their manner. They thrive on small talk to get a person to relax before target talk begins. Target talk is the topic of conversation you want to talk to the person about. Not all small talk conversations will lead on to target talk if the objective is just to get to know a person better.

Good small talk is a key networking skill. It is the warm up – the verbal limbering up exercise. It eases the way to useful talk. Without it, it can seem abrupt and off-putting to launch straight into a target talk topic. Small talk is like the birds' mating game. It tells you whether other people are worth pursuing as potential contacts. It tells you what interests them and helps you prepare what to say to encourage them to find out more about you and your firm.

Small talk topics include:

- weather;
- news items – providing they are light and humorous;
- sport;
- TV;
- hobbies;
- holidays;
- family – theirs;
- amusing things that have happened that day.

EXAMPLE **Small talk**

A news item in the local paper that said that Gloucester Hospital had changed the name of a pudding back to its original name. It had been changed previously as the powers that be thought patients would be embarrassed to ask for it. It changed from Spotted Richard back to Spotted Dick.

Small talk is not the time to offload the irritations of the day or to talk about gloomy topics, unless you end them on a humorous note that makes the other person laugh or smile.

Avoid 'earthquake' talk. These are opinions or facts that look at the darkest side of a topic or the worst case scenario.

Questioning and listening skills

To help put people at ease and to develop conversation, ask open questions that cannot be answered by 'yes' or 'no'. They encourage conversation and enable you to find out about other people. These questions generally begin with 'who', 'what', 'when', 'where' and 'how'. Avoid asking 'why', which may come across as confrontational if your tone of voice is wrong.

If closed questions are used, which can only be answered with 'yes' or 'no', this limits the conversation and makes it harder to get information from the other person.

Good listening skills show respect and interest in the other person. Good listeners are often rated more highly than people who dominate the conversation.

Use listening skills to find out about the person and what matters to them. This information is then used to create interest in you.

The hook – how to create interest in you

When a person asks you what you do, first think about what the benefits are to the other person of what you do. The more you know about the other person, the more you can tailor your reply to what interests them. Rather than saying you are a solicitor, word your reply in a way that makes them curious to find out more about you. The aim at this point is to make the other person ask the questions. This allows you to develop the conversation and to say more than if you had said the occasional conversation stopper of 'I'm a solicitor'.

You might consider saying:

- 'I help people move on to the next stage of their lives' (conveyancing or family solicitor).
- 'I help people live the lifestyle they want to live' (conveyancing solicitor).
- 'I help to cut costs and the time it takes to get planning consent in difficult situations' (planning solicitor).
- 'I help people change their domestic situation' (conveyancing or family solicitor).
- 'I help people making the biggest financial commitment in their lives take the right decision for them' (conveyancing solicitor).

When you are asked to explain more, express what you do in terms of the benefits to them. If, for example, it is an estate agent you have been introduced to, you could say:

You:	'I help make estate agents' jobs as hassle free as possible.'
Estate agent:	'How do you do that?'
You:	'As a solicitors' practice, we use case management systems which allow estate agents to access our mutual clients' files via the Internet. When their clients telephone wanting information, the agent can go straight to their file to get the information during the telephone call. It saves them having to telephone the solicitor to get the answers and then phoning back their clients. It gives a major benefit to estate agents and their clients.'

Business card

If you want to give someone your business card, ask for the other person's card and make a note on the back of the date and the place where you met, as a reminder. It can act as a good opening line in a subsequent letter to recall the occasion when you met. However, note that the Japanese consider it rude to write on a business card.

As you are handed a card, spend a few moments looking at the front of it, then make a favourable comment about it. A business card is a personal thing and respect is shown to the person by how it is handled and where it is placed.

Think about putting something on the back of the card that will help other people to remember you or be a talking point. Consider having your photograph on the back to remind them of who you are or list the legal services your firm provides.

Remembering names

The sound of our own name is said to be the sweetest sound. We all like to be remembered, but it is often difficult to remember other people's names. When you have been introduced to a person, either repeat their name several times when speaking to them to get their name to stick in your mind or to use the power of association.

The power of association is used to connect a person's name with something that stands out in the mind. It uses visualisation to picture something in the mind to help to remember the person's name. What stands out may be to do with:

- location;
- situation;
- event;
- who they remind us of;
- what they remind us of;
- use of the imagination – caricatures;
- movement;
- humour;
- interests.

The invitation

Have an event to which you can invite people you meet. It does not matter how far in advance it is. It provides the glue to bind people, the link to contacting and seeing acquaintances again. It gives an opportunity to gain their business card and to give your own.

The least likely people can often bring in business contacts that prove worthwhile. People seldom resent an invitation. They are more likely to warm to you for sending one.

Do not worry about whether you think people will get on – other people will often draw out aspects of people's personalities of which you may not be aware. In addition, an event to which you can invite people gives an excellent reason to contact them afterwards.

Circulating

'Working the room' is a key component of a successful networking event. The difficulty is sometimes being able to leave (graciously) one person and move on to another group or individual.

As a guide, try not to leave individuals standing on their own. Introduce them to someone else before you leave.

Never stand next to a wall, table or chair. It blocks off one side and does not allow people to approach you from that direction. It means that you limit the number of people you can catch the eyes of to draw them to you.

Do not sit down. It is very hard to get up and leave a person once you are sitting down.

Do not drink coffee. It makes the breath smell.

Avoid eating anything that crumbles easily. You may not notice that crumbs remain on your lips, chin and stuck in your teeth or have fallen down your front.

Useful partings

To leave people to speak to others, consider the following:

- 'I've really enjoyed talking to you. Thank you. I hope we shall see each other again soon.'
- 'I don't want to monopolise you all evening.'
- 'I must see XYZ before she leaves. Would you excuse me?'
- 'Can I get you a drink/food/top-up?' Have the aim of bringing someone back with you to introduce. If the other person doesn't want a drink excuse yourself to get one.
- 'Have you met XYZ? I must introduce you.'
- 'I must speak to our hostess/host, please excuse me.'
- Pretend your phone is ringing. Put your hand in your pocket or handbag and take out your mobile phone. Make a comment that your phone is on 'vibrate'. Pretend to look at the caller ID, apologise and say you must take it – and move away.
- 'I must get some fresh air.'
- 'I don't believe it. Have you seen who's just walked in? I haven't seen them for years/since . . . Would you excuse me?'
- 'I promised to telephone my daughter/son/spouse/office at xxx o'clock. I'm late already. Would you excuse me?'

The follow-up

Afterwards, reflect on the event. Make a note of who you spoke to and who you invited to your own event.

Go through the business cards you acquired and decide how you are going to follow them up. Add them to your database. Write on the back of each card and in the database where you met, specific items discussed and the date. Refer to this when you contact the person again.

Aim to contact everyone you met within one week of the event. This helps to reinforce the meeting in the other person's mind and may help to generate business leads.

As a follow-up do one of the following:

- write a letter, e-mail or telephone the people you met;
- make the follow-up contact personal in that it is not a standard letter that goes out to everyone. Remind them of something about the event, the conversation you had, or the weather or something they said. Make it chatty rather than formal;
- remind them of your invitation and ask them to let you know whether they can attend;
- invite them to your event;
- say how much you enjoyed meeting them (again) and talking to them and that you hope to meet again soon;
- suggest meeting for lunch;
- provide information or related information that you had discussed;
- send them something (an article for example) saying you thought they would be interested in it. If you send something substantial, a book, CD or video for example, give a date by which you want it returned. It provides a further reason to have contact;
- thank them for their comments or advice;
- thank them for inviting you;
- invite them to be your guest at an event you have been invited to attend;
- make it a policy not to be a '"Must do . . . " and rarely follow up on it'-type person. If you say you will do something – do it.

Further reading

Buzan, T. (1999) *Master Your Memory,* BBC Worldwide.

Carnegie, D. (1988) *How to Win Friends and Influence People,* William Heinemann.

Freemantle, D. (1998) *What Customers Like about You,* Nicholas Brealey Publishing.

Goleman, D. (1997) *Emotional Intelligence: Why It Can Matter More than IQ,* Bantam.

McCallister, L. (1994) *Say What You Mean, Get What You Want,* John Wiley and Sons.

Peppers, D. and Rogers, M. (1993) *The One to One Future,* Doubleday.

Stone, C. (2001) *Networking: The Art of Making Friends,* Random House.

Wiseman, R. (2004) *The Luck Factor,* Arrow Books.

9

Profile-raising activities

KEY POINTS

This chapter will

- suggest ways to raise your profile
- show you how to set objectives for getting better known
- explain the difference between public relations and advertising
- provide ideas for gaining free publicity
- describe how to write a press release and an article
- show you how to organise and speak in a radio interview
- explain how to plan seminars, entertain clients and sponsor events
- describe cause marketing and consider exhibitions

Solicitors' Publicity Code 2001

Solicitors' publicity-related actions are regulated by the Solicitors' Publicity Code issued by the Council of the Law Society. Reference to the regulations is recommended before undertaking profile-raising activities. See Appendix C for further information.

Introduction

Raising the profile of the firm among its existing and target clients is one of the foundations of marketing. Individual marketing actions rarely succeed. They need to be treated like an orchestra, where the conductor introduces each one to create and build a memorable, pleasing rendition. Marketing activities work best when they work together in harmony, each supporting and enhancing the others.

Figure 9.1 Profile-raising activities

Benefits

A positive higher profile increases awareness of the name of the firm and the services it provides. New potential clients are attracted to a firm because of its visibility and it reminds clients to use the firm in the future.

For individuals within the firm, an appropriate higher profile can lead to an increased perception of their expertise and knowledge; the authority and status of personnel may be raised. A high profile can attract more clients who want to use individual solicitors. It expands people's experience and knowledge by bringing them into contact with a wide range of other individuals and organisations, which is often very enjoyable, as well as being socially and commercially rewarding. In terms of personal career paths, it can aid promotion, salary and bonus negotiations.

EXAMPLE **Marketing**

Occasionally, using one marketing activity to raise the profile of a firm generates another, which may have a bigger impact. When Brookman Solicitors advertised its matrimonial services on posters placed in bathrooms in the City of London with a heading of 'Ditch the Bitch!', it attracted controversy. The amount of media coverage given to the poster campaign in the national press was worth thousands of pounds in equivalent advertising spend. It raised awareness of the firm far above what could have been expected from the poster campaign alone.

Objectives

It is important to decide what you want to achieve from your profile-raising activities. You may find the following questions useful:

1. How many times do you want to appear in designated media (in a positive light!) over the following year?
2. With regard to press articles about the firm over the previous year, what would it have cost the firm had it paid for the equivalent space in advertising? You may want to gain the equivalent of £20,000 advertising space for the following year.
3. Which charities do you want to support actively and publicly to encourage people to see the firm as a caring and active part of the community?
4. How many new clients do you want to attract?
5. What type of new clients do you want to attract, e.g. first time buyers; those of higher asset worth; 40–50-year-olds?
6. What fee income level do you want as a result of your combined activities?
7. Do you want to change your target clients' general perceptions of the firm from ABC to XYZ?
8. Do you want to be known as the local 'voice of authority' for virtually anything legal so that journalists will contact your firm for your opinions before they contact any other solicitors?

Evaluation

In order to be able to assess and cost actions against the results achieved, a method of evaluating the results needs to be in place before you begin.

The main benefit of raising your profile is that it supports and emphasises the other marketing activities you are undertaking. This can make it difficult to assess the results gained against the profile-raising actions taken, as they become entwined with other results. For further information on evaluating public relations activities, go to Chapter 10 on evaluating marketing activities.

Difference between public relations and advertising

The Institute of Public Relations in the UK defines public relations (PR) as 'the discipline which looks after reputation, with the aim of earning understanding and support and influencing opinion and behaviour'. Public relations is one strand of marketing. Another is advertising. Advertising is the paid-for promotion of the firm in the media.

PR includes:

- gaining positive media coverage of the firm;
- networking with potential and existing clients and referrers or professional contacts;
- holding exhibitions;
- sponsoring events and activities in the local, national or international community;
- entertaining clients;
- holding and attending seminars;
- encouraging staff to understand what the firm does and why it does it so that they speak well of it outside the practice.

Research into what influences corporate reputation by Corporate Advisory Services (CAS), which advises many FTSE and Fortune 100 companies, provided some noteworthy results. They found that television was the most powerful influence. Next came the attitude and behaviour of employees, which can influence positively or negatively how a firm or brand is viewed by its audiences or stakeholders (Barry, 2002). This emphasises how important it is to encourage staff to speak well of the firm inside and outside the office.

Table 9.1 Differences between public relations and advertising

Public relations	Advertising
Media space is not paid for	Paid-for media/advertising space
No control over if or when it appears	Total control over when it appears
No control over content	Total control over content, providing it is within the Advertising Standards Authority's Code
It may inadvertently result in damaging media coverage	It presents the firm in a positive light
Higher credibility than advertising	Lower credibility than public relations activities
Longer-term commitment to get media coverage results	Immediate results – an advertisement appears when you want it to
A lot of activity and effort may not generate any media coverage	Activity generates the production of the advertisement
The value is difficult to evaluate with precision	The cost is known and agreed before the advertisement is placed

Free publicity

There are many opportunities to gain publicity by sending press releases to the media with the aim of getting them published or broadcast. They do not all have to be related to the conveyancing department. Building recognition of the firm's name helps to encourage people to use the practice. Examples of opportunities and means to gain publicity are:

- proposed changes in the law – how they could affect local people, regardless of whether they become actual law or not;
- changes in the law;
- changes in regulations, i.e. Home Information Packs, environmental surveys, commonhold ownership;
- the Budget – how it will affect local businesses and people;
- major changes in the local economy – new firms joining or leaving the area – the impact on the housing market;
- comments on cases in the press related to property ownership – where allowed;
- perceived injustices in the law, where there has been strong national or local media coverage;
- supporting a local event or fight to save a local facility;
- charitable activities. For example, to target older clients for property downsizing, trusts, wills, long-term planning and probate, organise an 'Antiques evening' with a local auctioneer to raise money for the local hospice. Sell the tickets through clients, contacts, the hospice, the auctioneer's clients and the local paper. Ask the local paper to sponsor it as a joint event. Ask the local auctioneer to run a quiz to identify small items possibly provided by the auctioneer. The auctioneer could go through what the items are, award a prize for the best results and give a talk on antiques. Provide wine and cheese. Invite the local press photographer or take a photograph to send to the press immediately after the event;
- changes in the firm – where they are of interest to the publication's readers, e.g. for a local newspaper: long-service people retiring, new staff joining, a family day out, distribution of Easter eggs and toys at Christmas in the local hospital. As a rule, changes in the firm are not particularly of interest to a local paper, unless it has a business section;
- giving a present to the first born of the New Year at the local hospital;
- fund raising in the firm; get a monster cheque made – provided by the bank – and hand it over to the recipients, providing a photographic opportunity for the local press;
- an important anniversary – one year in business, 200 years established;

- sponsorship of anything from a park bench, flowers on a roundabout, productions at a theatre, school activities, sports events, exhibitions, etc.;
- a survey of local people's opinions of the Home Information Pack with the results broken down between first time buyers, the middle-aged and people downsizing plus gender differences. A survey of what men and women want when they look for a new home;
- whenever you do a good deed;
- using children and animals to get photographs published. Aim to link them to current affairs or take an alternative view or twist on them, e.g. Bill of Rights for Pets, with a picture of the office rabbit; sponsorship of an endangered species at a local zoo or safari park; a talk given to a school. Telephone the local paper and tell them there is a photographic opportunity at the local school (with the necessary school/parental agreements). The newspaper knows it will be able to sell the photographs to parents, aunts, uncles and grandparents, etc., and so will be more likely to print it;
- national day events: get on the bandwagon of 'day' events e.g. 'Take your Daughter to Work Day', 'Cycle to Work Day'. Make up your own day for the firm or make up a variation on the national day theme, for example, 'Take your Mother or "Gran" to Work Day' to show your opposition to ageism at work (that is if she is not already busy at work, or running your firm);
- history relating to your office building and a local famous event, or what happened in the town in the year that the building was built; the site may have been used for something of local interest, such as a local battle or hanging, an extraordinary case won or lost a hundred years ago;
- organising a fun quiz evening for teams from local businesses to develop better working relationships and strengthen existing ones;
- an article on changes to employment or tenant rights or changes to the ease or difficulty of selling property;
- supporting campaigns for the business and local community – to keep the local swimming pool open, to provide additional facilities for teenagers or to improve the road signage to encourage people to visit and stay longer in the area. Giving support to other businesses helps to engender good feelings towards the firm and the person who is giving the support;
- information on how to make it easier to sell your home (decoration tips, defined spaces in gardens) and tips on the kerb stop test (how to encourage prospective buyers to get out of their car and walk into the home, rather than drive by).

EXAMPLE **Using publicity**

One High Street firm successfully built its business with the help of publicity. It decided to actively pursue local publicity to raise its profile. When I first visited the firm, in the waiting room I looked through its thick album of press articles. One issue puzzled me. In no article could I see a refererence to how long the firm had been in business. The number and variety of press releases indicated that it had been going for some considerable time. When I asked one of the partners, he said the firm had been established for just four years.

To ensure that your publicity release gains exposure it is necessary to understand the perspective of a journalist. An item may appear newsworthy to you, but a journalist is interested in:

- location – if it is a local publication, journalists are generally only interested in news in the area where they sell papers;
- immediacy – a weekly paper will be interested in anything that happened in the previous week. A daily paper is only interested in the immediate days before. For some media, 24 hours ago may be considered old news;
- who – the more prominent or more authoritative the person in the news is, the more likely the item will gain media exposure. The views of the senior partner, who is chairman of the Chamber of Commerce, are more likely to be reported than those of a member of the public;
- human interest – such articles are more attractive to print than information on businesses. A story about one local couple's struggle to buy a home is more likely to achieve media coverage than bland statistics relating to numerous faceless people;
- change and suspense – major changes or unanswered questions, which leave people hanging on, attract news. New job creation or the possibility of redundancies attract coverage as long as they affect the readership and are of sufficient number to warrant interest. Most media are not interested in the internal changes of a practice, e.g. a move to a new building, people joining (unless it expands the business), or staff leaving;
- consumer affairs – matters that affect or could affect the 'man in the street' are of interest. Lifestyle issues such as makeovers, gardening and changing places have increasingly been covered. In terms of conveyancing, articles on how to prepare and decorate a home for a faster sale given the traditional style of houses in the locality, may attract readers. The potential impact of Home Information Packs on local people is also likely to appeal to the local media;

- surveys are often used to gain publicity, especially if they relate to the local audience for the media – a survey of the number of first time buyers helped by their parents to raise a deposit by remortgaging their own homes, is likely to gain coverage.

Writing a press release

A press release aims to make journalists' jobs as easy as possible. The more the press release is written to resemble the publication's style of writing and the more able the media are to use the press release with little amendment, the more likely it is that it will get published.

Gaining free publicity requires the agreement and cooperation of journalists. It is worth making the effort to get to know local journalists to find out what they are interested in and what you can do to help them. Call in to the local newspaper office and broadcast station to see the journalists. Introduce yourself so that they know you. This will generally help to encourage them to take more interest in the press releases you send to them. It also helps you to put faces to journalists' names.

Journalists work to tight deadlines. Respecting and understanding their work pressures will help to develop good, mutually useful working relationships. If a journalist contacts you to discuss a point, telephone her back immediately – her deadline could be within the half hour. If you leave it until the afternoon, for example, it could be too late. The lack of response from you puts extra pressure on the journalist, which may not be conducive to producing a favourable article. People are less likely to contact you in the future, if you do not return calls promptly.

Preparation for writing a press release

You should consider:

- Which publication?
- What interests their readers/audience?
- What interests the editor/producer?
- What is the house style (style of writing)?
- Why would they want to use your press release?
- What's in it for them?
- How many words do they want?
- Do they want a photograph? (Always include a 'happy' one if you can to attract attention and to get a larger article – but do not send it to radio stations!)
- How do they want the press release sent to them – e-mail, fax, post, etc.?
- What is their deadline?

Contact the journalist first to find the answers to these questions. Address what the readers, listeners or audience are interested in from their perspective, rather than from your perspective.

Avoid all legal jargon for a non-legal readership. Write short sentences. Get a non-legal person to assess and edit it critically. Decide what it is you want to achieve. Prioritise the points you want to make.

In the first paragraph, aim to include answers to 'who?' what?' 'when?' 'where?' 'how?' and 'why?'.

In the second paragraph, write the next most important point you want to make and so on for subsequent paragraphs. Relate the conclusion to the opening, where sensible.

Avoid self-congratulatory sentences such as 'XYZ Solicitors are delighted to announce . . .'. Include quotes from senior people in the firm and from external people to add interest.

Length

Preferably, do not write more than one A4 page. A second page of a press release can go astray. Write the name and the publication it is for in the top left corner of the page and the release date in the top right corner of the page. If it is on two pages, never finish a sentence at the bottom of the page, always finish on a 'cliff-hanger' to encourage the reader to turn to the next page.

Provide a potential heading – to attract the editor's or the journalist's attention to encourage them to read it.

Indicate at the end of the first page, which page it is and how many pages follow (e.g. '1/2' – meaning one of two pages). At the top of the following page, write '2/2', meaning the second of two pages and repeat the heading and who it is from, in case the sheets get separated.

At the end of the press release, write 'ENDS' and 'For further information, contact: name and telephone number'. Give the names of two people to contact in case one person is not available.

To include additional background information add 'Notes to the Editor'.

Photographs

Include a photograph if you can. Do not assume that a photojournalist will come to an event (called a photocall where journalists come and take photographs), even if interest has been expressed. A better photo opportunity may come up and yours may be dumped. Always plan to have your own photographer on hand and send in the photograph with the press release. The more unusual the photograph, the more likely it is to be used. A photograph will generally gain you more media publication space.

Writing an article

An article is written on the same principles as a press release. The key difference is that the publication's editor is contacted prior to writing anything to check whether an article would be of interest. Ask the same questions you would when writing a press release. The deadline is particularly important.

Keep sentences short and to the point. If the house style allows, include sub-headings and bullet points. Relate the final paragraph to the first paragraph if possible, to emphasise the key point or the purpose of the article.

Write double-spaced and send the hard copy with an electronic copy, for example on disk or by e-mail.

Write the article as an impartial report. Include authoritative individuals' comments to broaden its scope and depth. It should not be written with the typical wording used in a brochure or advertisement; it is also likely to be rejected if it is written in flowery, adjective-ridden language.

Advertising-led articles and advertorials

Local papers and magazines will occasionally run an advertising-led feature whereby they offer editorial space in return for you placing an advertisement. Publishers like these as they are good money spinners.

These features have a place in raising the profile of the firm, but their credibility tends to be lower than that of 'independent' features. The editorial may be written by the advertiser or by the newspaper. If it is written by the advertiser, there is control over the content. However, the total feature with a number of advertisers writing their own editorial may look amateur; the firm is effectively buying space for the editorial. The features are headed by the words 'advertisement' or 'promotion'. This tells the readers that they are not independent articles.

Networking

Networking can be a good way to raise the profile of the firm, particularly with bulk referrers (see Chapter 8).

Speaking

Giving a talk

Giving a talk to potential target clients and referrers can be a good way to become better known.

Prepare a presentation which you can give to several groups and which appeals to a wide audience. It could relate to humorous experiences inside or outside of work. Tailor the presentation to the interests of the particular audience. It does not have to be specifically about property transactions for you to be able to bring conveyancing into the presentation. For example, presentations on:

- how to keep your marriage/relationship fresh – and what to do if it goes off (brings in divorce, family law and conveyancing);
- stretching your income for older people (financial services, downsizing/conveyancing and tax implications);
- helping your children get on the property ladder (remortgaging, selling own house and buying two for self and offspring);
- developing your business (includes conveyancing and remortgages);
- higher asset worth, making it work for you (includes property investment or divestment and remortgages);
- moving home disasters – and how you helped to put them right.

Target the secretaries of interest groups from June onwards and follow up in September and October when most groups are putting their annual programme together. Examples of groups are given in Chapter 8 on networking.

To provide the breadth of information required to give justice to presentation skills is beyond the scope of this book.

Organise and speak in a radio interview

Local BBC radio stations have to fill many hours of broadcast time every day with local news and information. They are always willing to hear ideas that would appeal to their listeners.

Put forward suggestions to the manager of the programme you are targeting, relating to current issues and how they affect local people. Include how it could be broadcast, to give it some atmosphere, for example:

- phone-in: you answer questions live on air. Arrange to have friends and relatives ready to phone in with questions to get the ball rolling and to fill dry periods when no one else is telephoning. Supply them with suitable questions;
- round table discussion: you organise other professionals, such as accountants, surveyors, estate agents, etc., to have a discussion on air regarding a topical issue;
- one-to-one interviews;
- vox-pop: recording people's opinions from the street, in shops, offices, factories and farms.

Backgrounder

Prepare a backgrounder to give to the radio station or to a publication editor with a press release. A backgrounder is ideally no more than one sheet of paper with the background to the topic, such as:

- proposed changes in the law – the facts in plain English;
- how they would affect local families and people in different situations;
- why the topic is important to the listeners;
- who the proposed interview would be with;
- background on the person;
- extensive typical questions the interviewer could ask the interviewee;
- typical questions members of the public are likely to ask or want to know about;
- who else to contact for interviewing with their contact details;
- own contact details and dates you are available to be interviewed.

Preparation for the interview

Find out the name of the person who will interview you as this is unlikely to be the person with whom you arranged the interview. Ask whether it will be a live interview or pre-recorded, what it will be about, as it may not be about your press release, and how long it will be. This will help you decide and prepare what messages you want to give and the examples you want to use.

Think of the answers to the questions you are likely to be asked and be ready to answer easily the questions you have suggested are asked. The interviewer may not use them.

You can ask for the first question. The second question is likely to be based on your answer to the first question. Plan to give short rather than lengthy answers. Get straight to the point and keep it simple. If your answer is longer than approximately 25 seconds, you are likely to be interrupted.

Use anecdotes in your answers and make them personal to yourself or local people. Use 'I', 'me', 'we', 'you', 'your' in sentences. Refer to the effect on individuals rather than on the masses.

Think of the questions you definitely do not want to be asked and prepare answers for them.

If the interviewer starts to go off at a tangent use techniques like 'That's an interesting question but I feel that . . . (to go back to your point) . . .'.

Read the local and national press in the days before and on the interview day as an unrelated question regarding current events may be asked.

Be completely up to date with suggested discussion topics and tell the truth. Avoid legal-speak and do not get annoyed. Assume there is no such thing as 'off the record'. Be positive and avoid being defensive. Keep your tone friendly and bright. Use the interviewer's name from time to time.

When you go into the studio, make yourself as comfortable as possible. Take off your jacket and adjust the chair to suit you. If you do not feel comfortable with the headphones, ask whether you have to wear them as this may not be necessary. Treat the interview as if you were having a chat with a person in a small group of people rather than focusing on the thousands or more who may be listening.

You may be asked to do an interview over the telephone. If you do, use a landline rather than a mobile and do it in a quiet room. Keep the handset still and quiet. It can help to stand up when speaking by making your voice sound more authoritative and confident. Thank the interviewer at the end.

Seminars

Seminars can work well in terms of raising the profile with potential clients and referrers, especially when they are held in conjunction with other businesses. They can also be a good opportunity for low key cross-selling of services by introducing key clients or contacts to solicitors in other departments.

Where a joint seminar is held with accountants or surveyors, for example, invitations to the seminar are sent to both firms' client base. This makes the other firm's client base aware of your firm simply by sending them details of the seminar, even if they do not attend.

A short 60–90 minute seminar from 6.00 p.m. onwards makes it easier to attend than a half day or day event. Topics linked to conveyancing for the seminar may include:

- planning for retirement;
- inheritance planning;
- long-term care planning;
- buy-to-let or jet-to-let (buying property abroad to let out);
- funding children's education and first home;
- capital release schemes;
- landlord/tenant issues.

For a 90-minute seminar, have three topics with different people talking for approximately 20 minutes each with time for questions at the end of each presentation. Three topics provide a variety of subjects and so the seminar is more likely to attract a wider range of people. Practise the presentation in full, especially the handover between speakers.

Send out invitations four weeks before an event and again two weeks before as a reminder. On arrival, offer people a cup of tea or coffee and at the end a glass of wine with nibbles to encourage them to stay and meet more people from the firm.

After the event, write to each person who attended to thank them for coming and offer to discuss a particular issue raised at the seminar over the telephone initially. Write to those who did not attend and offer to send the handouts from the seminar.

Entertaining

Entertaining key clients such as developers and referrers helps to oil the wheels of the relationship. It gives people an opportunity to get to know each other better and to talk on a personal level. These are not necessarily the occasions to talk about business in depth.

More formal entertainment at corporate events helps to cement relationships. Such events can be a useful way to nurture longer-term relationships, particularly with referrers. Entertainment of this nature is often linked to the commercial side of the practice and is useful for cross-referring clients (see Chapter 6).

Sponsorship

Care needs to be taken when sponsorship opportunities become 'available', however worthy the cause. Good causes become better when the purpose of the sponsorship is seen by target clients and instils good feelings towards the sponsoring firm. For this reason, it is better to stay away from potentially controversial issues which the Senior Partner may avidly support but many of the firm's clients or referrers may oppose. Typical examples include political party fund raising and blood sport activities.

When offered a sponsorship opportunity, ask the following questions:

1. What publicity-related activities will the receiver of the sponsorship money do to help raise the awareness of the sponsoring firm?
2. What evidence is there of publicity gained from previous events?
3. Who will the publicity be targeted at and do they match the firm's target market? If not, should the firm act as a sponsor?
4. Who will manage the media to gain publicity? If it has to be the sponsoring firm, factor in the time and ability to do it.
5. What opportunities are there for the firm to tell its own clients and referrers about its good deeds?

6. Are there other sponsors bigger than the firm who will gain the publicity limelight and leave the small sponsoring firm with no publicity and feeling like sponsoring fodder?
7. What photo opportunities are there for the firm to raise its profile through innovative thinking or a publicity stunt, even though it is not the biggest sponsor?
8. How will you evaluate the results?

If the firm attracts conveyancing clients from a reasonably close catchment area, then only sponsor local activities. If its target market is people with growing families, approach the local schools to see what sponsorship activities it can undertake, or else sponsor the local children's football and other sports teams. If the target market is wealthier young families, sponsor local gymkhana events in more rural areas or consider sponsoring youth orchestras.

If the target market is aged 50 plus, consider sponsoring activities such as a local theatre production, a flower show or an antiques evening. For referrers arrange an inter-firm quiz between a number of referrer and potential referrer businesses.

Cause marketing

Cause marketing is linking your firm to a good cause, e.g. raising money for the local children's hospice. This aims to encourage people to see the firm in a favourable light.

Cause marketing needs to be done on a drip-drip approach over a period of time. An example of cause marketing is selecting a charity to support for a year and to commit to raising funds for it through a series of events. This could be a charity raising funds to send deprived children on holiday. If staff are involved in choosing which charity to support, they are more likely to be willing to organise fund raising events which will encourage them to spread the word and enhance the firm's image.

With the charity's permission, the words: 'Sponsors of XYZ Charity (using their logo) for 200X' could be printed on all letter-headed paper, posters, invoices, advertisements and newsletters.

Exhibitions

Exhibitions should be treated with caution. Unless the exhibition organisers spend significant sums to attract the firm's client types to an event, it is likely to give a poor return to the firm.

Typical examples are the local Council or Chamber of Trade and Commerce organising a trade exhibition of local businesses where the main people who attend and visit a stand are other exhibitors. Do be clear about the reasons for attending and the likely costs of creating a professional exhibition stand to show the firm in its best light.

When making up panels for the exhibition stand, keep wording to a minimum. The panels are effectively wallpaper and tend not to be read in any detail.

If you commit the firm to an exhibition stand, do not staff it with junior people. Exhibitors can spend thousands of pounds on a stand to get it looking just right and then completely fail because the most important aspect, the people staffing the stand, do not reflect the firm in the best way.

The stand needs to be staffed by solicitors and partners. If the feeling is that their time is too valuable to be spent on an exhibition stand, then seriously question whether the stand should be taken. There is nothing worse when visiting an exhibition stand than to ask a fairly basic question and the member of staff having to ask another person to find out the answer – that is, if there is anyone there to ask.

Further reading

Barry, A. (2002) *PR Power,* Virgin Books.

Bradbury, A. (2002) *Successful Presentation Skills,* Kogan Page.

10

Evaluating marketing activities

KEY POINTS

This chapter will

- recommend ways to set objectives against which to assess activities
- explain methods of evaluating press coverage
- describe how to work out market share
- encourage the use of new client enquiry research
- show you how to evaluate direct marketing
- suggest ways to assess customer satisfaction
- provide ideas to help increase the response rates of client questionnaires
- suggest the use of a 'mystery shopper'
- explain why it is good to welcome complaints

Introduction

It can be particularly difficult to assess the results of individual marketing activities, as few function in isolation. Most tactics support or work to enhance others. Taking key clients or referrers to lunch oils the relationship, but is unlikely to provide additional business if the level of service given is poor and the advice offered questionable. Sponsoring a local theatre production is unlikely to bring in new clients, if nobody has heard of the firm. For marketing activities to be effective, they need to work in harmony with each other.

Objectives

Before results can be measured, they must be assessed against clearly defined objectives which are agreed before the marketing activities are initiated. Objectives which follow the SMART criteria (Specific, Measureable, Achievable, Relevant and give a Timescale – see Chapter 1), provide a control mechanism to assess results at different times, e.g. quarterly or monthly.

Sample marketing objectives might be:

- to increase fee income by 16 per cent from clients with properties over the value of £500,000 by 31 December 200X;
- to gain £X fee income to set up commonhold ownership agreements with six developers by 26 September 200X;
- to gain X volume of remortgage work from three building societies by 30 June 200X.

Use the SMART method as a control tool. Assess results from turnover figures broken down according to the objectives.

Objectives achieved

Assess whether the objectives have been achieved within budget at the quarter, half and three-quarter way points as well as at the end of the full year or selected time period, i.e. has fee income increased in line with the objectives? If there is a variance between actual and planned objectives, consider what steps have to be taken before the final date.

Awareness/perception surveys

If the objectives are to do with building awareness or changing perceptions of the firm, an awareness or perceptions survey is needed before the marketing activities begin. A firm would want to discover what clients actually thought of the practice before making decisions about how to change perceptions, if this was needed. A further survey after the marketing programme has finished will enable the two studies to be assessed against each other to determine whether the objectives have been achieved.

There are two ways to measure attitudes. Quantitative techniques measure numbers – they will tell you how many people feel a certain way. Qualitative methods will tell you why the interviewees feel in a certain way. Quantitative methods tend to be the favoured route as they can easily be carried out using questionnaires with a large number of people. Qualitative techniques require usually one to one or small group discussions (focus groups) with a skilled interviewer.

Observing client behaviour

Client behaviour is often a better indication of what clients think than what they say. Behaviour can be observed when people first come into the office, in reception, in the waiting area, in a fee earner's office and when they leave. Although subjective and potentially misunderstood, indications can be taken from their body language of posture, eye contact, facial expressions, hand and arm movements, tone of voice as well as from what they say.

Press coverage

If the objective is to gain print space in terms of articles or broadcast airtime, one method of evaluation is to measure how many single column centimetres (number of centimetres per single column) or minutes on air are achieved. The problem with this method is that the publicity may be in publications or on broadcast stations that are not read or listened to by typical clients and hence have limited value. In addition, the coverage may not have been favourable and so may be damaging to the practice.

The key is to assess changed attitudinal behaviour towards the firm. Again, surveys need to be carried out both before and after a programme of activities to assess the changes.

Advertising Value Equivalent

The AVE (advertising value equivalent) method is used to measure the editorial print space gained against the amount it would have cost to buy that same space as advertising. This is a simple measure, and so has its followers, but it is fundamentally flawed.

Editorial coverage has a higher credibility value because it cannot be bought. With some exceptions, people tend to buy publications for the information contained in the articles, not for the advertising (although it is the advertising that subsidises the cost of the publication). It is the editor's and the journalist's decision whether to use the press release, so it carries more weight than a paid advertisement.

AVE does not measure the relevance of the media to the target market. The article could appear in a publication which is unlikely or very likely to be read by many of the target market. The measurement is the same regardless.

The tone of the article could be recommending or ridiculing, but the AVE method does not distinguish between the two. Nor does AVE measure the real value of public relations through the media, which is to influence attitudes and behaviour.

For public relations activities, there are three elements to assess:

- the media used;
- do they reach the target market?
- do they influence attitudes and behaviour?

Journalists need to be on the target market list of people to influence. Others on the list will include clients, referrers, professional contacts, estate agents, developers and building societies, for example.

Media tracking analysis

To minimise the drawback of the AVE method, media tracking analysis can be used.

Assessment

Are key marketing messages in the article? The analysis might include the following:

- Has a new service been mentioned?
- Is it written in a favourable light?
- Has a quote from a partner been included?
- Has the website or a telephone number been given?
- Has the address or location been included?
- Did a photograph appear?

The relevance and prominence of the media to the target market

The publication the article appears in is assessed. If it is in the property section of a leading broadsheet Sunday newspaper that you know many of your target market reads, it will carry more weight than if it appears in a local free paper.

Where the article appears in the publication also matters. If it is at the bottom of page 22 next to a dominating sale advertisement for computer equipment, it will have less impact than if it appears on the front page.

Circulation and readership of the publication

Circulation and readership indicate how many people may have seen the article. Circulation is the number of copies sold. This is audited by the ABC bureau, the official industry standard. If the publication tells you how many copies are printed, this is of no real value in assessing effectiveness as it does not indicate how many people will read it. It could be distributed free (or not at all) and immediately be thrown away by many recipients.

Readership is the number of people which the publishers estimate read the publication. The industry standard is to multiply up the circulation figure by 2.5 to 3 to get the readership figure. This figure should be treated with reservation.

Market share

To measure behaviour in terms of whether more people have used the firm for property transactions compared to the competition in a specific area, work out the firm's market share and if it is increasing or decreasing over time.

From the Land Registry, find out the number of properties sold in the previous quarter in a particular area. Divide it by the firm's number of conveyancing transactions in the geographical area covered by the Land Registry. Multiply the figure by 100 to give the firm's approximate market share as a percentage:

Number of sales your firm has acted on in the quarter:

$$\frac{124}{\text{386 properties sold (Land Registry figures) last quarter}} \times 100 = 32.12\% \text{ of market share}$$

Direct marketing, flyers and newletters

When a newsletter or flyer is issued or a direct marketing letter is posted, invite people to contact the firm quoting a reference number to receive an offer or discount for example. This makes it easier to monitor the response to the specific marketing activity.

The beauty of direct marketing as a one-to-one marketing medium is that different messages can be sent to different people to assess their responses. If, for example, information given in a personal letter sent to clients has a better response than the same information written in a newsletter article containing several articles, then send more personal letters.

Other response levels to advertising, for example, are measured by inviting people to telephone a different number from the main office number. With the increasing use of direct dial telephone numbers, it would be relatively easily to count the number of calls to a particular line.

Website hits

Website hits, which broadly indicate the number of times people visit a website, are sometimes used to assess the effectiveness of the website. In reality, this is not very significant. What matters is whether the website caused someone to take action to contact the firm and fee income generation was the result. This information can be gained from the new client enquiry research.

By counting the number of people who request an online quotation and assessing those against the number who convert into business, the effectiveness of the online service can be evaluated. What it does not measure, however, is how many people tried to request an online quote but gave up because of a difficulty. A poor online facility can result in potential clients not using the firm because of their bad experiences.

Client feedback

New client enquiry research

To discover how a new client found out about the firm, ask during the initial discussion, or early on. The findings are recorded, then assessed against the marketing budget allocated for different forms of communication. All new clients should be asked this question, but the results should be treated with reservation.

It can be very difficult for people to remember precisely how they heard of the firm. Perhaps they:

- drove or walked past and saw the firm's name outside the office;
- saw the advertisement in Yellow Pages;
- received an invitation to attend a seminar, but did not go;
- spoke to a friend who had used the firm (but did not actively recommend them);
- were recommended by an existing client.

Where the client has come to the practice as a result of a recommendation, it is useful to find out who recommended the person to offer thanks and so encourage more of the same. If certain clients recommend many people it helps to show gratitude by inviting them to an entertainment event and developing closer relations.

It is of practical benefit to know why the client gave the recommendation. When a picture starts to emerge why, those are the issues on which to focus in order to encourage more recommendations.

Clients' responses will give an indication of which marketing tactics are more useful than others.

Client mid-way comment research

Client surveys are used to assess clients' views of the service they receive from the firm. After an appropriate period of time, approximately half way through completing a matter, consider asking clients how (well) they think you are meeting their expectations. By the end of the case, it is too late to make changes, but you may be able to identify any problems before they become significant if clients are asked midway through a matter.

Client exit, comment or satisfaction surveys

These are commonly called client satisfaction surveys, although this implies a bias that there is a level of satisfaction. A clients' comments survey is a better description. A survey is carried out at the end of work completed on behalf of the client.

A couple of firms have told me that they have around 80 per cent of the client survey forms returned when they are sent out with the final bill and a prepaid envelope. Other firms quote a much lower response if the forms are sent out separately. According to Hill, Brierley and MacDougall in *How To Measure Customer Satisfaction* (1999) customer survey response rates of around 30 per cent can be expected in closer business relationships and below 20 per cent in mass markets.

Improving response rates

The following methods will help to improve response rates:

1. The inclusion of an introductory letter explaining why the survey is being done and how it will benefit clients can increase response rates on average by 30 per cent.
2. A postal reminder sent 10 days after the original mailing, including another questionnaire can boost the return by a further 25 per cent.
3. For the determined, a telephone call to remind clients to return the form should provide a further 25 per cent response.
4. To add around 20 per cent to the response level, have a user-friendly questionnaire which begins with a couple of easy questions and isn't too long. Always leave more personal questions to the end as it can put people off even starting to fill it out if they are put at the beginning,
5. An advance letter sent out before the questionnaire to advise people that it is on its way will increase responses by a further 15 per cent.
6. Incentives, whether coupons or donations to charities, tend to have little or no effect and can actually have a detrimental effect if they make respondents think the firm is trying to sell something.
7. To avoid the risk of clients thinking this is just another mailshot, it is best to keep envelopes plain and personally addressed. If the solicitors' firm's name is printed by the franking machine, this should increase the chances of the envelope being opened.

Table 10.1 Techniques for maximising response rates summary

	%
Introductory letter	30
First reminder letter	25
Telephone reminder	25
Respondent-friendly questionnaire	20
Advance-notice letter	15
Incentive	minus 15
Second reminder letter	12
Envelope	+/− 10

Source: Hill, N., Brierley, J. and MacDougall, R. (1999) *How to Measure Customer Satisfaction*, Gower

While it would be unrealistic in most instances to do all of the above, an introductory letter with the user-friendly questionnaire sent in a plain envelope is likely to increase responses from, say, 30 per cent to 52 per cent – quite a significant amount.

Client satisfaction questionnaire's content

The sample client satisfaction questionnaire in Appendix D is for a High Street firm with a range of legal services. In addition to assessing clients' views of the firm, further questions can be included for marketing purposes. For example:

- to assess which promotional activities are better than others, include a question on how the client first heard of the firm;
- to evaluate whether clients know what other services the firm provides (and so increase their awareness at the same time) ask if they are aware that the range of services are available – then list them;
- to encourage clients to recommend the firm to others, consider including a question on whether the client has recommended or would be willing to recommend you to another. This can help to prompt them without actually asking them to do it.

Mystery shopper

To assess the people aspect of marketing, ask someone to act as a 'mystery shopper' to assess how well the firm's staff respond to a potential new client. For further details, go to Chapter 13, 'The client's perspective'.

Welcome complaints and demanding clients

A person who complains provides an opportunity for the firm to gain a more loyal client once the problem is resolved. Demanding clients may set the standard which average clients are likely to expect in the future. They prepare your firm for the future.

Rather than taking a defensive view about clients making complaints, treat their concerns as possibly the tip of the iceberg. From the clients' perception, they are right. See things from their point of view and make any appropriate changes.

Clients are more likely to indicate their dissatisfaction to support staff than to their solicitor or in writing. Encourage support staff to pass on what clients have said and treat it seriously. Many unhappy clients will vote with their feet by not using the firm again. They may say more to other people (potential and possibly existing clients) than to the solicitor they are displeased with. Support staff are the antennae for the early warning signs of annoyed clients. Use them to help assess how the firm is seen by clients and whether it lives up to its promises. For further information, see Chapter 14 on complaints avoidance.

Act on results

It is one thing to evaluate the results of marketing activities, but this is to little purpose unless the knowledge gained is used to make changes to how the marketing budget is spent. If the evaluation results are only glanced at, there is little point in doing them.

If there is no follow-up action, it can affect clients' opinions of the firm detrimentally when deficits are highlighted, but continue to be made.

Further reading

Barry, A. (2002) *PR Power*, Virgin Books.

Hill, N., Brierley, J. and MacDougall, R. (1999) *How to Measure Customer Satisfaction*, Gower.

Leland, K. and Bailey, K. (1995) *Customer Service for Dummies*, IDG Books.

11

Converting telephone callers into clients

KEY POINTS

This chapter will

- explain how to use the influencing arrowhead to convert more callers into clients
- encourage you to make better use of tone of voice in conversations
- describe how to talk in terms of what matters to clients
- show you how to deal effectively with objections
- advise using closing techniques to gain instructions

Introduction

Clients are increasingly shopping around to get the best quote. Of the calls your firm received over the last week, how many of them converted into business? Could this be improved?

Craig *et al.*, found that 33 per cent of conveyancing clients had shopped around and that:

> While the majority of clients had not shopped around before selecting their solicitor, a greater number of younger clients had done so. For clients who had shopped around, other important reasons for deciding between firms were the telephone manner of the solicitor and details given about the experience and expertise of the firm.
>
> Craig, R., Rigg, M., Briscoe, R. and Smith, P. (2001) *Client Views: Experiences of Using a Solicitor for Personal Matters*, Law Society Strategic Research Unit

The same research found that when conveyancing clients were questioned about the importance of price in the decision to choose a solicitor, 32 per cent considered it to be not very important or not at all important.

Table 11.1 Client views – importance of price in the decision to choose a solicitor

	Conveyancing
Sample size	587
	%
Extremely important	9
Very important	18
Quite important	39
Not very important	18
Not at all important	14
Don't know	1

Source: Craig, R., Rigg, M., Briscoe, R. and Smith, P. (2001) *Client Views: Experiences of Using a Solictor for Personal Matters*, Law Society Strategic Research Unit.

Conveyancing is the one legal service where clients can easily compare quotes on price with other firms. For many people, it is the legal service where they have a better understanding of what they are getting than in other areas of the law. This means that it is a short step from plucking the service off the supermarket shelf, hence the interest of other non-traditional service providers in the market sector. The challenge, therefore, is to differentiate your firm from others and to use telephone techniques to encourage clients to use you.

Research by Craig *et al.* also found that over 90 per cent of clients had made telephone contact with their law firm. Of those, 78 per cent considered the ease of contacting a solicitor by telephone to be very good or good. On the other hand, 11 per cent considered it to be very poor or poor. The majority of potential clients will initially make contact with your firm by telephone. How people in the firm responds to callers will influence whether potential clients place their business with you.

It is not just the first time a person telephones the firm that counts though; it matters every time they contact you. How people in the firm react will underline or change the caller's attitude towards the firm. Each call is therefore equally important.

We are all salespeople

Do you consider yourself to be a salesperson?

My experience of asking delegates this question in seminars is that few people raise their hands. I would argue that we are all salespeople to some degree. Solicitors may sell their time by the six minutes. The support staff sell their time to their employer every day. If employers are not happy with what they are buying, they will take steps to cease to buy an employee's time.

When telephoning a firm, potential clients may be told that they will be put through to a 'fee earner'. Consider how that sounds to lay people. Perhaps their understanding of the jargon is that it is a 'person who sells legal services on a commission/fee basis'. That sounds like a salesperson working on commission. It may sound better to use the words 'legal adviser' rather than 'fee earner'.

There are two types of salespeople. Those belonging to the first type want to make the sale primarily to benefit themselves. Perhaps their income depends on sales being made or on attaining targets to gain a bonus. Salespeople of the second type help customers come to the right decision for themselves regarding a purchase. These salespeople are there to assist customers with their knowledge and understanding.

It is this second type of salesperson who is the subject of this chapter – the salesperson who acts as an adviser.

Skills and attributes of a salesperson/influencer

People with good influencing skills tend to possess the following key attributes.

Attitude

They will be:

- client service orientated;
- good listeners;
- thinking from the client's perspective;
- self-confident.

Questioning

They will:

- ask questions about the client's current situation;
- ask questions about clients' needs and wishes or how they want to change their situation.

Analysis and product knowledge

They will also be able to:

- analyse the client's situation in terms of legal issues and implications;
- talk knowledgeably about the service and processes involved;
- approach the problem from the client's perspective.

Selling/influencing skills

Their selling and influencing skills lead them to:

- present the benefits of the services that will solve the problem from the client's point of view and resolve the client's concerns;
- ask for the instructions or allow the client more time to think about it, then follow up.

Training

Ultimately, people can have sound knowledge of their firm's services, ask the right questions and provide answers in an understandable way, but still not get the instructions. Unless members of staff actually know how to sell, the client is likely to thank them at the end of a telephone call, put the receiver down, then phone the next firm on the list. Your firm might have been the best one for that client, but because your staff didn't know how to get the instructions, the client ended up worse off.

Few of us are natural salespeople. Basic training in influencing skills for all staff who give quotations will assist clients to make the right decision – and increase your fee income. Lessons learned from good influencing training will stay with delegates for the rest of their lives. They can use such training to gain cooperation from everyone they have contact with, from work colleagues, clients, suppliers, to partners or spouses and children; and it also helps to make life smoother.

The process of influencing people

Converting telephone callers into clients can be viewed as a process. Figure 11.1 demonstrates the steps. You may not need to go through all the steps every time, but understanding them and being prepared for them will considerably help your conversion rate of turning callers into clients.

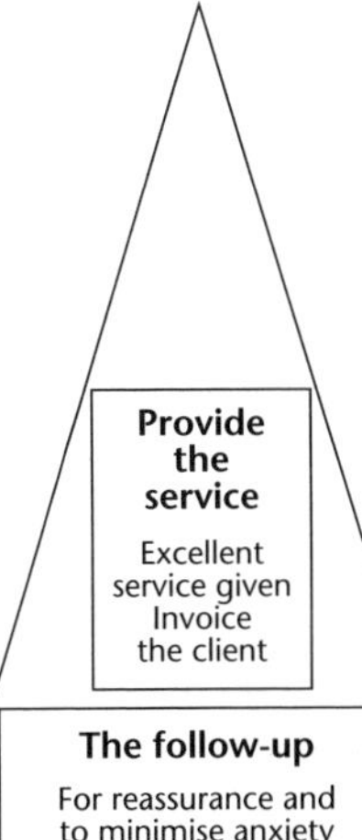

Figure 11.1 The influencing arrowhead figure

Preparation for telephone calls

Preparing for telephone calls from clients includes thinking about your services from the client's perspective. Clients are concerned about how much the service is going to cost them, how long it will take and what they have to do.

Think about typical questions clients are likely to ask and practise giving answers from the client's point of view. Use plain English to explain complex legal and procedural issues.

Words and knowledge

The words you use need to be understandable and jargon free to help the caller feel comfortable with your firm. It is easy to slip into conveyancing jargon, particularly when dealing with fellow professionals all day. We can forget that the words used actually are jargon and that lay people (clients) may only have a hazy understanding of what they mean.

Many clients will only see a solicitor a handful of times in their lifetime. Although they may have bought a property before, this does not mean that they can remember the exact meaning of the words involved. Their understanding may be inaccurate. If words are used that are not understood, this can help to alienate callers who may feel reluctant to ask questions because they don't want to reveal their lack of knowledge.

EXAMPLE **Mystery shopping**

When conducting 'mystery shopping' research by telephone, on one occasion I was put through to the probate department. I asked what probate was. The lady answering said, 'Well, it's probate.' I said 'But I don't understand what probate means', so she repeated in a much louder voice 'It's PROBATE.' She hesitated, then said 'I'll put you through to the solicitor.'

Jargon

Support staff are the first point of contact for most clients and they have a critical influential role to play in encouraging the callers to use the firm. Anyone who speaks to a client in a department should be trained and skilled at putting jargon words into plain English.

When speaking in plain English, the skill is to put across the points without sounding patronising. This can be avoided by asking callers how long ago it was that they last bought or sold a property. This is likely to indicate their level of understanding of expressions and words used.

Some jargon used regularly by solicitors in conveyancing transactions includes:

- disbursements;
- searches;
- exchange of contracts;
- completion.

These are described for the benefit of clients in plain English below.

Disbursements

These could be described to clients as: 'expenses that other organisations charge you for information we need for your home purchase/sale. The local authority charges for giving information on planned developments near your home, for example.'

Searches

Searches can be described to clients as follows: 'We search for information which could affect the purchase and subsequent resale of your home. We contact the coal authority, for example, to ask them to search through their records to find out if any mines were located under your home which could affect the foundations in the future.'

Exchange of contracts

Exchange of contracts can be described to clients as: 'a legal step which commits both you and the other person to buy or sell your home. Your home does not change hands at that point. It is the legal commitment made on both sides to buy or sell at an agreed future date.'

Completion

Completion can be described as: 'when ownership of the property changes hands. It is the day you have to move out if you are selling, or have the right to move in, if you are buying. It is the day the balance of the money is paid or received.'

Telephone voice

Tone of voice

A person's attitude is demonstrated through their tone of voice. In a telephone conversation, communication is through the words used and the tone of voice conveyed.

According to professor of communication Albert Mehrabian, with face-to-face communication, 'body language' and tone of voice accounts for some 93 per cent of a communication. Over the telephone, the conversation is 'blind'. There is no visual reference to support the tone of voice and words used. While Professor Mehrabian's research has been challenged, what it does emphasise is that greater consideration needs to be given to the tone of voice used over the telephone.

People may think about the words they are going to use, but not how they are going to say the words. Trust is partly built on feeling at ease with the other person. Tone helps people to feel at ease and have confidence in the firm.

Tone comprises:

- inflection;
- volume;
- speed;
- pitch;
- intensity;
- enthusiasm;
- self-belief supported by knowledge.

People's tone of voice can reveal how they are feeling. A person with a monotone or flat sounding voice communicates boredom and a lack of interest in what the caller is saying. An abrupt tone tells the caller that the person on the other end is angry or impatient. An enthusiastic and warm tone conveys confidence and interest in helping the caller.

Answer the telephone with a welcoming tone that tells callers you are glad they rang your firm. Then let the caller set the tone.

Client's tone	Your tone
Friendly	Warm
Sad	Understanding
Worried	Reassuring
Angry	Concerned
Enquiring	Helpful
Shocked	Sympathetic

Inflection

Inflection is the highs and lows of the pitch of a person's voice that shows that you mean what you say. They tend to tell the caller how uninterested or interested you are. Without inflection, the result is a monotone.

To improve the quality of the inflection, try:

- smiling when you are on the telephone – it helps the voice sound more welcoming;
- standing up when speaking – automatically the shoulders go back so more air fills the lungs and the voice generally comes across as stronger. Standing up also helps many people to feel more confident and so sound more authoritative;
- stressing key words by pausing before and after saying them – it slows the words down and gives people more time to absorb them. It also highlights certain expressions you want to emphasise;
- changing the volume: saying key words louder or quieter – it encourages the caller to listen with more attention.

Speed

The rate at which a person speaks can reflect the part of the country where they grew up. When nervous, we tend to speak more quickly. As a rule, aim to slow down what you are saying, to give the caller more time to take it in. This is particularly important where English is not the other person's first language.

Enthusiasm and confidence

Enthusiasm and confidence are linked, in that it is hard to be enthusiastic if a person is not feeling confident. A confident person sounds more authoritative and knowledgeable about what he or she is saying.

Self-confidence tends to go in waves to some degree during the day. If a person does not sound confident on the telephone, this will not encourage a caller to want to give instructions to the firm. Confidence is gained through having a thorough knowledge of the answers to most of the questions a caller is likely to ask. The ability to speak from the perspective of the client and knowing how to explain the fee in an authoritative manner aids confidence.

Confidence also comes from within a person, so how people feel about themselves, the feel-good factor, has a direct impact on how confidently and therefore authoritatively, they come across.

See Chapter 8 on networking for ways to increase confidence.

The greeting

Give your name when you answer the telephone. The client will often not remember it, but it is the first step in building trust.

If the person who answers does not give his or her name, it tells callers that the firm expects personal information from them (name, the property they want to buy, the amount of the purchase or sale price, etc.) but that the person in the law firm does not trust them enough to reciprocate. When I have conducted mystery shopper research across a range of firms (see Chapter 13 'The clients' perspective'), I have often been surprised at how infrequently people in law firms give their own names when they answer the telephone in their departments.

Gathering information

Wants, needs and problems

The next stage is to find out what the client wants and needs and to highlight any problems. What often happens is that the client says, 'I want a quote for doing the conveyancing to buy/sell a house with a purchase price of £x,000.' If a quote is given at this point the client is unlikely to use the firm unless it is the cheapest.

The aim is to develop rapport by getting the client to do the talking. Generally, the more clients talk, the more they build trust with the person they are speaking to and hence with the firm. By encouraging clients to speak through the use of open questions, it is hoped that clients will reveal the golden nugget of information that can then be used to persuade them to use your firm.

There are two skills used in this stage: questioning and listening skills. Part of encouraging clients to do the talking is to ask the right kind of questions.

Questioning skills

The ability to ask questions and to encourage the caller to talk are skills that are critical to the process of helping people make the right choice. They help to develop rapport and trust and build confidence in clients' minds that you are the right person to use. They give a taster of how well they think you will work together and whether you are on the same wavelength.

These skills communicate to callers that you will treat them as individuals and not just as another case. They provide the information that is needed for you to see the uniqueness of their situation and respond accordingly.

Background questions

Use background questions to establish a context for the client. These are information-gathering questions; establish the client's background, history and experience.

Try to make the majority of the questions open questions. These are questions which cannot be answered by 'yes' or 'no'. They begin with, for example, 'who', 'what', 'when' 'where' and 'how'. Try to avoid asking 'why' questions. With the wrong tone of voice, it may appear attacking and put people on the defensive. Instead use 'for what reason . . .' or 'tell me more about . . .'.

Table 11.2 Background or information-gathering questions

Question	Information
When do you hope to move in?	Tells you the timescale to work to or if you need to amend the client's expectations.
Is this your first home/Do you have a home to sell?	Tells you how experienced the client is at using solicitor firms.
When is the most convenient time to contact you?	Leads into the times when you are available.
Do you use e-mail?	Tells the client that you do and can therefore be contacted at the client's convenience.
What kind of things are important to you when choosing which solicitor to use?	Tells you the client's expectations of your firm.

Questions which seem irrelevant to the client will cause antagonism, so you need to be ready to give a reason for asking a particular question.

The other half of asking questions is the essential skill of listening.

Listening skills

The ability to listen well over the telephone is one of the most important skills a person can have. Many things can hinder our, and the prospective client's, ability to listen, such as:

- wanting to ask a question;
- being distracted by another person or thing;
- associating in our own minds with something the other person has said and allowing thoughts to go off at a tangent;
- wanting to say something which we think is more important than what the other person is saying;
- not hearing what the other person said;
- not understanding their accent;
- background noise;
- writing notes at the same time as listening.

Active listening is shown over the telephone by:

- giving vocal encouragers, such as 'and then . . .', 'yes', 'uh-huh';
- not interrupting;
- asking relevant questions;
- summarising back for clarification.

Quotations, benefits and credibility

Craig *et al.* in a study on clients' perceptions found that the perception of 'value for money' has a greater influence on the commitment of clients involved in conveyancing cases than in other areas of the law. However, solicitors involved in these cases are not viewed as performing well in this respect. Priority should be given to improving clients' perceptions that they are receiving value for money. This will increase the likelihood of their using the firm again or recommending it to others.

Clients often do not appreciate what work solicitors have to do during the conveyancing transaction. For this reason, they may think that it is expensive. While estate agents' fees will be substantially more, it is easy for the client to see what they do to earn their fee.

The person giving the quote therefore needs to build value into the fee, rather than just give a bland figure.

EXAMPLE **Building value into the fee**

The fee is £XXX plus VAT for our time to act for you.

For this fee we confirm to you in writing your instructions. We use our specialist legal knowledge to check and agree, subject to your instructions, the terms of the contract with XYZ's solicitors.

We apply to the regional authority for the local search which tells us if there are any plans to build major constructions nearby which could affect the value of the property and your ability to sell it in the future. We analyse the answers and report back to you.

We apply to the Coal Authority for a coal mining search to find out if any mines went under the site of your new home which could affect the structure in the future. We then advise you accordingly.

We also send off for a Land Registry search to check the title of the property, and ensure that the person selling it has the legal right to sell it. We receive from your lender a copy of the mortgage offer if you are having a mortgage and we send you a report on the title of the property.

We fill in Stamp Duty Land Tax forms, which can take up to half an hour.

The local authority, Land Registry, and Coal Authority charge you for giving the information needed. These charges have to be paid separately from our time fees.

BOX 11.1 Courage on costs

John Bott reckons that few conveyancers will have the courage to increase their fees to cover the work involved in completing the new Stamp Duty Land Tax (SDLT) forms (see [2003] *Gazette*, 11 December, 12). I think he is wrong. My firm is charging an extra half an hour's time for dealing with the new form in residential cases and I have heard of a number of others in my area that, like us, are not prepared to absorb the extra cost. Conveyancing lawyers need to recognise that they now do a good deal of additional work compared with, say, five years ago. Examples include ID checking, environmental and water searches, dealing with additional enquiries (which have proliferated in the past couple of years), dealing with building regulations enquiries, obtaining defective title indemnity polices (post-Council of Mortgage Lenders handbook) and now the SDLT forms. They should also not forget that many clients and solicitors now communicate by e-mail, which results in time being spent (usually by the lawyer rather than the secretary) in typing and then printing off for the file. The SDLT return forms mark an interesting stage in the history of residential conveyancing. Lawyers are suddenly waking up to the fact that basic laws of economics do not allow them to absorb the increased work and responsibility that is imposed on them by government, mortgage lenders and the like. Those lawyers who are not brave enough to charge extra for doing significant amounts of additional work will put themselves out of business in the next three to five years, perhaps sooner. Conveyancing charges will rise over the same period but will still be a bargain when compared with the fees charged by most of our European counterparts.

Letter to *The Gazette*, 15 January 2004 from David Briffa,
Warners Solicitors, Tonbridge

Present the service from the client's perspective

The key is to use the information gleaned from asking questions to present the benefits of using the firm's services to match the exact needs identified by the caller. Benefits are phrased from the caller's perspective.

General statements such as the following tend to have a low impact on prospective clients:

- we've been established since 1854;
- we have conveyancing specialists;
- we're open until 5.00 p.m.

Statements which describe how a benefit meets an explicit need will have the highest impact in influencing callers to use your firm. By using link phrases such as 'which ensures that . . .' or 'so you can then . . .' or 'which will enable you to . . .' information is phrased in terms of the benefits to be gained by the client.

Table 11.3 Key features and benefits

Features		Benefits
We work quickly	which means that. . .	It keeps your costs down
We allocate two people to your file	which means that. . .	Whenever you telephone with an enquiry, there should always be someone who can answer your query
We keep you informed throughout	which means that. . .	You won't have to worry about having to chase us

If clients raise a problem, the same approach is used in presenting the benefits which will solve the problem from their perspective.

If the problem is 'I cannot see you during normal office hours', the answer could be:

> 'Because we do virtually all the legal paperwork by letter, telephone and e-mail (if you use e-mail) *this means that* you don't have to take valuable time off work to visit us to sign the paperwork. If we do need to see you, we can arrange it at a time that is convenient to you outside of work hours so that it does not cause you a problem.'

If the problem is 'I am a teacher. I cannot make or receive telephone calls at work', the answer could be:

> 'We recognise that it's not always easy for people buying a home to telephone their solicitor from work or inside office hours at a time that suits their solicitor. We're open all week until 6 p.m. and on Saturdays from 9.00 a.m. to 12.30 p.m. *which means that* you can contact us when it's convenient for you. Using e-mail, you can send messages 24 hours a day.'

Establish the firm's credibility

The same technique is used to establish the firm's credibility in the client's mind. Features are translated into benefits that have a direct meaning for the individual client.

Put yourself in the position of a client: why would you use your firm? Very few firms, in my experience of doing mystery shopper exercises, ever attempt to differentiate themselves from other practices by establishing their credibility.

When asked during mystery shopper exercises on behalf of firms, 'why should I come to you rather than to another firm?', many respondents don't know what to say with any ease. Very few have been able to say what their practice's competitive advantage is. While some have said what they consider themselves to be good at doing, such as 'we have conveyancing specialists' this does not differentiate the firm from another practice that is likely to say exactly the same.

Think of your own firm's competitive advantages for the client. Describe what they mean rather than just stating what they are. If you are going to use figures, do not use whole numbers ending in nought or five. It sounds more exact to say 83 per cent rather than 80 per cent or 85 per cent, but be accurate in what you say. Some suggestions follow:

> '76 per cent of our business comes from existing clients or from clients who have been recommended to us. *This means that* it is particularly important to us that we give you an efficient and friendly service because we hope that you will want to recommend us to others.'

> 'XYZ recommend us to people like yourselves because they know through experience that we make buying a home as hassle free/as smooth/as straightforward/as uncomplicated as possible *so that you will* enjoy the whole experience of moving home from the day your offer is accepted to the day you settle in.'

Clients are predominantly concerned with the two-pronged issues of time and cost. It is likely to have the greatest impact if you can word your credibility so that it saves the client one or both of these.

Dealing with objections

Handling objections is part of the influencing process. When a person presents an objection, this does not necessarily mean that they do not want to 'buy'; it often means that they are using your reaction to the objection to justify using you and to satisfy themselves that they are going to make the right choice. Treat objections as positive signs.

The objections put forward may mask the real objection. Some objections are trivial. By asking open questions, you can help to establish the real objection and address that.

Objections tend to comprise two issues: the practical and the emotional. No one likes to be proved wrong. To lose 'face' antagonises the caller, causes resentment and rarely wins a client. The key is to answer both the logical and the emotional questions. The logical may be a legal procedure issue. The emotional may be that clients need reassurance about something.

Sometimes objections are raised because callers know their partner is likely to want to know the answer to that question. They themselves may be convinced, but they want to know what to say in answer to their partner's questions, hence they ask.

There are two approaches to use: 'agree and counter' and 'answer a question with a question'.

EXAMPLE **Dealing with objections**

Client: 'We'll probably use the solicitors we know.'

Agree and counter

Use active listening skills without interruption to show that you are taking the objection seriously and are treating the client with respect. Then agree with the client's viewpoint before putting an alternative view forward.

Solicitor: 'I can understand you wanting to use a solicitor you know; what can happen, though, is because your solicitors may not be familiar with the development at [site name] there can be delays moving in due to the time it takes to get the information they need . . . [and other reasons] . . . which can mean missing the deadline set by the builder's own solicitors for exchange of contract and the sale possibly falling through. When do you hope to move in? [and other questions].'

Answer a question with a question

- How long have you known the solicitor?
- How important is it to you that you use a solicitor you know?
- What things matter most to you when choosing a solicitor?

Objections to the cost

Suppose you receive an objection to the price such as, 'I wasn't expecting it to be that much!' What could you say?

Take care not to put any other solicitor down. If the name of another firm has been mentioned, do not imply that it would give anything but a good service.

When you receive an objection, ask questions:

'The price is important, but is it your only issue?'

'What matters most to you when buying a home?'

'We're not the cheapest because we give a good service. In life, you generally get what you pay for. For most people buying a home, it is the most expensive purchase they have made to date. People know that they are likely to sell their home at some stage in the future. To give a cheap quote, corners may have to be cut and this could mean vital issues are overlooked, which only come to light when you want to sell your home – and prevent you from selling it. Would you want that to happen?'

'You are guaranteed always to find a cheaper quote somewhere else. We give a value for money quote for the extensive work we do for you. We . . .[lead into the benefits of using your firm from the perspective of the client] . . .'

If your quote is the lowest and the caller asks why it is less than others, you can say:

'We give a value for money quote by keeping our costs down and passing the savings on to our clients, as we want you to come back to use us when you need legal help in the future. For routine parts of the conveyancing process, we use experienced staff who are closely monitored, rather than high cost solicitors. A qualified solicitor supervises your conveyancing and checks everything is done properly. This is how we give you a good value for money quote.'

Try to find out what the core objection concerns. Is it the total cost or when the disbursements or the deposit have to be paid?

Do you accept credit cards and is that a way to help a client pay up front for disbursements?

Specify which part of the fee goes to the firm for overheads and time spent on the case and which part goes to pay other organisations (disbursements, VAT, etc.).

Encourage clients to think of the fee from a different perspective. You will enable them to achieve the change they want (moving home, starting a new life, completing a divorce, buying a business). Lead into reiterating the benefits to them of using you.

Get the instructions

The one area of skill which many staff lack is the ability to encourage the potential client to actually give the instructions to the firm – to 'close the sale'.

BOX 11.2 Closing the sale

Before running seminars in house for firms, delegates are frequently asked to complete pre-course questionnaires. This encourages them to think about the course topic and makes sure the content reflects what actually happens in practice in their particular firm.

Answers to the question 'what do you tend to say at the end of a telephone call with a potential client who has asked for a conveyancing quote?' typically include the following:

- Thank you for calling. I will send confirmation of the quote in the post.
- I'd be pleased to act for you.
- Please come back to me if you have any questions.
- I give them my direct dial telephone number, in case they want to call me, and I tell them my name again.
- I look forward to hearing from you.

The response of clients to any of the above, after they have put the telephone down, is likely to be to telephone the next firm of solicitors on their list.

Clients want to make a decision that is right for them. They want to get the legal ball rolling. They want to know that the legal steps have started and that this is one less issue they have to think about, one less decision to make. Telephone calls finished with the typical responses given in firms are not going to take the weight off clients' shoulders by making the decision of which law firm to use.

Ultimately 'selling skills' are needed to help clients come to the right decision for them.

Buying signals

The first step in closing the sale is to recognise the buying signals given by potential clients to indicate that you have convinced them and that they have come to a decision. They may include:

- 'That sounds fine to me.'
- 'I like the sound of that.'
- 'Uh huh.'

As soon as you hear the signals, ask for the business. If you continue to sell the benefits of using your firm, you may talk the caller out of using you. 'Zip the lip.' Do not say any more to persuade – it will do the reverse.

Closing methods

Once you hear the buying signals, use a closing method that is right for the situation and one that you feel comfortable saying with confidence and ease.

Simple

'Can we act for you?'

Summarise then close

'Well, as long as there are no hold-ups outside of our control, we should be able to do everything for you in the timescale, so would you like us to act for you?'

Reiterate the key benefits and ask for the order

'By using us, you will not have to take any time off work. We can see you at a time that is convenient to you in the evening or on a Saturday morning by arrangement. You can contact us when it's convenient to you by e-mail. Just about everything can be done by e-mail, telephone and post so can we act for you?'

Sharp angle close

- 'If we could start today on the legal aspects, would you be happy to use us?'
- 'If we could negotiate a moving in date of XXX, would you be happy for us to act for you?'
- 'If . . . then . . .'

The assumption close

This assumes clients are going to use you and that the only decision they have to make is about something of minor importance:

- 'I could see you at 4 o'clock this afternoon or would 10 o'clock on Thursday morning suit you better?'
- 'I could contact the agents straightaway and ask them to fax the details to me to save you from doing it, then I'll be able to make contact with the other solicitors. What's the agent's telephone number?'

If staff handling telephone enquiries for quotations ask for the instructions at the end of their telephone calls, they will increase their conversion rate of callers into clients.

EXAMPLE **Influencing techniques**

After delivering a seminar inhouse for one large conveyancing firm using the influencing techniques in this chapter, the practice manager e-mailed me to say:

> 'As feedback, I received a call from one of the delegates, who confirmed that she has used the techniques learned and a client both complimented her on the firm's approach and said that he chose us because of it.'

The follow-up

From doing mystery shopper exercises, I found that firms rarely follow up the enquiries they receive and often do not even send the quotes or information requested.

Think how much it costs your firm to actually get potential clients to contact it in the first place. It is said to cost many times more to gain a new client than to retain an existing one. If enquiries are not followed up and are allowed to go cold, all the marketing activities and costs, both direct and indirect, are wasted. Not all enquiries should be followed up. It may be obvious that some callers will never become clients. Select the 'cherries', the clients who are likely to be more profitable to the firm and follow up their enquiries.

Action agreement

If it is not possible to get the instructions, get an 'action agreement' on when you will next contact the caller or what you will do, with the caller's agreement. If callers say they need to discuss the matter with their spouse or partner, express understanding and suggest that if their partner has any questions, you would be pleased to speak to him or her. Offer to call the spouse or partner, if that would help the caller.

If you say you will send the written quote, ask if you could telephone in a couple of days to see if they have come to a decision. Emphasise that you appreciate that this is a significant decision to make and that they do not want to make it in a hurry. The follow-up is only done with callers' agreement. If callers do not want it, the firm does not want to annoy potential clients and waste time.

Thank clients for their enquiry and use their name.

If callers have instructed the firm, follow up with confirmation details on the day the instructions have been given. This helps to minimise anxiety and gives reassurance to clients that the firm acts as quickly as it says it does.

Regulations

Accepting instructions is regulated by professional rules and guidance and by statute. Readers are directed to the Law Society's *Conveyancing Handbook* and *The Guide to the Professional Conduct of Solicitors*.

Provide the service

The final part of the influencing arrowhead (see p. 193) is to provide an efficient and friendly service. To do everything the client expects and to be proactive in keeping the client informed.

Further reading

Johnson, K.L. (2003) *Selling with NLP*, Nicholas Brealey Publishing.

Johnson, S. (2004) *The One Minute Sales Person*, HarperCollins.

The Law Society (2004) *Money Laundering: Guidance for Solicitors* (pilot – January 2004) (published by the Law Society at www.lawsociety.org.uk).

Leyland, K. and Bailey, K. (1995) *Customer Service for Dummies*, IDG Books.

Mehrabian, Albert, and Ferris, Susan R. (1967) 'Inference of Attitudes from Nonverbal Communication in Two Channels', *Journal of Consulting Psychology*, 31(3) 248–258.

Silverman, F. (ed.) (2004) *Conveyancing Handbook*, 11th edn., Law Society Publishing.

Timm, P. (2002) *50 Powerful Ideas You Can Use to Keep Your Customers*, Career Press.

12

Managing clients' expectations

KEY POINTS

This chapter will

- show you what clients like and dislike about the actions of solicitors
- enable you to take steps to avoid problems which give rise to complaints
- provide suggestions for a client care charter to manage expectations
- recommend the content of a minimum standards statement for staff
- help you manage expectations before people become clients
- encourage you to monitor clients' expectations and satisfaction levels

Introduction

Many clients' expectations of law firms have changed over the last twenty years. Previously when a client went to see a solicitor, the solicitor was deemed to have the higher status of the two and the client was often treated in a way that emphasised the point. If there was a master–servant relationship, the solicitor was definitely in the position of the master.

This relationship has changed substantially for many. While solicitors are still held in high esteem by many, their role may now be seen more as suppliers of legal services. Solicitors may consider the relationship to be one of equality with their clients, yet some clients may view the relationship as one where the client is now the master. After all, who is paying whom?

Other businesses have helped to raise clients' expectations of the level of customer service. We have been told repeatedly that 'the customer is king' and 'the customer is always right' and that business is about meeting customers' wants and needs. This has encouraged a belief that all businesses will treat us as 'king'. The disappointment hits when clients experience for themselves that many businesses do not live up to their preconceived expectations.

Clients' views

Clients rarely complain about the quality of the legal work they receive, probably because they are not qualified to assess it. Nor do they generally ask for a second opinion to be able to compare the advice given. They are aware, though, of how they are treated. Certain solicitors' actions are highly rated by clients and others are likely to lead to complaints.

BOX 12.1 Customer satisfaction

Solicitors rated highly by their clients:

- have good listening skills;
- show genuine interest in the clients' wellbeing;
- take time and care to ensure that the client fully understands the key legal issues and their implications;
- are open and approachable;
- speak and write in plain English;
- are accessible and respond quickly to calls;
- are efficient and do not delay;
- keep the client informed without needing to be chased;
- provide good information on the likely costs;
- discuss the costs regularly;
- never surprise the client with the amount of the bill;
- make regular checks to gauge the client's satisfaction with the service;
- make clients feel valued;
- leave clients feeling happy to recommend the practice;
- are good at communicating the value of their service.

From Anne Rigg 'How to deliver customer satisfaction'
([1999] *Gazette,* 1 December, 46)

Of respondents to a survey who had used conveyancing services, 79 per cent gave an overall rating of their firm as 'very good/good' while 8 per cent of clients who had conveyancing cases gave an overall rating of 'poor/very poor'. The respondents were taken from a nationally representative sample, who had sought legal advice in the previous twelve months (Craig *et al.*, (2001) *Client Views*, Law Society Strategic Research Unit).

BOX 12.2 Reasons for satisfaction with the firm

Base: All rating as very good, good or fair (1,351)

When the reasons for favourable overall ratings of the firm were analysed, the following factors were apparent:

	%
Very professional/experienced	29
Did everything I wanted	27
Very efficient	23
Good service in general	22
Very helpful	10
Achieved a good result/got the outcome I wanted	10
Provided clear explanations	8
Kept me informed	7
Did what they said they would do	6
Were very approachable	6

Clients with conveyancing cases were most likely to mention being kept up to date (12 per cent).

Craig *et al.* (2001)

Problem areas

Turning to the issues and actions that commonly lead to complaints, it is no surprise that costs are a dominant issue. Anne Rigg, in her research on 'How to deliver customer satisfaction', explains:

> . . . research shows that there are key parts of the client–solicitor relationship that consistently cause problems . . .These are:
>
> - Poor handling of the initial cost discussion.
> - Failure to provide a good estimate of the total cost.
> - Poor billing procedures leading to unpleasant or alarming surprises when bills are presented.
> - Poor explanations of the legal process and its implications.
> - Poor or no management of clients' expectations of the outcome of the legal process.
> - Intimidating, patronising or arrogant manner of the solicitor.
> - Poor client handling by other staff in the law firm.
> - Solicitors not listening or involving the client in the decision-making process.
> - Lack of accessibility at times convenient to the client.
> - Lack of progress and communication in line with client needs.
> - Slow progress or delay.

BOX 12.3 Reasons for dissatisfaction with the firm

Base: All rating as poor or very poor (142)

When the reasons for dissatisfaction with the firm were analysed, the following factors were highlighted:

	%
Provided poor service	29
Inefficient	24
Took longer than necessary	20
Did not seem interested in the case	19
Didn't keep me informed	15
Didn't have enough experience to handle the case	13
Did not look after my best interests	12
Too expensive	10
Did not do what I wanted	8
Could have worked harder	7

Craig *et al.* (2001)

Avoiding the causes of dissatisfaction

To analyse the issues in the lists above, consider how stress can affect clients' emotional and mental wellbeing.

For many, moving home can cause considerable stress. People may feel anxious, irritable, frustrated, angry, insecure, depressed and powerless. Their mental symptoms may include poor concentration, wavering attention span, an inability to listen well, procrastination and poor memory recall. Stress may, in part, explain why clients perceive some of the poor actions by solicitors.

Fee information

The Guide to the Professional Conduct of Solicitors states in detail the information solicitors must give to clients at the start of the case and when it should be updated. However, in the survey by Craig *et al.* (2001) 13 per cent of survey respondents using conveyancing services stated they did not receive a cost estimate at the start of the case.

It can often be very difficult to estimate the likely costs as solicitors may not know what is involved until they get into the details of the case. This may be true for conveyancing services, but when was the last time you bought something where:

- You did not know for certain how much it was going to cost you personally?
- You could not compare against a competitor's service?
- You did not want what you were buying?
- You got no pleasure from the process of buying it?
- The salesperson said that even though you were paying, it was not certain you would get what you wanted, or how long it would take to get it?
- You had difficulty understanding the language the salesperson was using?
- There was no after-sales service?
- There was no guarantee?

These questions reflect how a client may view buying some legal services. It is easy to understand, therefore, how misunderstandings occur, particularly regarding the price. With such apprehension, clients welcome regular discussions regarding the fee. With fixed-price conveyancing, this is less of an issue, unless the figure given allows for an increase in the fee for unexpectedly complicated matters.

When I started in business in 1987, one of my first clients said to me, 'When you are about to tell your client what you are going to charge, look them straight in the eyes. If you look away at that point, they know they can negotiate.'

This is good advice to anyone who gives a fee rate face to face.

Explaining the legal process

If clients do not understand an issue because it has not been explained well enough, given their level of knowledge, they may feel annoyed and frustrated.

A client with a probate case he wanted to handle himself said:

> The solicitor didn't try to help me. He just said it was too complicated for me to do it myself and I'd have to come back to him anyway. If he'd just pointed me in the right direction, I'd have gone back to him. As it was, I lost respect for him. I do still occasionally use the firm, but only for simple things. I don't think they can manage anything too complex.

A good way to explain the conveyancing legal processes, and to help educate clients regarding the likely timescales in order to manage their expectations, is to produce a flow chart. It is often easier to follow a flow chart than read prose.

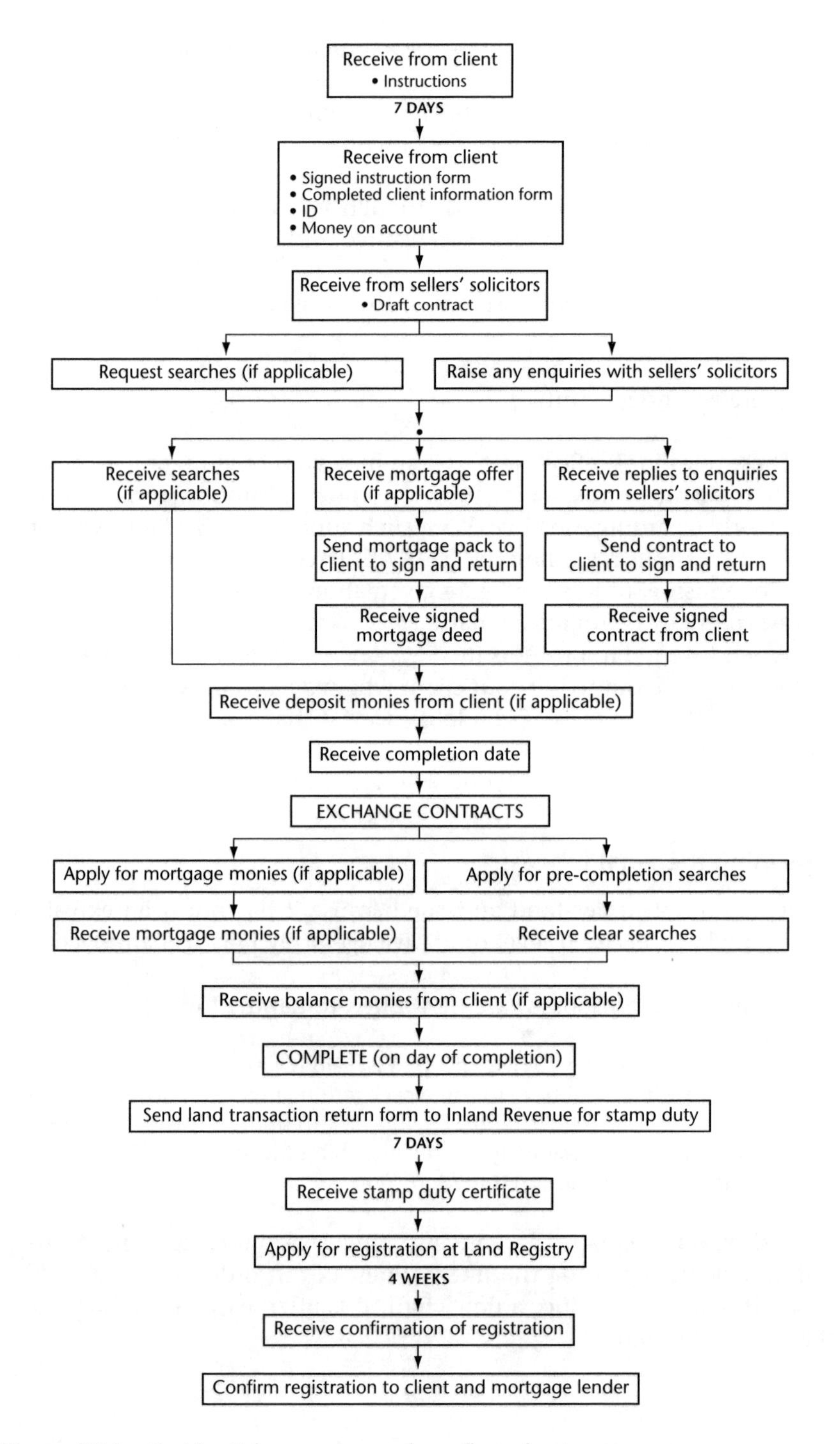

Figure 12.1 Residential property purchase flow chart

Use of a flow chart can help clients to understand what has to happen at every stage and what can go wrong and cause delays. Given that clients under stress may have poor memory recall and an inability to listen well, you need to repeat issues and follow them up in writing. A flow chart can be a useful reference source for clients. The skill is to get the balance right and not risk being patronising.

Tone and manner

Jenkins and Lewis, in their study on clients' perceptions found that 'a small but significant number of recent clients also thought solicitors were pompous and had a condescending manner' (Jenkins and Lewis (1995) *Client Perceptions*, Law Society Strategic Research Unit).

A successful arable farmer said he moved to another solicitor because the previous one was so pompous and arrogant when he was dealing with him. 'He just didn't know how to treat people,' said the farmer. 'He acted as if he was being benevolent by coming down from his lofty perch to your level.'

We are all aware of how we are treated by others and whether they show us respect. When we are paying someone to do something for us, sensitivity to the issue may rise. While using the services of solicitors may not remotely fall within the concept of 'retail therapy', we generally want to feel happy with a buying experience.

Clients should never be 'sent' to the solicitor's office. The solicitor, not the secretary, should always go to them. You should always greet clients personally, however long you have known them or however many times they have come to the office. This emphasises the person's importance and the balance of the relationship. It shows respect.

Ideally, solicitors should always be on time for a client's appointment. If the solicitor cannot help but be delayed, a secretary should inform the client and give an estimate of how long the wait will be, offering the option of making another appointment if no one else can see the client. The secretary should apologise for the delay and offer a drink. When the solicitor sees the client, he or she should also apologise for the wait and offer an explanation as a common courtesy.

Poor client handling by other staff in the law firm

Clients may have an excellent relationship with their own solicitor, but not be happy with how other people treat them.

Q: From the client's perspective, how many cases has your firm got?
A: One.

Q: Which is the most important case?
A: Theirs.

The reason why a client is seeing the solicitor is likely to be the biggest issue in that person's life at the time. It may be causing sleepless nights, and may be the only thing the client can think or talk about.

Clients need to feel that the legal adviser they are using to help resolve the issue appreciates its importance to them. They need to be shown through words and actions that they are the most important people to the firm. If other staff in the firm ignore them, this is likely to be taken as a sign of disrespect. Respect is fundamental to our sense of self-esteem.

One way to avoid this happening is when the client is waiting in reception or the waiting room. If another member of staff goes into the room, as a matter of courtesy, clients should be acknowledged with a nod of the head and a 'Hello' or 'Good morning/afternoon' and possibly an enquiry as to whether they are being seen to. You will know that they have been seen to, but this is a way of showing respect and recognising their importance to the firm.

Involving the client in the decision-making process

When people are under stress, it is harder to take in and remember information given. If clients think that steps are taken without their agreement or understanding, they are likely to feel dissatisfied.

A client with a probate case said 'I'm a working man. I saw one solicitor and he treated me as if I had no brains. He wouldn't explain to me what the process was. He just said it had to be done in the way he said. He wouldn't discuss it. I think he looked down on me.'

Accessibility and communication

People's expectations of accessibility have been raised by other businesses. We see businesses where clients can buy their groceries or use banking services 24 hours a day, seven days a week. Yet their local solicitor may not be available at lunchtime and may close at 5.00 p.m., which is just when clients may be free. Increase in competition is likely to encourage more solicitors to be available outside office hours.

Npower's launch into the conveyancing market was heralded with the statement 'We believe that the working hours of solicitors have left a gap in the market that we hope to exploit' ([2002] *Gazette*, 5 September, 3).

Managing clients' expectations of solicitors' availability has led one solicitor to tell his clients, right from the beginning of the relationship, that he will be available to take calls after 11.00 a.m., with the implication that he is not available before then. His view is that this enables him to work more quickly in the mornings with fewer interruptions, and clients have generally accepted this.

When clients were asked for their reasons for satisfaction with the firm they had used, 12 per cent of conveyancing clients mentioned being kept up to date (Craig *et al.* (2001)).

One of the key reasons why clients complained to the Law Society was because they felt they had not been kept informed. Clients need to be contacted even when there is nothing new to tell them. If they are not, they are likely to feel that the solicitor has put their case to the bottom of the drawer and forgotten about it and them.

The use of case management software where clients have access to a secure area on the web to view the progress made on their case (case tracking), enables clients to gain much of the information they require when they want it. It also leads to fewer telephone interruptions by clients or their estate agent to gain updates from their solicitor.

EXAMPLE **Conveyancing computer system**

STARS (Supplier Tracking and Reporting System) web-based computer system was developed by Legal Services Marketing (LMS), which operates one of the largest networks of solicitors and surveyors. According to its website, it handles over a quarter of a million transactions a year and completes in the region of one in five of all remortgages in the UK. STARS enables clients to track their cases online 24/7. They can gain access to a secure site on the web to see details of their case and get an up-to-date progress report.

Managing expectations early

Clients often do not know what their expectations are until things go wrong. Underlying expectations may not surface until problems appear. One of the reasons why people may choose a branded product is because if it goes wrong, they think they will get a better service to put it right than from the suppliers or manufacturers of an unbranded product. The same occurs when clients are disappointed with the service given by a law firm. Disappointment is likely to be caused by unrealistic initial expectations. Yet the client does not know that they are unrealistic.

The average client, excluding commercial and criminal clients, is likely to see a solicitor only a handful of times in his or her life. With such limited experience, the clients' expectations may be built on what they have seen on television and at the cinema, where everything happens in double-quick time. Part of managing clients' expectations begins with educating them to avoid the risk of disappointment at a later date.

Advertising

For conveyancing clients, recommendation and being cheapest were the more common reasons for choosing a firm (Craig *et al.* 2001). Some clients will come through advertising or walking past the office. Where advertising is used, whether it is in Yellow Pages or other directories when people are telephoning around, or in the local press or on posters, this presents the first opportunity of managing expectations.

The use of a strap line to go with the firm's logo and name can be used, for example: Smith & Jones Conveyancing Solicitors 'We act quickly'. British Gas, in an advertisement to encourage people to visit its conveyancing website, used 'Find a solicitor who won't leave you in the dark when you move.'

Wording in the advertisement can educate potential clients about what to expect from the firm. It can also define the limits of what the firm will do.

Smooth Move Conveyancing Solicitors
'Keeping you informed on the move'

When you become a client we promise to ...

- Provide a fixed price quote
- Listen to what you want
- Take time and care to ensure you fully understand the legal issues relating to your home move
- Be friendly, professional and accessible - we open until 6 pm on weekdays
- Respond to your telephone calls within 4 working hours
- Keep you updated via the internet

'We keep our promises'

94% of our clients in a recent survey said they would recommend us to others

Telephone **Smooth Move Conveyancing Solicitors** on ...

Figure 12.2 Sample advertisement

First contact

To find out clients' expectations of you and your firm, ask them when they first instruct you what these expectations are. Most probably clients will not have many fixed ideas at that time, so ask them again part way through the case to gauge their expectations and satisfaction levels. Talk through the firm's client charter and explain what you will do for them and what you will not do. Take the time early on to avoid misunderstandings and potential difficulties later. Some expectations may need to be lowered and others raised.

Client care charter and minimum standards statement

The development of a client care charter helps to manage clients' expectations provided it is actively used. A minimum standards statement for internal use by staff can mirror the client care charter to ensure that the points made in the charter are carried out.

The client care charter can be printed on a large poster and framed. It can be placed on the wall opposite where clients sit in the reception and waiting rooms. A copy can be placed in each room where clients see solicitors. The best position is on the wall behind but to the side of where the solicitor generally sits. This will enable clients to see it easily.

A copy of the charter can be printed on one side of a card the size of a small postcard. On the other side, the name of the conveyancer and the contact details can be inserted for reference. This can be given to clients with the Practice Rule 15 client care letter.

The charter becomes the 'terms of engagement' that the client can expect from the firm. The minimum standards statement is used as a benchmark for staff within the firm to adhere to at all times in order to deliver the promises of the client care charter. Solicitors may wish to distribute copies of the Law Society's client care charter (see Appendix E) to their clients or may develop their own charter and minimum standards statement.

Staff–client relationships

People are the business. How staff respond to clients and potential clients will encourage or discourage clients from choosing the firm. It can be a sobering experience to think of the last time you visited a business where the staff seemed genuinely pleased to see you and made you feel welcome. Consider your own firm. How are clients greeted in the reception and on the telephone? Are they made to feel they made the right decision to come to your firm by the way they are treated?

The most important person in any firm initially is the first person the potential client speaks to. That person has the power to make or break the relationship. Good receptionists are worth their weight in gold.

I have had an opportunity on a number of occasions of delivering training courses to see an excellent receptionist at work in a leading firm of solicitors in Bristol. She is always elegantly dressed, has a warm smile and a welcoming tone. Clients are offered a tea or coffee. She combines being knowledgeable and professional and remains friendly. She helps to put clients at ease.

Additional statements in your client care charter might be:

- All members of staff will greet and treat clients as 'honoured guests'.
- We will listen to what you have to say and what you want.
- We will take the time to explain the issues, the implications and potential outcomes.
- We will advise a range of options and recommend the best one to take.
- We will help you make the best decision for you.

The minimum standards statement, which is for staff, will include the above and add:

- Initially, greet all clients with a smile. If you know them or have been given their name, use the formal version, i.e. Mr, Mrs, etc., unless they have indicated that you may use their first name.
- To gain information, particularly where the client has not decided whether to use the firm or not, ask mainly open questions which generally begin with 'who', 'what', 'when', 'where' or 'how'. Avoid the 'why' question as it can come across as challenging what the client has said. Instead ask 'What are your reasons for . . .' 'Tell me more about . . .' 'Please expand on . . .'.
- Use plain English to explain issues and the implications of decisions made. Use examples of what can happen to explain points and to manage expectations.

Specialist solicitors

This relates to the range of services the firm provides. The client care charter may include:

> The law is complicated enough so we will introduce you to a solicitor who specialises in the area of law related to your situation. This will ensure you get the depth and breadth of knowledge required to give you sound advice.

The minimum standards statement may add the following:

> Do not be tempted to give advice in an area of the law in which you do not specialise. If asked, always recommend the client sees the person who specialises in that legal area. Complaints of negligence can follow where a solicitor gives advice in an area where he or she is not completely up to date.

The impression given by the person who answers the telephone is likely to influence the caller to use the firm or not. The telephone is often the first means of human-to-human contact a potential client has with the practice. If a potential client telephones and asks whether the firm covers a particular area of law, the person answering the call should be able to give an immediate answer. No one should be allowed to answer the telephone until he or she is familiar with the range of services the firm provides.

EXAMPLE **Poor responses**

I contacted a life assurance company to find out about their ethical fund as a potential place to invest a pension contribution. I was eventually put through to the marketing department. The person who answered the telephone said 'What's an ethical fund?' When I explained and asked the question again, the response was 'Oh, I dunno'.

I conducted a 'mystery shopper' research exercise to assess the sales assistants in a furniture store. While I was looking around, a shopper came in to ask the assistant if he had a dressing table with drawers. The assistant said 'No, sorry'. The shopper left the store. I was standing next to one at the time.

Processes

When people choose a firm, it may be due to a recommendation, yet it is the processes that are likely to let them down. The processes relate the time it takes to:

- have the telephone answered;
- negotiate the telephone menu system and the frustration caused;
- make an appointment (and the time the client is kept waiting after the allotted time of their appointment has passed);
- return clients' calls or respond to their letters and e-mails;
- receive information or a bill.

When clients are stressed, their perception of time changes. Waiting for a returned telephone call can make every hour seem like a day.

EXAMPLE **Returning calls**

A client telephoned her solicitor first thing in the morning. She received a message that he would phone back. She telephoned again just before 5.00 p.m. to find out when he would call her as she had waited by the telephone all day. The telephone was in a kiosk on a street corner.

From the client's perspective, the issue the solicitor is dealing with may be the biggest event in their lives, yet for the solicitor, it is likely to be only one of a number of equally important cases.

Expectations may need to be lowered. The client care charter can be used to raise or lower clients' expectations. For example:

1. All telephone calls will be answered the same day. Where the solicitor is at court or out of the office, his or her secretary will inform the client and arrange a time when the call can be returned.
2. All e-mails will be responded to within 24 hours.
3. All letters will be answered within three working days.
4. Ground floor interview rooms are available for wheelchair users and the elderly.
5. Clients can contact us 24 hours a day using e-mail.
6. We will see clients in their homes, if they are not able to come to us.
7. We can see clients out of office hours, if necessary.
8. We are available at lunchtime for appointments to fit in with clients' needs.

The minimum standards statement will include the above and add:

1. Clients must not be kept waiting longer than five minutes for a prearranged appointment. If there is a delay, the secretary will explain the reasons for the delay and offer refreshments and make a later appointment, if required.
2. All telephone calls and e-mails are to be returned within the same working day and preferably within four hours by the solicitor, assistant or secretary.
3. All letters will be answered within two working days, even if it is only to give an acknowledgement of the letter and explain that it will be responded to in detail within a stated timescale.
4. Encourage clients to see you during normal office hours. Be flexible to see clients out of those hours.

Quotations and costs

Costs are the area which can cause anguish for clients paying their own bills. The Solicitors' Costs Information and Client Care Code states that solicitors must:

> . . . make sure that clients are given the information they need to understand what is happening generally and in particular on:
>
> (i) the cost of legal services both at the outset and as a matter progresses; and
> (ii) responsibility for client matters.

The main causes for concern are escalating costs and misleading costs information. The Law Society has prepared some additional notes to the Solicitors' Costs Information and Client Care Code on these subjects (*Guide to the Professional Conduct of Solicitors 1999*, 13.03):

> 2. Wherever possible, a solicitor should give an estimate of the likely cost of acting in a particular matter. When giving such an estimate or forecast, regard should be had to Part III of the Consumer Protection Act 1987 which deals with misleading price indications. To give an estimate which has been pitched at an unrealistically low level solely to attract the work and subsequently to charge a higher fee for that work is improper because it misleads the client as to the true or likely cost.
> 3. Oral estimates should be confirmed in writing and clients should be informed immediately it appears that the estimate will be or is likely to be exceeded. In most cases this should happen before undertaking work that exceeds the estimate. Solicitors should not wait until submitting the bill of costs. The Office for the Supervision of Solicitors deals with many complaints that have arisen simply because the solicitor does not have a system for tracking costs, and estimates are exceeded without the client's authority.
>
> . . .
>
> 8. Where clients want to set a limit on costs solicitors should warn of the consequences before accepting instructions. Any limit cannot be exceeded without the authority of the client. Further, where the limit imposed on the expenditure is insufficient the solicitor must, as soon as possible, obtain the client's instructions as to whether to continue with the matter.

The client care charter may state:

- We will give an estimate of the costs where possible.
- We will keep you informed of the costs on a regular basis.
- We will discuss payment terms to help you budget for the cost (this is for non-conveyancing services).

The minimum standards statement can include the Solicitors' Costs Information and Client Care Code. In addition:

1. Discuss costs openly with your clients when they first appoint you and at appropriate times as the matter proceeds.
2. Send a Client Care Practice Rule 15 letter stating the costs, disbursements and hourly rate or fixed costs on the same day the client gives instructions. Use plain English and avoid small print to negate any potential criticism of trying to disguise the costs.
3. Where an estimate has been given, keep a careful track of the costs. If you realistically think the estimate will be exceeded, advise clients at least seven days before the estimated figure is reached and ask for their specific instructions to continue or otherwise. Confirm

telephone instructions by letter on the same day the instructions are given.

4. Where relevant, agree payment terms with the client when instructions are given. Depending on the type of legal service provided, encourage clients to pay monthly amounts to help them budget and to assist the firm's cash flow where it is appropriate for the work type.

Costs are dealt with in more detail in Chapter 2.

Monitoring clients' expectations

It is prudent to monitor clients' satisfaction levels with the service they are receiving. It also helps to prevent potential problems developing that could become costly and time consuming.

Use support staff to help keep a finger on the pulse of clients' satisfaction levels. Clients often complain that their expectations have not been met to support staff before they say anything to their solicitor. Many will freely complain to support staff and say little to their solicitor.

Encourage support staff to tell the solicitor if the client has not been happy, even if it is a complaint or irritation that the solicitor does not think is valid. It is the client's perspective that is important at this point. Problems nipped in the bud prevent time-consuming complaints developing later.

Clients' opinions of the service received can provide invaluable feedback to the firm. It is a wasted opportunity if a client comments questionnaire is not sent out to discover what is going well (clients' expectations met) and what needs to be improved (where clients are disappointed). Craig *et al.* (2001) found that 'clients were asked whether the firm of solicitors they had used had asked them to express their views on the service provided. Only one in ten had been invited to do so'.

At the end of the case, send a client comments questionnaire out with the completion statement in a stamped addressed envelope.

See Chapter 10 on evaluating marketing activities for further information on client comments surveys.

Further reading

Craig, R., Rigg, M., Briscoe, R. and Smith, P. (2001) *Client Views: Experiences of Using a Solicitor for Personal Matters*, Law Society Strategic Research Unit.

Jenkins, J. and Lewis, V. (1995) *Client Perceptions: Existing and Potential Clients: Experiences and Perceptions of Using a Solicitor for Personal Matters*, Law Society Strategic Research Unit.

The Law Society (1999) *The Guide to the Professional Conduct of Solicitors 1999*, Law Society Publishing.

Rigg, A., 'How to deliver customer satisfaction' [1999] *Gazette*, 1 December.

SOURCES OF INFORMATION

For further information on the Law Society's Strategic Research Unit visit: **www.research.lawsociety.org.uk**.

For the latest version of the Solicitors' Practice Rules go to **www.guide.lawsociety.org.uk**.

13

The client's perspective

KEY POINTS

This chapter will

- explain the differences between buying a product and a service
- describe the clues clients look at to give an indication of service quality
- show why process issues matter
- explain why people are the most important element of giving a service
- advise how to be a mystery shopper
- help you decide how you want clients to see your firm

Product and service

What is the difference between buying a product and buying a service, especially when that service is from a solicitor? Most products have an element of service in the buying process. An assistant serves you, even if it is just to take payment and, if requested, help you with your choice and purchase.

There are four key differences between buying a product and a service. One is that you can generally see, touch, taste or try a product before you buy it. With a service, you cannot. The service experience is *intangible*.

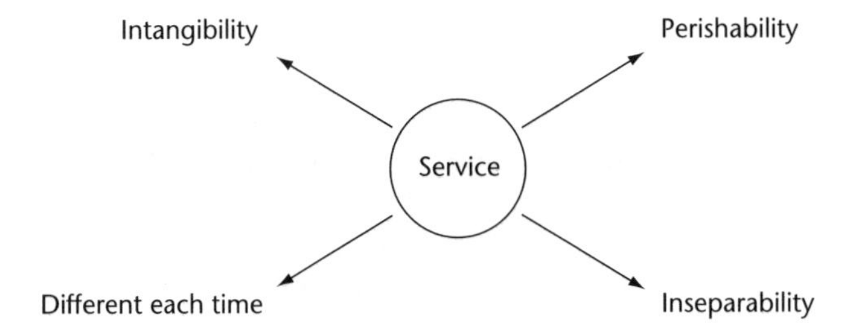

Figure 13.1 Services compared to products

A product is made prior to use. With a service, consumption is at the point of production. As a solicitor gives advice, that advice is 'consumed'. As a person has a haircut, the hairdresser 'produces' the haircut at the same point that the client receives it. There is *inseparability* between the producer and the consumer.

This also means that the consumer is integral to the production of the service and may play a part in the experience of receiving it. If clients are very stressed when receiving legal advice, they may not be able to listen with a clear head or understand the advice as well as if they had not been stressed.

When a product is manufactured, it can be made to be exactly the same each time. This means that buyers have a high level of certainty in what they are buying. As a service is produced at the point of consumption, it is likely to be *different each time* it is produced. This creates uncertainty in the buyer. It can make it difficult to standardise the service given. When there is high demand for the service, the saying 'when the heat is on, the service is gone' is always a danger for firms delivering services.

There is an element of *perishability* when buying a service. Where the service is time constrained, such as buying a seat on a flight or a hotel room, when the time has passed to receive that service, it cannot be regained. A service cannot be stored to be given before or after the consumer receives it.

These key differences between buying a product and a service mean that clients are faced with greater uncertainty, which leads to greater anxiety when they are buying a service. They need more reassurance from the people within the law firm that they have made the right decision to use that firm.

People are the linchpin in the delivery of services. Staff at every level can make or break the relationship with clients. They are the firm's greatest asset and, potentially, its biggest liability.

Service delivery

People

People are the most important element in delivering a service. The style of service delivery and the processes involved are a major part of clients' buying experience. The attitude of the people the potential client has contact with, not just initially, but throughout the client's dealings with the firm, will initially influence then underline or change impressions of the firm. How the service is delivered shows the quality of the firm.

As clients participate in the delivery of the service, clients' perceptions – of receiving personal respect, of service quality and of ultimately being willing to recommend the firm to others – depend on their interaction with staff.

It is the active willingness of staff to be flexible and to recognise further needs of clients that help to give the firm the edge over competitors and increase turnover. People within the firm represent the whole firm. How other people in the firm, in addition to their solicitor, treat clients has a significant influence on clients and their attitude towards the practice.

EXAMPLE **Disrespect**

A colleague went to see a solicitor about an employment issue. She arrived at 9.05 for a 9.15 appointment. She said people walked past her in the reception without enquiring who she was. She was not greeted. She was not offered a cup of coffee or tea during the three-quarters of an hour meeting at which she was being charged £178 an hour. Although she thought the advice was good, she left the office with a feeling of not being valued or treated properly.

Key role of support staff

The communication routes between clients, legal advisers and support staff are shown in Figure 13.2. This emphasises that support staff often have a pivotal role in the client's relationship with the firm as a whole. They are in a strong position to influence clients' attitudes towards the firm, both positively and negatively. They are often the oil that lubricates the relationship between clients and the fee earners dealing with their matter. The interaction of support staff is as important as the relationship of the client with solicitor.

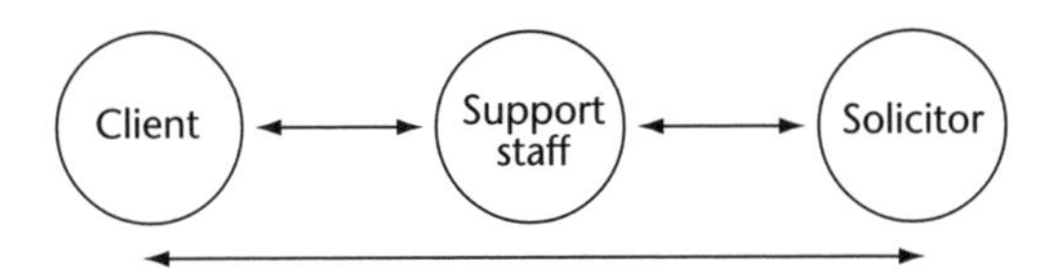

Figure 13.2 Communication channels

While the people element is critical to the impression clients gain of a firm, there are other clues, both physical and process related, that clients look for to decide whether they want to use the firm in the first place, and if they do so, decide the impression they develop of the firm over time.

Premises

Consider this. You are in an unfamiliar town one weekend with a friend. You are feeling hungry and spot a restaurant from across the road. Consider the impressions the restaurant gives from the outside to encourage or discourage you from using it. Perhaps you would decide not to eat there if the paint was peeling, windows were dirty and the door was partly boarded up. When we select a service, before we make the decision to buy, we tend to look for clues to give an indication of whether we think the service is going to be at the standard we expect and want.

EXAMPLE **First impressions**

I went to see one firm to give advice on the impression the firm gave to clients, following a telephone mystery shopper exercise I had conducted on their behalf. When viewing the premises from the outside, I commented that they gave a reasonably good impression, with the exception of some broken paving slabs in a small pile at the front. I suggested they were removed as they looked untidy.

The following Monday, I received an e-mail from my client to thank me for the advice and to say that the paving slabs had been removed. They had been thrown through their shop-front style of office window on the previous Saturday night!

The outside of a solicitor's office, including its immediate surroundings, gives an impression of the firm. Inside the office, this impression is further developed by all manner of physical features, quality of fittings, and décor of reception, waiting room and interview room. A firm's marketing materials – brochure, leaflets, advertisements, and website – will also contribute to the overall impression clients have of your firm.

EXAMPLE **Premises**

The chairman of a business decided to change solicitors. He visited a couple of firms unannounced to assess their reactions. His first impression of one was of weeds growing in the path leading up to the locked front door. He had to say who he was in the entry phone before he was allowed in. The receptionist advised him that no one was available to see him and asked him to come back later. At the next firm, the receptionist explained that although no one could see him for long, a solicitor would speak to him for a few minutes. The chairman chose the latter firm. As soon as he returned to his own business premises, he called his managing director to come to see the weeds on their own pathway, realising the poor impression they gave. Together, on hands and knees, they pulled up the weeds.

Firms need to consider what their clients expect from them. For some clients, a highly stylish and polished entrance, reception and other public rooms, may be alienating and make them feel that this must be an expensive firm – or one which overcharged. Other clients would expect to see up-market surroundings with the latest office décor.

It is the clients whom you want to attract and retain who will guide your firm into providing those critical physical clues. The impression given of the practice before, during and after clients receive a service should give comfort and reassurance to them that they are making and subsequently have made the right decision to use the firm.

Take into account all the areas clients may visit and ensure a consistent message is given. A client walking into an untidy solicitor's office where files are piled up around the walls of the room and where the colour of the top of the desk is hard to establish, may get the impression of disorganisation and the solicitor not really being up to the job.

Do not forget the toilet if it is one clients may use. A dirty towel, sink, or worse, pan, may make clients recoil as much as if they had seen this in a restaurant's wash room.

Process issues

It is often the process issues that lead to clients developing a poor impression of the firm – see Chapter 12, 'Managing clients' expectations'.

Process issues will flavour how clients view the firm. They will encourage or discourage clients from using the practice and recommending it to others.

Be your own 'mystery shopper'

Asking for a quote

Imagine you are a client and see your own firm from a client's perspective. Flick through Yellow Pages or the most commonly used local directories for your area. See which advertisements attract your attention. Assess how your own firm rates. If it has the website quoted in the advertisement, assess how long it takes to appear on screen and how useful and up to date the information is. Does it inspire you to want to contact the firm and use it?

Ask a friend to telephone the firm so that your voice will not be recognised. Listen in on another line to see how people respond and what they say to give encouragement to use the firm. Start off by telephoning the firm to get a quote for buying and selling a house:

- How many rings does it take to get through?
- Telephone at different times of the day and week.
- What is the response on a Friday at 4.30 p.m. and between 1.00 p.m. and 2.00 p.m.?
- How does it compare to other times of the week?
- If the person you want is not available, are you asked to telephone back or are you told that a named person will return your call?
- Does the person call back in the time frame specified?
- Does the person give their name?
- Do they engage the mystery shopper in conversation to build rapport, or is it a minimal question and answer session?
- What is the attitude of the person who answers towards the caller?
- Does the member of staff ask for the instructions?
- Does he or she offer to send a quote in the post?
- If a difficulty is mentioned in the purchase, such as a dispute over the boundary line, is any allowance made for it in the conversation and the quote?
- Ask for a written quote if one is not offered.
- How long does this take to come? If it was received the following morning, you would probably be pleased. If it was two days later, would it be acceptable to you when you wanted it urgently? Longer than two days is likely to indicate that the firm will not get the business as the client may well have gone elsewhere by then.

Use your own website. Assume you have little knowledge of the workings of the Internet and computer use or, better still, ask someone who has limited experience to request a quote online:

- How easy was it to understand what to do and how to do it?
- How quick was the response?
- Is there sufficient information to make a decision and would you want to give your instructions to the firm?

If you have asked for the quote by post, when you receive the envelope, consider the impression it gives:

- Are your title, name and address written correctly?
- What impression does the feel of the envelope give?
- Does the paper feel thin and limp or crisp and clean?
- As you open the envelope, what is the first thing you see on the page?

Tip: where window envelopes are not used, always fold an envelope with the words facing outwards. Insert it into an envelope so that the first words the recipient sees on opening it are their name, address and the sender's name on the letterhead. This gives reassurance.

- Is the language used understandable from a lay person's perspective?
- Does it provide the information requested and include all the additional information it says is enclosed?
- Does it encourage you to use the firm?
- Does it tell you what to do next?
- Is a map provided or directions given, including where to park?
- If you do nothing, is your enquiry followed up by someone in the firm or is it ignored?

Few solicitors follow up enquiries, even when the business could be particularly profitable. For more information on following up enquiries, see Chapter 11, 'Converting telephone callers into clients'.

Visit your firm as a client

Next, assume that an appointment has been made for you to see a solicitor. Follow the map or the directions provided to find your office. Assume you do not know the area, and assess whether your office is easy to find – given a one-way system, for example. Can you park near by at different times of the day? Do you need to improve the instructions or give locations of additional places to park? If the instructions are not crystal clear and easy to read, clients will arrive both annoyed and late.

On a number of occasions, I have been sent directions to a firm's offices that are printed in a small font and as one long paragraph and are hence impossible to follow when driving. Have a large scale, simple to use map, with one-way systems clearly marked. Print directions in a 12-point font. Use simple sentences. Start each change of direction on a new line.

This will help visitors to arrive at your offices in good time and with praise for the excellent directions.

Stand across the street from your office building. See it as a new client would see it for the first time:

- What impression does it give?
- Is the sign showing the name of the firm easy to read?
- If there are signs on the windows, can they be read?
- Do the signs say what you do?
- If your address has a street number, is the number easy to identify on or near the door?

Black or dark print on a white background shows up well, but is not easy to read when used on window signs. White print against the windows, which from the outside generally show a darker interior, stands out more and so is easier to read. Gold print may look good to you, but can also be difficult to read on window signs. For legibility, use predominantly lower case rather than block capitals.

If there are stickers on the windows of associations that you are a member of, do those associations mean anything to the person in the street? Ask your clients what they mean. If they do not know their significance, do not have them in your windows and consider not putting them on your letter-headed paper. They distract from the messages you want to put over to clients.

EXAMPLE **A downward spiral**

There is a story of man who had a caravan roadside café parked in a lay-by. It did good trade and was popular with passing lorry drivers and motorists. He had several signs from half a mile along the road leading up to his café telling people of his famous all day breakfast rolls, tea, coffee and sandwiches.

His son went to business school and came home to tell his Dad that there was a recession on and that people had stopped spending as much. He told him that he may as well take down his furthest signs because they weren't needed. His father thought his son must be right because he'd been to business school, so took his signs down. He found his son was right. Business started to tail off. He agreed with his son that people weren't spending as much, so he took more of his signs down as business dwindled. Eventually he had to close his business.

Try to make it as easy as possible for your clients to find you. Prominent signage helps to draw attention to the firm and hence will attract more passers-by:

- Is the paintwork of the door and windows clean and fresh?
- Have the door, windows, window sills, entrance door step and mat been cleaned recently?
- If you have window boxes, are the flowers alive and healthy looking?
- When you walk through the door, is it easy to see where to go?
- Is the reception welcoming?

Public areas

A number of firms have a box of toys for children of different ages. Harassed parents are unlikely to have a good meeting with their solicitor and make well thought out decisions. Clients come as a package and helping to entertain their children shows that the firm understands their pressures and is family friendly.

Many firms routinely offer coffee to waiting clients. Clients are aware of how much the visit is going to cost them. The offer of a tea or coffee is a simple and appreciated courtesy.

EXAMPLE **Music**

One firm has classical music playing in the background in the waiting room. This has two benefits. It helps to screen out the voice of the receptionist taking calls and revealing the names of callers. In a small town, clients waiting may know the name of a caller and with a little knowledge of the specialisation of the solicitor they are put through to, they may be able to deduce the confidential business of the calling client. The second benefit is that it can relax clients and help to make them more at ease.

Is there anything to indicate what the firm does in the reception or waiting rooms? It is very easy to assume that clients know nearly as much about your firm as you do, in terms of the range of services offered. We tend to have selective retention of the information to which we are exposed. We often need to see or hear information on a number of occasions before we remember it. This is the reason why advertisements on television often appear frequently in a short period to get the message across.

While you may have informed clients of your range of services in a client care letter or in a brochure, to remind them in subtle ways will encourage the client to see the firm as providing a range of services and not to compartmentalise it as just a conveyancing firm (see Chapter 6, 'Relationship management and building brands').

Next, watch what your clients do when they come into the reception area:

- What do they look at?
- Do they sometimes go through the wrong door because they do not know where to go?
- Are they given immediate eye contact, a smile and warm welcome?
- Is the receptionist knowledgeable and discreet?
- Does he or she offer a cup of coffee to clients to help to make them feel welcome?
- Where do clients sit mainly?
- Are the chairs tatty or do they look appealing to sit on?
- Are there sufficient chairs so that people do not have to sit next to each other for the majority of the time? Given a choice, people will leave empty chairs either side of themselves and only sit next to another client if there is nowhere else.
- What do clients do when waiting for an appointment?
- If you have leaflets or brochures in a rack, do people ever pick them up? Is it easy to read what is in the brochures when they are in the rack? If clients rarely take the literature, consider spreading them on an easy to reach table.

People may have a fear of touching items that do not belong to them and so will not pick up leaflets that are on a rack and out of the way. Leaflets need to look inviting and easy to read, with pictures (see Chapter 7, 'Brochures, flyers and newsletters').

Ask your receptionist to make a note of how often clients' appointments start after the allotted time and whether solicitors always go to the reception to greet clients or whether clients are 'sent' to the solicitor. If clients are kept waiting for more than a few minutes after an arranged appointment time and if clients are 'sent' to the solicitor, it gives the message that solicitors and their time are more important than clients and their time.

Monitoring what actually happens in practice will help to give an indication of how the firm comes across to clients, and how you would feel if you were paying for a service and treated in the same way.

All of these points are the evidence that clients look for when deciding whether they think they will get a good service from the law firm. When we are paying for a service, we expect to be treated well and with respect.

What impression do you want to give?

There are two aspects to consider when you are thinking about the impression you want clients to have of the firm. First, what do you think your existing clients expect of the firm? How do they see the practice and is that how you want them to see it? A note of caution: it is easy to think we know what our clients think of us and, quite simply, be wrong. The only way to really know is to ask a representative sample of them using a questionnaire (see Chapter 10, 'Evaluating marketing activities'). The second aspect to consider is how you *want* clients to see the firm.

Opticians' premises used to be seen as somewhat dreary places on a par with dentists. Their waiting rooms were dull. People were patients rather than customers. They had specific places to sit and were not invited or encouraged to touch and try out different frames without being invited. That has now changed in many firms with the introduction of a fashion mentality to buying glasses.

If, for example, your target market is people aged 20s to mid-40s because they are likely to move more often with career and family changes, the impression of the firm needs to reflect what they may expect to see and how you want them to see the practice. Modern décor, light airy colours, bright lighting, wooden floors, a children's play area or box of toys, a coffee machine, modern chairs and possibly modern art on the walls, help to promote an up-to-date ambience to people with little time and high expectations.

If the target market is older or conservative people, they may expect to see a traditionally decorated solicitors' office environment of possibly darker colours and carpet.

Most firms do not have the luxury of being able to start from scratch. The impression given to new clients has to meet the expectations of clients with a range of legal needs. As other departments may target different client types, a firm may want to give a diversity of impressions to a variety of clients, yet there also has to be consistency in the messages provided.

Name of the firm

To avoid the potential mismatch of different target clients' perceptions of the firm, some firms have taken the step of creating a new brand with a different name which is aimed at conveyancing clients only.

Solicitors have traditionally had the names of their partners in their business name. As the number of partners has expanded and the firms developed, the original partners' names are often retained or a new name created. The more the name says what it does, the easier it is to remember and it provides its own marketing message (for further information, see Chapter 6, 'Relationship management and building brands').

Recommendations for public areas

Reception and waiting rooms

The reception is the 'shop front' of the practice – it helps to form and establish impressions in clients' minds. Partners' time and thought needs to be given to the overall effect of the space. The ambience created by the reception area will differ according to the expectations of the types of clients the firm wants to attract.

The following are suggestions for all firms:

1. Ideally, the waiting room should be separate from the reception area so that the details of clients telephoning cannot be overheard by waiting clients.
2. Signage directing people to the reception should be at eye height.
3. Lighting needs to be bright and airy.
4. Background classical music can help to relax clients and cover the voice of the receptionist answering telephone calls.
5. Seating arranged in pair groupings with space between them will encourage people to feel more comfortable (rather than having seats close to each other where people have to touch). Chairs need to be comfortable. Avoid too many low sofa-type seats that can cause problems for older people.
6. Light-coloured walls which have a new coat of paint when they start to look tired are clean, welcoming and inviting.
7. Fresh flowers give a colourful appearance. Well cared for, healthy looking plants (rather than the dusty artificial variety) help to create a pleasing ambience.
8. The receptionist's desk ideally will have no barriers in front of it making it difficult for clients to see the receptionist. Many firms have bookcase-type structures attached to the receptionist's desk to separate the reception from clients. While there may be individual reasons for installing fortress-type reception areas, they can give the impression of wanting to keep a separation from clients that may not be encouraging. If a barrier is desired, consider the use of one with a glass front.
9. On the walls opposite where clients sit, place a large framed poster of the range of services that the firm provides and a similar one of the firm's client care charter.
10. The receptionist should immediately greet clients as soon as they enter the room, even if it is by eye contact and a nod of the head, if the receptionist is answering a telephone call at the time.
11. Telephone calls should be answered between the second and third 'ring'.
12. Clients should be greeted warmly and given eye contact. They should be offered a coffee or water while they are waiting.

13. A box of children's toys can be offered to clients with young children. Toys are tidied up immediately clients have left the reception.
14. Solicitors should always go to reception to greet the client. The client should never be sent to the solicitor.
15. Clients should never be kept waiting more than five minutes beyond the time of the appointment. If an unexpected delay does occur, the solicitor's assistant should see the client and explain the delay or take some details down from the client that will assist the solicitor.

Interview rooms

Interview rooms ideally should have a round table and proper height chairs for the table.

EXAMPLE **Putting people at ease**

I went to see a doctor. He indicated where to sit. When I sat down, I could only see the furrowed forehead of the doctor as he kept a wooden box file of forms directly in front of where his patients sat. The impression was most off-putting, as if he didn't want to catch anything from his patients.

On another occasion when I saw a medical consultant, the seat opposite his desk was of the low armchair variety. When I sat in it, it reminded me of being seven years old again and being peered down upon by the terrifying headmaster – probably an impression the consultant wanted to give to help him feel superior. It was not one that encourages the patient/client to want to engage the consultant, though.

There should be natural light, but solicitors should not sit with their backs to a window. This can make it more difficult to read someone's lips, if the client is hard of hearing. On the wall behind where the solicitor sits, there can be an A2 framed poster of the firm's range of services on one side, then a similar poster of the firm's client care charter on the other side.

Clients should be offered a hot or cold drink (for which they are not charged), at the beginning of the meeting and again part way through, if the meeting is likely to be a long one.

Interview rooms on the ground floor should be available for wheelchair users and access provision should comply with disability regulations.

For information on using publicity literature to create impressions in clients' minds, see Chapter 7, 'Brochures, flyers and newsletters'.

Further reading

Chernatony, L de. and McDonald, M. (2003) *Creating Powerful Brands,* Elsevier Butterworth Heinemann.

Johnson, K.L. (2003) *Selling with NLP,* Nicholas Brealey Publishing.

Johnson, S. (2004) *The One Minute Sales Person,* HarperCollins.

Timm, P. (2002) *50 Powerful Ideas You Can Use to Keep Your Customers,* Career Press.

14

Complaints avoidance

KEY POINTS

This chapter will

- discuss the potential cost of complaints
- recommend sound risk management to reduce complaints and professional indemnity premiums
- show the anatomy of a complaint
- give reasons why clients complain
- explain how to identify the early warning signs of a complaint

The cost of complaints

Complaints are not a major issue in the majority of firms. The Lander Report ([2003] *Gazette*, 22 October) said that 'on average, solicitors will only encounter one dissatisfied client a year. The vast majority of law firms have a positive attitude to complaints handling and adequate procedures in place – but a small minority are letting the side down . . .'.

Up to two-thirds of complaints (4,220) regarding poor service closed by the Law Society were upheld in 2003 ([2004] *Gazette*, 21 May).

Although complaints may be few and far between, the cost of them can be significant. Solicitors can be ordered to pay compensation to clients who receive poor service. Where solicitors' services are found to be inadequate, the firm can be asked to pay up to £840 of the cost of their investigation by the Consumer Complaints Service, formally the OSS (Office for the Supervision of Solicitors). Furthermore, solicitors who consistently ignore their responsibilities for handling complaints can be fast-tracked to the Solicitors' Disciplinary Tribunal.

Complaints can lead to the reduction of bills already charged, reductions in the amount to be charged to clients, waiving of the costs of work done, free future work to rectify the problem, the loss of valuable clients and increases in the cost of professional indemnity insurance.

Furthermore, according to the Consumer Complaints Service, a dissatisfied client can lose the firm up to 23 new clients. The amount of time spent on complaints which could have been spent on fee earning varies from case to case. Anecdotal comment is that an average of six hours is needed to resolve each complaint. Other effects on the practice are harder to quantify financially, but can have a major impact. These may include:

- low morale;
- lower productivity;
- poor atmosphere;
- stress;
- anxiety;
- increased sick leave;
- staff turnover;
- staff retention problems;
- difficulty in hiring high calibre staff;
- poor reputation.

At the extreme, complaints may lead to dissolution of the partnership and loss of the practising certificate. These are painful and generally unnecessary costs that could otherwise potentially be profits.

Risk management

Sound risk management and good client care not only help to retain clients and encourage recommendations from existing ones, they also help to minimise the risk of receiving complaints.

Professional indemnity premiums are linked to the active use of risk management systems. Systems are designed to minimise errors being made which could damage the reputation of the firm and result in serious complaints.

Time spent on implementing risk management procedures is an investment in the future prosperity of the practice. Good quality risk management leads to efficiency of service for clients. This in turn will encourage clients to recommend the firm to others.

Lexcel

Lexcel is the Law Society's quality standard for legal practice management administered by their Practice Excellence Unit. The standards, office procedures and assessment guide are published in a kit and solicitors' firms can seek accreditation by the Society under the scheme. Lexcel helps to reduce complaints by having procedures in place to manage risk. This in turn can help to reduce professional indemnity premiums.

Practice Rule 15

Under Solicitors' Practice Rules 1990, Rule 15 requires all private practices to have a complaints procedure. Clients need to be informed from the start that there is a complaints procedure and told whom to contact if they are not happy with the service given. If a client makes a formal complaint, that is the time to send a copy of the complaints procedure together with a letter acknowledging the complaint.

Complaints, perceptions and causes

Many service complaints seem to stem from a difference in the perceptions of the client and the solicitor. A client as a lay person, often with little experience of dealing with legal matters, may have perceptions of how long processes will take and what is involved which are quite at odds with a solicitor's knowledge of what actually happens in practice. The lack of understanding of the legal processes and differences of perception are often at the root of complaints.

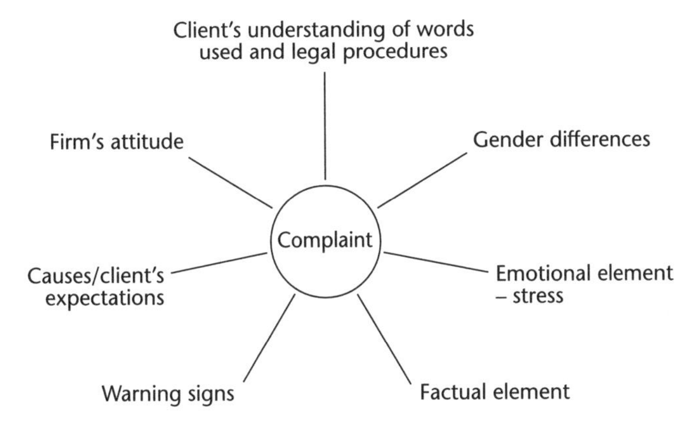

Figure 14.1 Anatomy of a complaint

According to the Consumer Complaints Service, the causes of service complaints include:

- not returning telephone calls;
- not replying promptly to letters;
- unexplained delays;
- unclear communications;
- not keeping the client informed of progress;
- not checking regularly that you are still working towards the solution the client wants or that the solution is achievable; and

- not giving the best information possible and regular updates about likely overall costs.

EXAMPLE **Stress**

A friend was trying to sell her house in Northern Ireland. She said that her whole life felt in limbo. She didn't know whether to put plants in the garden as she didn't know whether she would be there in the summer. She didn't know whether to redecorate to not. She didn't want to look for another property and risk the awful disappointment again of losing her dream house because she could not find a buyer for her own home. She said 'I just can't get on with my life.'

For average residential conveyancing clients, the reason why they are seeing their solicitor is likely to be the biggest issue in their lives at that time. They are likely to be suffering stress with the thought of it. People tend to respond to stress in a number of different ways and how they respond on one occasion may be quite different from how they respond on another. Clients may feel that events are out of their control. How clients respond to a solicitor may be influenced by their emotional, mental and physical state.

Types of complaint

Complaints fall into either the service complaint category, where clients believe they have not received the proper level of service, or the negligence allegation category. If it is a negligence allegation, the firm's professional indemnity insurers need to be informed and the client told that the firm has insurance in place to deal with claims of negligence. The client should be advised to seek alternative legal advice to pursue the claim.

The largest number of negligence complaints relate to conveyancing work, which is a reflection of the volume of conveyancing instructions compared to other areas of legal work. The main causes of complaints, according to articles in the *Law Society Gazette* ([2003] 25 April, 4 July) are:

- failure to make the correct searches and enquiries;
- failure to investigate title and charges;
- failure to advise on the possibility and consequences of co-ownership;
- missing the priority period deadline for registering titles and charges;
- delays;
- bad communication with parties; and
- disorganisation.

The initial problem can be escalated if the solicitor thinks it is a negligence allegation and immediately takes a defensive or confrontational attitude, while the client is actually annoyed about the level of service given.

A complaint will have two sides: the one the client experiences and the one the solicitor sees. Both aspects need to be addressed to avoid complaints and to handle them sensitively, should they arise.

Clients are likely to complain if they feel their expectations have not been met or if they have been given poor advice and service. They are likely to give early warning signs that not all is well, and if these signs are overlooked, the problem will grow.

The complaint is likely to have a factual side, to do with what went wrong and an emotional component, to do with how the client felt. Both aspects need to be addressed. Male and female clients generally deal with problems differently, which implies that alternative problem resolution techniques may be required.

From the solicitor's perspective, he or she may feel exasperated that the client has unreasonable expectations that cannot possibly be met. The firm's culture may be to take a confrontational approach to any hint of criticism. It may have a blame culture which encourages fee earners to hide problems rather than admit a mistake or that they are out of their depth with a file. The words a solicitor uses to clients may be perfectly understandable to the solicitor and an assumption may be made that clients know more than they actually do. This can result in complaints when misunderstandings surface. Both the clients' and the solicitors' perspectives need to be analysed to assess the root of a problem and to understand how to avoid it happening in the future.

Clients' expectations

To avoid potential complaints or the risk of having a disillusioned client at a later stage, have a frank and open discussion about the level of service the client expects as soon as possible. Getting clients actively to think about what they want and being open helps to establish a healthy relationship right at the start.

It may be that some of the client's expectations are too high and that you need to lower them. One of the main causes of service complaints by clients is unreturned telephone calls. Where the client may expect to have calls returned within an hour, for example, consider telling them that the firm's policy is to return phone calls within the working day or within 24 hours (explaining that you may be out of the office). This helps to make their expectations more realistic. For further information on managing expectations and the use of a client charter, see Chapter 12, 'Managing clients' expectations'.

Retainer letters

Retainer letters or letters of engagement also help to manage clients' expectations. They are particularly important as evidence in a solicitor's defence against a claim of negligence. Such letters can be sent separately or included with the Practice Rule 15 Client Care letter.

All the following areas can result in complaints unless they are clearly stated and understood by the client.

Costs information

Poor costs information is one of the key underlying reasons for claims.

EXAMPLE **Costs**

A complicated conveyancing matter went on for four years. The original estimate was for £500. The final cost was over £2,000. At the end of the first year, the client was sent a bill for £250.00. At the end of the second year, it was for £500. The client complained. The solicitor protested that the client must have known that costs were being incurred, but there was no evidence on the file that the client had been informed of this

[2002] *Gazette*, 30 May

Where an estimate rather than a fixed cost is quoted, it is better to overestimate than underestimate. If an estimate cannot be given because of the nature of the work, explain why and give the hourly rates.

A common cause of complaint is when the original estimate is exceeded, but the client is not informed. *The Guide to the Professional Conduct of Solicitors 1999* states that clients must be kept informed about costs as a matter progresses. Clients should be told what costs have accrued at not more than six monthly intervals. Clients should also be told in writing as soon as it is known that an estimate will be exceeded.

Instructions

Detail the client's instructions in plain English and make it clear what the solicitor will and will not do. It is the solicitor's responsibility to ensure that the client understands everything in the retainer letter.

Timing

Timing is another area that often results in claims. Be realistic about the timescales, rather than promise that you can do something in the time the client wants; be clear when pointing out the potential reasons for delay (see Chapter 12, 'Managing clients' expectations' for an example of a flow chart providing likely timescales to manage clients' expectations).

Client service questionnaires

Consider using a client service questionnaire for existing clients to complete at the end of a matter. This is to research whether you are actually giving the level of service you think the practice is providing. Asking clients what they think of the service can help to identify potential problems early and prevent them from becoming a cause for complaint.

Communication and understanding

Level of understanding

It is often a mistake to make assumptions about what a client knows: 'We don't know what we don't know.' Clients also do not know that their expectations are unreasonable. It is a good idea never to make assumptions about clients' level of understanding or knowledge. When dealing with fellow professionals all day, it becomes easy to think that lay people have the same ingrained knowledge that you have. What may be commonplace to a solicitor in terms of legal processes, timescales and procedures is unlikely to be known by a typical client.

In terms of knowledge of procedures, conveyancers may find themselves exasperated: 'Surely he knew it couldn't be done as quickly as that!' Why would clients know if it had not been explained to them? Lay clients have little or no understanding of legal procedures, the likely delays and the reasons for them.

The words used need to be understandable and jargon free to help the client feel comfortable with the firm. It is easy to forget that the words used actually are jargon and that lay people (clients) may only have a hazy understanding of what is being said, or may have a completely different understanding. Even when something has been explained once, this does not mean that the client will fully remember it at a later date.

Complaints can arise due to misunderstandings about what has been said and agreed between a solicitor and a client. It is up to the solicitor to show that clear advice has been given. If the solicitor cannot give evidence to that effect, any finding is likely to go against the solicitor and in the client's favour. Words used can still lead to misinterpretation by the client.

Words such as:

- disbursements,
- searches,
- trusts,
- joint tenancy and tenancy in common,
- covenants,
- exchange, and
- completion

are typical jargon words which clients may not fully understand. It is worth practising explaining these words in plain English to people of different ages and educational levels so that there is little risk of not being understood (see Chapter 11).

Early warning signs

Clients are likely to give early warning indications that they are not happy with the level of service provided. The ability to recognise the early warning signs of a complaint, then to take positive action, can avoid the costs involved in handling a formal complaint.

Typical early warning signs of complaints brewing are:

- clients are likely to express their dissatisfaction to support staff before telling the fee earner;
- poor tone of voice used by the client;
- body language and facial expression revealing annoyance;
- a client chasing up phone calls not returned;
- sarcastic comments made by the client;
- comments beginning 'But I thought . . .' 'Why hasn't . . .' 'You said it would be . . .';
- personality clashes or antagonism at an early stage;
- the fee earner not showing the client respect;
- clashing styles of verbal communication causing antagonism;
- the client telephoning the partner when the assistant solicitor is dealing with their file;
- clients not paying interim bills, where required.

Attitude

The firm's culture and individuals' attitude to clients are likely to reflect how they respond when clients complain. If the firm's culture is such that problems are swept under the carpet and ignored rather than dealt with immediately, complaints are likely to erupt into major problems.

A client may respond to the subtleties of non-verbal communication we are emitting and be prickly or easygoing in response. Clients who subsequently complain to a firm may have had their sensitivities raised at an early stage by the reaction they encountered from their solicitor and other people in the firm, to them.

Complaint handling

The Law Society provides materials on client care and complaint handling procedures which can be viewed and downloaded from the Law Society's website (see below).

Practical research

Use the information gained and the experience of receiving and dealing with complaints as practical research to improve methods of working within the firm. Issue a report of the points learned to all who could benefit from it and consider using it as the basis for internal training or improving the office manual to avoid similar problems arising in the future.

Further reading

Frith, M. (2001) *Complaints Avoidance and Handling: A Solicitors' Guide*, Emis Professional Publishing.

Hannan, G. (1991) *Equal Opportunities*, Gender.

SOURCES OF INFORMATION

For the latest version of the Solicitors' Practice Rules go to **www.guide.lawsociety.org.uk**.

To download the Law Society's guidance *The Client Care Guide to Keeping Clients* (second edition, 2004) and *Handling Complaints Effectively* (third edition, 2004), or to order the *Practice Excellence Training Package*, go to **www.clientcare.lawsociety.org.uk**.

15

The Internet and e-conveyancing

Rupert Kendrick

KEY POINTS

This chapter will

- outline the legal framework for e-conveyancing
- identify the key electronic developments
- explain the proposed model for conducting e-conveyancing

E-conveyancing

Origins

The Land Registration Act 2002 (LRA) contains the origins of e-conveyancing. The aim of the LRA is to create a register that is an accurate reflection of the true state of the title to a registered estate at any given time, so far as it can possibly be. This will come about through the introduction of electronic conveyancing over the next few years.

The LRA creates the legal framework for electronic conveyancing. The detail will be governed by regulations in the form of the Land Registration Rules 2003. The legislative provisions which provide the framework for e-conveyancing are contained in ss.91–95 in Part 8 of the LRA.

The provisions which govern the operation of the Land Registry's network are set out in Schedule 5 to the LRA. These include provisions for access to the network; terms of access; termination of access; network transaction rules; the overriding interest of the network; and the management of transactions.

Framework

It is presently anticipated that e-conveyancing will be introduced on a voluntary basis in 2006. The infrastructure for e-conveyancing is found in s.92 of the LRA 2002 and Sched. 5. It provides that e-conveyancing will be conducted by means of a secure electronic communications network.

Access to this network will be authorised by the Land Registry through a contract called a 'network access agreement' made with the intending user (for instance, a law firm, licensed conveyancer or other authorised service providers, including lenders and estate agents), under the LRA, Sched. 5, para. 1.

The network will be linked to the National Land Information Service (NLIS) so that virtually all enquiries relating to title can be conducted online in accordance with the underlying principle of the LRA – that it should be possible to investigate title to the land with the minimum of additional enquiries.

The network will not just be employed for the 'legal' stages of the conveyancing process, but will also be capable of being used for the provision of information about property to those who need to know. Under the LRA, Sched. 5, para. 9 it will be used to manage 'chains' of domestic sales.

It is intended that, in due course, the electronic communications network will be capable of being used to conduct all stages of the conveyancing process.

The e-conveyancing provisions will not become operative for some time. They are subject to further subordinate legislation. The LRA obliges the Lord Chancellor to consult 'as appropriate' on almost all the subordinate legislation that will be required.

The Land Registry

Certain electronic developments have already been introduced into the conveyancing process.

Land Registry Direct

This is the Land Registry's own system that enables account holders to view registers and title plans from their PCs, make searches online and other similar services. Enhancements to these services are expected to include moving from dial-up to an Internet-based system, the ability to view online documents referred to on the register and the possibility of printing official copies via the practitioner's own printer.

Land Register Online

This is primarily aimed at members of the public and will enable them to view registers and title plans via the Internet. A small fee is payable by credit card. If clients are able to obtain information electronically from the Land Registry, they may well expect professional advisers to be able to do the same.

Procedural developments

A trial of electronic discharges (EDs), the possible successor to the END (electronic notification of discharge) system of mortgage discharge, has been carried out. Currently, when the END system is used, a member of staff at the lender's office sends what amounts to a formalised e-mail to the appropriate Land Registry office. When the END message is received, staff act upon it in the same way as if it were sent by post.

The new system known as EDs is a fully automatic system whereby an electronic message is automatically generated by the lender's computer which instructs Land Registry computers to cancel the relevant charge entries. A prerequisite for a lender to join the scheme is an undertaking to confirm to the conveyancer that the charge has been discharged.

The Land Registry is also looking into a system of direct electronic charges whereby lenders would be able to lodge a mortgage document and an application to register it electronically. The transaction has certain security implications, in particular the need to consider how an electronic document should be signed. Would an electronic signature be required or could the lender just lodge an electronic scanned copy of a standard paper document?

From October 2004, the Land Registry has used e-mail to send requests for information arising during a title registration under a new system that is to be rolled out across the country. The Registry will automatically send requisitions by e-mail where an e-mail address is provided on the application form.

The Registry has also launched a variable direct debit scheme for payment of registration service fees, with notification of the amount to be debited e-mailed in advance.

The Land Registry is also looking at electronic lodgement of other applications. The simplest of these will be those applications that do not contain deeds. The existing caution is a good example. Most conveyancers have electronic versions of such applications that they complete on their PCs. They print off the completed application and send it to the Land Registry, where the information on the form is uploaded on to the Land Registry's system. It would be quicker and simpler if such an application could be forwarded electronically by the conveyancer. Eventually, the Land Registry will be looking at electronic lodgement of applications containing title deeds.

PISCES

PISCES stands for the Property Information Systems Common Exchange Standard. This is a set of definitions and rules aimed at facilitating the electronic transfer of data between different businesses and different software packages used in the property sector. It is technology that enables software solution providers to offer solutions that can transfer data between databases – and therefore between systems and organisations.

It is hoped that the standard will eventually apply to all transfers of data in the property sector, worldwide. Representatives from legal and residential working groups are participating in the Land Registry's workshop to agree data transfer requirements for the e-conveyancing system.

The eventual benefits are claimed to include: the saving of cost and time of re-keying data from incompatible systems; reduced data transfer errors; integrated data in organisations; faster transactions; and freedom of choice of solution providers. Executive law firm members of the scheme include, primarily, large city firms, such as Clifford Chance, Linklaters and CMS Cameron McKenna. See **www.pisces.co.uk** for further information.

Electronic developments

NLIS

NLIS (**www.nlis.org.uk**) is an e-government service that provides online information on land and property. It allows users to obtain a variety of different searches through one online service provider. NLIS comprises:

- Information House – its regulatory and quality monitoring role;
- NLIS Hub (MacDonald Dettwiler) – a link between the providers and service channels maintaining the Hub catalogue in respect of price, maintenance times, etc.; and
- NLIS Channels – NLIS Searchflow (**www.searchflow.co.uk**); TM Property Service (**www.tmproperty.co.uk**); Transaction online (**www.transaction-online.co.uk**).

The main data providers are local authorities, which provide replies to enquiries through NLIS by various channels of communication. Other data providers also support NLIS, including the Land Registry; the Coal Authority; the water service companies; the Environment Agency; water companies; Companies House; and the Valuation Office Agency. Other key data providers, including public and private sector services, are being asked to participate and data provider user groups are being held.

Online search providers

Aside from NLIS, there are other commercial enterprises and public bodies (such as **www.coalminingreports.co.uk**) that offer search services online. A number of the commercial enterprises belong to a trade association called the Council of Property Search Organisations (**www.copso.com**).

Online instructions and quotations

Conveyancing case management software often has a module that enables a law firm both to accept instructions online and, if required, to provide a quotation in respect of the services required.

A typical example of a solution is that provided by ConveyanceLink from SellersLink Ltd. This unusual model is based on a 'pay as you go per case' basis – sometimes referred to as 'pay as you convey'.

Commenting on its advantages, Ingrid Hindle, partner, Middleton & Upsall, says:

> ConveyanceLink enables us to send out client quotes in seconds, generate letters from pre-installed templates with ease and even send our clients text messages automatically once key milestones have been reached.

An early adopter of this strategy has been Fidler & Pepper, who recognised it as a valuable marketing strategy. Most obviously, the benefit lies in convenience to clients. Less obviously, but just as importantly, there are clear advantages in introducers (estate agents) and strategic allies in the process of the transaction (lenders) having a perception that the firm is modern and forward looking.

Online case tracking

An early technological 'service' development has been the emergence of online case tracking facilities. These facilities enable appropriately authorised parties (e.g. clients, estate agents and lenders) to access a confidential area of a law firm's website (an Extranet) and view the progress of a particular transaction.

One example of this technology is the solution from Easyconvey.com developed by Easy Convey Ltd. The solution is designed for sole practitioners and small firms. At its heart is CASA, which is automated technology governing workflows, letters and documents, all of which can be tailored to preferred styles.

Parties to a transaction view progress through Track-a-Matter, which provides password protected access to enable authorised parties to check the status of ongoing instructions. Workflow details from CASA are automatically updated to Track-a-Matter and the site is secure and information passing over the Internet is automatically encrypted.

The strategy is now being developed by some law firms on a collective basis, most notably the Solicitors' Tracking and Reporting System – widely known as STARS. The technology requirements for participation are relatively straightforward – Internet Explorer: version 5 or above; an e-mail system; and a basic CM system. Legal Marketing Services (LMS) has integrated its STARS software with over 40 other systems, so it is unlikely that many firms' systems will be incompatible.

Membership of LMS requires conformity with certain benchmarks. LMS's team of panel development managers carry out regular performance and development reviews with all panel firms. Through a documented process of file reviews, management interviews and dialogue with key members of staff, an audit looks at whether key objectives are being met. Performance and development review findings are documented then recorded and shared with panel firms (see **www.trackmycase.com**).

However, not all clients may require this service. Charles Christian, Editor of *Legal Technology Insider* says:

> One of the volume conveyancing market leaders had invested in a very sophisticated web-enabled case management system that allowed clients to submit instructions online and monitor the progress of individual conveyancing matters via a secure extranet link on a 24/7 basis. The firm in question had no doubt that possessing this technology and its ability to offer online facilities was a key factor in helping it differentiate itself from other firms in beauty parades and go on to win new business. Yet, despite the apparent enthusiasm of clients and prospective clients for these technologies, very few actually made use of them; in some instances, this was because the clients themselves lacked in-house systems to access them as many financial institutions still have 'green screen' or dumb terminals in their branch offices or stand alone PCs with no Internet access.

Firms contemplating offering this service should consider undertaking a client survey before doing so.

The trend now is for the various separate stages of the conveyancing transaction to become linked seamlessly – so that a suitable CM solution will perform a variety of functions, such as online quotations, online instructions, online searches and online tracking and reporting facilities. Links to the Land Registry already enable certain formal transactions to be performed, eventually developing into a complete electronic service.

One example of this development is law firm Dickinson Dees, which claims to be the first to link up a CM system to an NLIS channel, using the PISCES standard (**www.dickinson-dees.co.uk/e-commerce/mbrf156.asp#555**).

Portal services

An example of this is the recent launch of what is claimed to be the UK's first Internet-based service where a complete end-to-end conveyance can be transacted and completed through a secure portal. Called Transact Direct, it is the product of a joint venture between Scottish law firm PSM

(Peddie Smith Malaco) and CM specialists Visualfiles (the parent company of Solicitec).

The system, which has been undergoing trials since June 2003 and is currently handling over 1,500 property transactions each month, is initially being focused on the Scottish conveyancing market, with plans to widen it to the broader English market.

Stamp Duty Land Tax

The Inland Revenue allows commercial suppliers to integrate SDLT forms into their forms and CM software packages. The Stamp Taxes unit also provides an online service for the submission of a return (at **https://www.ir-online.gov.uk/stamps/**).

Home Information Packs

At the time of writing the Housing Bill is completing its passage through Parliament with a view to Regulations in 2005 and possible implementation in 2007. Sellers will be obliged to provide certain information in advance in a Home Information Pack when selling a property. It is expected that this will include local searches; office copy entries; property information and other information traditionally supplied in the pre-contract stage. A Home Condition Report Steering Group of key stakeholders is advising on research into the development of a certification scheme; the development of a home condition report and recruitment of home inspectors.

The proposed model for e-conveyancing

In the context of current developments, the model for e-conveyancing is likely to have the following features:

- an electronic communications system linking every conveyancer to the Land Registry's system and possibly to other government departments, such as the Stamp Office (for automatic stamping of electronic documents) and Companies House (for automatic registration of company charges);
- a system of electronic funds transfer running parallel with the e-conveyancing system;
- a repositioning of the Land Registry in the conveyancing process. If all conveyancers were linked to the Land Registry via the proposed electronic communications system, the contents of contracts could be compared with the appropriate register at every early stage – possibly before the contract is sent electronically by the seller's

conveyancer to the buyer's conveyancer. Any discrepancies could be identified and rectified at that stage, so eliminating the need for requisitions on title later;
- if all such problems can be eliminated before completion, it follows that changes in ownership could be made at the same time as electronic completion of a transaction – one seamless process entailing completion by registration eradicating the gap between completion and registration;
- a 'chain management' system for domestic conveyancing which could be used to make the conveyancing system more transparent by revealing to practitioners the progress of other transactions in a chain. This could show the stages reached in a particular transaction identifying what is delaying exchange of contracts throughout the whole chain. The LRA obliges conveyancers to provide information on the progress of any transaction in a chain. In the event of a conflict arising, the duty to the electronic system overrides the duty of confidentiality. It is also possible that a chain management system might provide a safe and efficient method both of exchanging contracts simultaneously and of completing transactions simultaneously.

Launching the new e-conveyancing model at the Law Society on 18 June 2004, Steve Kelway of the E-Conveyancing Task Force took a hypothetical example from the perspective of both seller and buyer. As far as technology is concerned, all that is required is a CM system compatible with the Land Registry's service. It was emphasised that the Land Registry did not want to involve suppliers in significant additional expenditure in order to be eligible for the network access agreement. The CM system should be capable of storing documents, particularly contract, transfer and letter templates.

Draft contract

The transaction begins with the seller's conveyancer obtaining electronic versions of the office copies, including the file plan and any other relevant items, and saving these to his/her PC.

The contract template is then completed by the seller's conveyancer. It is envisaged that there will be complete interoperability as between the different systems, standards and templates, with the arrival of PISCES and XML schema. The contract is sent by E-DX to the buyer's conveyancer.

Agreeing amendments

The seller's conveyancer logs on to Land Registry Direct – identified by firm member and password, and for whom there may be graduated ranges of access. The contract is then uploaded on to the system and a validation message is issued. At this point, the opportunity may be taken by the Land Registry to raise any requisitions, which are dealt with electronically.

The buyer's conveyancer receives notification of the contract from the Land Registry. After taking instructions, any amendments can be introduced and the contract can be returned to await validation.

Pre-signature

At this point, both parties can view progress by entering the system and viewing the chain management matrix. The matrix identifies steps so far taken, with green buttons indicating completed stages and red buttons identifying outstanding stages. If there is a conflict of interest with a client in respect of disclosure of information to the chain management matrix, the duty to supply information to the chain management matrix prevails. The matrix is updated on the completion of each stage.

The concept of a 'notional register' is introduced. The seller is able to view this. It represents how the Register will appear if the transaction proceeds to completion. The seller's access is restricted purely to the changes that will result. The buyer's conveyancer sees much more information on the notional register and will likewise see how the Register will appear after the transaction is completed.

Signing contracts

When the contract has been agreed, the proposal is that both the seller's and buyer's conveyancers will obtain their clients' electronic signature from an authorised storage resource and apply this to the electronic contract. As in the traditional process, even at this stage, the contract remains in the system – still unexchanged.

Exchange

When ready to exchange contracts, the buyer's conveyancer will check the daylist to ensure that there are no matters that will prejudice exchange. He or she may also need to check the chain management matrix in the case of a contract race – in which event a subsidiary matrix will have been created.

Consideration is being given to whether the chain management matrix might be a suitable mechanism for exchanging contracts. Once exchange has occurred, a unilateral notice will appear on the Register of the formation of a contract and the Register is then 'frozen'.

Transfer

The procedure for drafting, agreeing and executing the transfer will broadly follow that of the contract, in terms of agreeing amendments and the application of electronic signatures. Until the date of transfer is agreed, and the transfer document becomes operative, the draft will sit in the system.

The buyer's conveyancer will attend to the buyer's financial arrangements and once these are finalised, will check the updated chain management matrix with a view to completion.

Completion

The mechanism for completion will be the Electronic Funds Transfer System. Once completion has taken place, an automated message will be issued by the Land Registry to confirm completion of the transaction. The notional register ceases to be 'notional' and becomes the final Register.

Just one of a number of key issues exercising practitioners' minds is the viability of electronic signatures, and particularly their vulnerability to fraud or theft. Nicholas Bohm is e-commerce consultant to Fox Williams and a member of the Law Society's Electronic Law Committee. Writing on this subject in the summer 2004 issue of *Managing Risk*, he says 'The risk is the insecurity of the computers and networks used for electronic conveyancing . . . value exposed to the risk is the value of property which might be fraudulently transferred by the misuse of an electronic signature.'

It was emphasised that this was a hypothetical example of the operation of the e-conveyancing process and that further work, including informal consultation, is still taking place. Nonetheless, it is a revealing concept of how the eventual model might emerge.

E-conveyancing marketing strategies

Websites

There are many publications offering advice on developing websites and the law, regulations, and best practice governing their development and use (see the further reading list at the end of the chapter).

Law firms offering conveyancing services over the Internet will need to consider carefully the nature of their websites, security issues, and compliance with the law. Depending upon the range and extent of services offered, firms may like to consider the inclusion of:

- online quotation forms;
- online instruction forms;

- online case tracking facilities;
- a flow chart of chronological steps of the transaction;
- FAQs on the conveyancing process;
- client care standards (e.g. Law Society's Client Care Charter);
- links to related conveyancing sites giving relevant help and information.

As a marketing strategy, the firm may want to indicate any quality and professional standards to which it conforms (such as Lexcel), and membership of other relevant associations such as the Law Society's Property Section or Clarity.

Legal marketing sites

Some websites offer marketing services to law firms as an outlet for lawyers wishing to market their firm's services, but who may not have the time, expertise, or, perhaps, the inclination to undertake this themselves. Each firm must judge for itself how far a marketing site is likely to be effective in terms of the firm's marketing plan.

Delia Venables (owner of Legal Resources in the UK and Ireland – **www.venables.co.uk**) conducted an e-mail survey of law firm use of legal marketing sites. She reported:

> In carrying out the survey, I e-mailed 800 firms . . .The 70 responses I received were overwhelmingly sceptical, saying either that they had not tried these marketing sites or that they had tried them and found them of very little use. [Of the few positive responses, the] interesting comment made by one of them was that, because two sites are run by a solicitor . . . who 'weeds out' useless prospects at an early stage, the enquiries sent to the firms are indeed quite likely to turn into real business.

She concludes with some advice:

> Before paying over real money to any of these sites:
>
> - ask for validated figures for web site traffic;
> - ask for details of how many firms are on the panel;
> - ask for figures of how many contacts are passed on to each member of the panel on average;
> - talk to other solicitors on the panel to find out how many of these contacts turn into real clients;
> - do not forget the free listings available, including the Law Society's own listing – check your entry.
>
> *Internet Newsletter for Lawyers*, July/August 2002

Functional domain names

Some practices have opted to use 'functional' domain names (as opposed to the name of the firm) to indicate conveyancing services. They are intended to inform prospective clients of the nature of the services offered (in the hope that this will attract more attention and therefore site visitors), rather than the less informative name of the practice.

Examples include:

- **www.changing-homes.com** (Larcomes LLP);
- **www.cheapconveyancing.co.uk** (Heron);
- **www.conveyancing.co.uk** (Howard Schneider Spiro Steele);
- **www.conveyancingquotations.com** (Hamers);
- **www.e-conveyancing-solicitors.co.uk** (Jarian);
- **www.goconveyancing.co.uk** (Mason Bullock);
- **www.legalmove.com** (Hammonds);
- **www.movingahead.co.uk** (Pryse Jones);
- **www.onlineconveyancing.co.uk** (Drummonds);
- **www.quickconveyancing.co.uk** (R. Lewis Jones & Co).

CASE STUDY **Fidler & Pepper**

Fidler & Pepper is one of the 'small firm' pioneers of e-conveyancing. As long ago as 1998, the firm provided a facility for clients to track the progress of their conveyancing transactions online. Partner, Mark Slade, offers his views on e-conveyancing:

> Firms must embrace the change. It's no use either resisting or ignoring it. It won't go away. Visit firms already involved in the process and think how your own firm could become involved.
>
> We recognised at an early stage that estate agents would only refer work to those law firms which were efficient and competitive in terms of their processes and pricing. I think they are the leverage for the use of IT. We realised we had to use IT in order to compete. In the commercial sector, the change is driven by clients and the competition of their business.
>
> I don't see e-conveyancing as a switch-over from a paper-based process to an electronic process. It's really a seamlessly developing process, step by step, until all the steps in the conveyancing process are conducted electronically. It involves the use and manipulation of data in the conveyancing transaction – ultimately, totally electronically. A case management system is necessary, enabling online tracking and online search facilities. Land Registry Direct allows certain steps to be performed electronically.
>
> One of the biggest problems is the question of culture. A firm needs 'can do' people at all levels. It's all very well buying a brand new computer system, but if it isn't used properly, the exercise becomes purposeless. You'd be much

better off with an older and cheaper system which can be used by someone with real expertise. It isn't just a matter of IT kit. You need committed personnel – committed to learning and providing a better service, not necessarily the most expensive system.

Make sure the financial commitment is right for your firm. Make sure your people are involved; that they are willing to learn; that they are properly trained and educated in the new systems and procedures; and that they have the right attitude and want to do the job in a better way.

IT can be an excellent client relationship tool, offering, for instance, the generation of letters to keep clients informed, and the ability for clients to track their own instructions. In the face of the coming changes to the conveyancing process and the profession itself, surely no law firm can afford to ignore it.

Further reading

Archbold, C. (2003) *E-Business Basics for Law Firms*, Law Society Publishing.

Holmes, N. and Venables, D. (1999) *Researching the Legal Web*, Lexis-Nexis.

Joseph, M. (2003) *Small Firms' Attitude to E-Business* (Research Study 47), Law Society Strategic Research Unit.

Kendrik, R. (2002) *Managing Cyber-Risks*, Law Society Publishing.

The Land Registry (2003) *E-Conveyancing Consultation Report.*

The Land Registry (2003) *E-Conveyancing Consultation Document.*

Webb, N. (2003) *Internet Marketing*, Law Society Publising.

Appendix A

Typical layout for a business plan

Cover

Details
Circulation
Contact details, address, telephone numbers
Prepared by
Approved by

Executive summary and reasons for the business plan

Contents

1. Definitions and time period covered

Background information on the firm, mission, values, history, organisational structure and services provided at locations/branches

2. External marketplace

Political, economic, social and technological influences – opportunities and threats
Client/market analysis
Competitor analysis
Competitive advantages

3. Internal influences

Internal strengths and weaknesses of the firm in relation to the external opportunities and threats it faces
Key factors
SWOT
Limiting factors
Assumptions and impact of alternative scenarios

4. Strategy

Firm's objectives
Business strategy
Operating plans

5. Financial analysis

Break-even analysis
Turnover forecasts
Capital expenditure
Operating costs
Profit and loss account
Balance sheet
Cash flow
Funding needs

Appendix

Detailed financial data
Marketing strategy
IT plans
HR and training plans
CVs of senior management

Appendix B

Summary of marketing-related legislation and rules

Data Protection Act 1998

This Act was implemented following the European Data Protection Directive which requires member states to 'protect the fundamental . . . right to privacy with respect to the processing of personal data'. It covers all personal data in whatever form it is held, whether electronic, paper or CCTV. Individuals have a legal right to access all personal data held on them.

Data protection principles

1. Data must be processed fairly and lawfully.
2. Data must be processed for specific purposes and not in any manner incompatible with those purposes.
3. Date must be adequate, relevant and not excessive.
4. Data must be accurate.
5. Data must not be kept for longer than is necessary.
6. Data must be processed in line with the data subject's rights.
7. Data must be kept securely.
8. Data must not be transferred to countries outside the European Economic Area unless they can provide adequate protection.

Privacy and Electronic Communications (EC Directive) Regulations 2003

These came into force on 11 December 2003. They cover commercial communications by fax, telephone, e-mail, SMS and the telephone and fax preference service. For further information go to **www.informationcommissioner.gov.uk**.

Preference services

The telephone preference service (**www.tpsonline.org.uk**) and the fax preference service (**www.fpsonline.org.uk**) enable people and businesses to put their names on the register not to receive marketing communications. It is mandatory for marketers to check their lists against the registers. If a person or business has registered its name (unless recently) and has marketing communications sent to them by fax or telephone, criminal sanctions in the form of fines apply.

The Direct Marketing Agency (DMA) has run the mailing preference service (MPS), which is voluntary, since 1983. Customers can ask to have their names and home addresses deleted from mailing lists. The British Code of Advertising, Sales Promotion and Direct Marketing and the DMA's code of practice make it obligatory for list owners and users and DMA members to check their lists against those registered with the MPS. Although there is no legal sanction, bad publicity can result (see **www.dma.org.uk**).

Advertising and marketing codes

The Advertising Standards Authority (ASA) administers the British Code of Advertising, Sales Promotion and Direct Marketing which was created and is revised by the Committee of Advertising Practice (CAP). It is referred to as the CAP Code. While the ASA does not have legal sanctions, it can put pressure on members to refuse to give advertising space and commission to bodies that do not comply with the code. It also uses poor publicity to make its point (see **www.asa.org.uk**).

Electronic Commerce (EC Directive) Regulations 2002

These require that the providers of any service which is normally provided for remuneration, at a distance, by electronic means should clearly state that any commercial communication is easily identifiable as such.

Consumer Protection (Distance Selling) Regulations 2000

The Consumer Protection (Distance Selling) Regulations 2000 came into effect on 31 October 2000. The regulations apply to contracts with consumers made 'at a distance', for example, by telephone, mail order and the Internet.

BOX Telephone ordering – guidance

A1.4. Instructions taken by telephone, etc.

1.4.1. If instructions are received by telephone, e-mail or by any other non-face-to-face method, consideration must be given to the Consumer Protection (Distance Selling) Regulations 2000 (SI 2000/2334). [. . .]
1.4.2. The Regulations apply where a 'supplier' (the solicitor) is providing services to a 'consumer' (an individual instructing the solicitor on personal business). Corporate clients instructing a solicitor on company business are not consumers within this definition.
1.4.3. A 'distance contract' is one which is concluded under 'an organised sales or services provision scheme' e.g. in response to an advertisement or where there is no physical communication up to and at the moment when the contract is concluded. Instructions received by letter or e-mail may fall within this definition of a distance contract.
1.4.4. Contracts relating to financial services are exempted from the regulations but contracts to provide conveyancing services are not currently exempt.
1.4.5. Where the regulations apply certain information must be supplied to the client in writing (regs. 7 and 8). Most of the information required would be contained in a client care letter (e.g. name of solicitor, price, description of service to be provided) but in order to comply with the regulations it is suggested that, in cases

where the regulations do or might apply, a clause is included in the client care letter to state that the contract between the solicitor and client will not be concluded until the client signs and returns a copy of the client care letter to the solicitor.

1.4.6. Further, the client care letter must exclude the client's right to cancel the contract once work under it has commenced, otherwise a right to cancel and to recover money paid exists under reg. 10. The client care letter should also seek the client's agreement to the contract coming into force from the moment the signed client care letter is returned to the solicitor.

1.4.7. It is also essential for the client care letter to obtain the client's agreement to exclude reg. 19 which provides that if the services provided under the contract are not performed within a maximum of 30 days from the date of the contract, the contract is treated as if it had not been made.

1.4.8. Where the client has been referred to the solicitor under an agreement covered by section 2A Solicitors' Introduction and Referrals Code 1990, the client must be told the details of the agreement and the level of payment made by the solicitor.

Silverman, F. (ed.) (2004)
para. A1.4, *Conveyancing Handbook*, 11th edn., Law Society Publishing

Money Laundering Regulations 2003

The Money Laundering Regulations 2003 came into force on 1 March 2004 and replace the 1993 and 2001 Regulations. They are relevant to this book in terms of training staff, identifying the client, and accepting instructions.

Discussion of these regulations is outside the scope of this book and solicitors are directed to *Money Laundering: Guidance for Solicitors* (Pilot – January 2004) published at **www.lawsociety.org.uk** by the Law Society.

Note

This list is not exhaustive. Research should be undertaken regularly into existing and new laws and directives to ensure marketing activities comply.

Appendix C

Solicitors' Publicity Code 2001

(last amended 13 January 2003)

Code dated 16 November 2001 promulgated by the Council of the Law Society with the concurrence of the Master of the Rolls under rule 2 of the Solicitors' Practice Rules 1990, regulating the publicity of:

- solicitors, registered European lawyers and recognised bodies practising in England and Wales; and
- registered foreign lawyers practising in England and Wales in partnership with solicitors or registered European lawyers.

Section 1 – General principles

(a) Misleading or inaccurate publicity

Publicity must not be misleading or inaccurate.

(b) Clarity as to charges

Any publicity as to charges or a basis of charging must be clearly expressed. It must be clear whether disbursements and VAT are included.

(c) Name of firm

A private practice must not use a name or description which is misleading. It would be misleading for a name or description to include the word 'solicitor(s)', if none of the principals or directors (or members in the case of a limited liability partnership) is a solicitor.

(d) Unsolicited visits or telephone calls

(i) Practitioners must not publicise their practices by making unsolicited visits or telephone calls to a member of the public.
(ii) 'Member of the public' does not include:

(A) a current or former client;
(B) another lawyer;
(C) an existing or potential professional or business connection; or
(D) a commercial organisation or public body.

(e) Addresses to the court

It is not proper for practitioners to distribute to the press, radio or television copies of a speech or address to any court, tribunal or inquiry, except at the time and place of the hearing to persons attending the hearing to report the proceedings.

(f) International aspects of publicity

Publicity intended for a jurisdiction outside England and Wales must comply with:

(i) the provisions of this code; and
(ii) the rules in force in that jurisdiction concerning lawyers' publicity.

Publicity intended for a jurisdiction where it is permitted will not breach this paragraph through being incidentally received in a jurisdiction where it is not permitted.

(g) Practitioners' responsibility for publicity

A practitioner must not authorise any other person to conduct publicity for the practitioner's practice in a way which would be contrary to this code.

(h) Application

This section of the code applies to all forms of publicity including stationery, advertisements, brochures, directory entries, media appearances, press releases promoting a practice, and direct approaches to potential clients and other persons, and whether conducted in person, in writing, or in electronic form.

Section 2 – Professional stationery

(a) The letterhead of a private practice must bear the words 'regulated by the Law Society'.

(b) (i) The letterhead of:

(A) a sole principal must include the name of the sole principal;
(B) a partnership of 20 or fewer persons must include a list of the partners;
(C) a recognised body which is a company with a sole director must include the name of the director, identified as director.

(ii) The letterhead of:

(A) a partnership of more than 20 persons must include either a list of the partners,
(B) a recognised body which is a limited liability partnership must include either a list of the members, identified as members,
(C) a recognised body which is a company with more than one director must include either a list of the directors, identified as directors,

or a statement that the list is open to inspection at the office.

(iii) (A) On the letterhead of a recognised body which is an unlimited company; or
(B) in the list of partners referred to in sub-paragraph (i) or (ii)

above, if a partnership has an unlimited company as a member; or

(C) in the list of members referred to in sub-paragraph (ii) above, if a limited liability partnership has an unlimited company as a member;

it shall be stated, either as part of the unlimited company's name or otherwise, that the unlimited company is a body corporate.

(c) In a private practice, if the partners (or directors in the case of a company, or members in the case of a limited liability partnership) comprise both solicitors and foreign lawyers, the list referred to in (b)(i) or (ii) above must:

(i) in the case of any solicitor, identify him or her as a solicitor;

(ii) in the case of any lawyer or notary of a state (other than the UK) covered by the Establishment of Lawyers Directive 98/5/EC:

(A) identify the European jurisdiction(s) – local or national as appropriate – under whose professional title he or she is practising;

(B) give the professional title, expressed in an official language of the European state(s) concerned; and

(C) if the lawyer is a registered European lawyer, refer to his or her registration with the Law Society; and

(iii) in the case of any registered foreign lawyer not included in (c)(ii) above, indicate his or her professional qualification(s) as a lawyer and the country or jurisdiction of qualification.

(d) Whenever a registered European lawyer is named on the letterhead used by any private or in-house practice, there must be compliance with paragraph (c)(ii) above.

Section 3 – Interpretation and repeal

(a) In this code, words have the meanings assigned to them in rule 18 of the Solicitors' Practice Rules 1990, except that:

(i) 'letterhead' includes a fax heading; and

(ii) 'solicitor' means a solicitor of the Supreme Court.

(b) This code replaces the Solicitors' Publicity Code 1990.

Appendix D

Client satisfaction questionnaire

Bloggs & Co. Solicitors have a policy of constantly reviewing the quality of service we give to our clients. *We want you to recommend us to others.* To help us improve the service we give to you, please would you complete the following short questionnaire. Your answers are confidential. Thank you.

1. How did you originally hear of Bloggs & Co.? Please tick

Recommendation	
Yellow Pages	
Walking past the office	
Advertisement in XYZ paper	
Radio advertisement	
Article in a newspaper	
Back of a bus advertisement	
Other? Please state	

2. Which legal services have you used?

   ....

   ....

3. Are you aware of the following legal services Bloggs & Co provides? Please tick only if your answer is 'Yes'.

   a. Divorce or separation ....
   b. Personal injury ....
   c. Commercial conveyancing ....
   d. Will ....
   e. Trust ....
   f. Civil dispute ....
   g. Children's matters ....
   h. Sale or purchase of home ....
   i. Landlord/tenancy dispute ....
   j. Probate ....
   k. Neighbour disputes ....
   l. Criminal law ....
   m. Other – please state ....

4. How satisfied were you with your initial contact with the firm? Please tick:

	Satisfied	Fairly satisfied	Not very satisfied	Not satisfied
a. The welcome given by the receptionist				
b. Promptness in taking or receiving telephone calls				
c. Friendly and approachable				

5. Do you have any comments you would like to add regarding your initial impression of the firm? Please state.

   ....

6. With regard to the list below, how satisfied were you with your solicitor's actions? Please tick:

My solicitor:	**Satisfied**	**Fairly satisfied**	**Not very satisfied**	**Not satisfied**
a. Initially saw or spoke to me within an acceptable timescale				
b. Had an initial cost discussion				
c. Estimated likely costs				
d. Keeps me informed of the costs				
e. Discusses costs regularly				
f. Sends me bills at agreed times				
g. Explains the legal processes				
h. Explains the legal implications				
i. Manages my expectations of the outcomes				
j. Involves me in the decision-making				
k. Listens to me				
l. Has a genuine interest in how I am feeling				
m. Treats me with respect				
n. Doesn't keep me waiting when I have an appointment				
o. Does what he or she says he or she will do				
p. Is open and approachable				
q. Is accessible when it is convenient to me				
r. Responds quickly				
s. Keeps me informed				
t. Returns my telephone calls within 24 hours				
u. Other staff treat me with respect				
v. Please add any additional points here:				

7. With regard to any of the above, would you like to give your reasons in support of your views?

   ....

   ....

   ....

8. What improvements do you think could be made to give our clients a better service?

   ....

   ....

   ....

9. Have you ever recommended Bloggs & Co to anyone else? Please tick:
   a. Yes ....
   b. No ....
10. Would you be willing to recommend us to others?
   a. Yes ....
   b. No ....
11. Do you have any final comments you would like to add or any person you would like to mention?
   ....
   ....
   ....
   ....
   ....

If you would like us to respond to any of your comments, please would you give us your name and contact details.

Name ....

....

Address ....
....

Telephone number ....
....

Please return the completed questionnaire to Bloggs & Co. at..............................

THANK YOU FOR YOUR TIME AND FOR HELPING US TO IMPROVE OUR SERVICE

Appendix E

Law Society's Client Care Charter

Whatever legal service you need, you have the right to be treated with care and professionalism by your solicitor. The Client's Charter is your guide to what to expect from your solicitor in terms of customer care.

Working together

Whilst your solicitor has various duties to you as their client, they can only give their best advice and service if the information you give them is accurate and complete.

A solicitor will:

- put your interests first when representing you;
- be polite and considerate in their dealings with you;
- find out from the start what you are hoping to achieve, and aim to make sure that your expectations are realistic;
- make every effort to explain things clearly, and in terms you can understand, keeping jargon to a minimum;
- agree with you the type of service you can expect to receive;
- tell you who will be handling your work;
- explain what the costs are likely to be;
- keep you informed of costs throughout so that you can work out if a particular course of action is worth following financially;
- respond to your letters and phone calls;
- tell you about any developments and update you on progress as work proceeds;
- give you a clear bill which shows the work done and the amount charged;
- treat all clients fairly, and not discriminate against anyone; because of his or her race, sex, sexual orientation (sexuality) or disability; and
- keep what you tell them confidential, and refuse to act for anyone else if doing so could compromise that confidentiality.

This is a summary of the main rules and principles that apply to all solicitors.

PLEASE NOTE: Other legal and professional duties may occasionally affect the ability of your solicitor to meet all these standards. For example, the legal duty to release information about money laundering or the solicitor's duty to the court can override the duty of confidentiality or the duty to put your interest first.

What to do if you have a complaint

Most people have a good experience with their solicitor, but things do sometimes go wrong. That is why there is a clear and effective complaints procedure in place.

Every solicitor's firm has to have their own complaints procedure, and you should use this procedure first before going elsewhere.

If this does not provide a satisfactory resolution, you should complain to the Consumer Complaints Service, Victoria Court, No 8 Dormer Place, Leamington Spa, CV32 5AE. Phone: 0845 608 6565.

After this, if you are still not satisfied, you can take your complaint to the Office of the Legal Services Ombudsman, 3rd Floor, Sunlight House, Quay Street, Manchester M3 3JZ. Phone: 0161 839 7262. Email: **lso@olso.gsi.gov.uk**

For a list of solicitors in your area and lots of other information on legal issues, visit the Law Society's website at: **www.lawsociety.org.uk**

You can find details of the rules which apply to solicitors, including the circumstances when your solicitor may not be able to meet all the terms of the Charter, at **www.guide-online.lawsociety.org.uk**

Index